Messages *from the* Universe

Seeking the Secrets of Destiny

CRAIG HAMILTON-PARKER

CRAIG HAMILTON-PARKER

Copyright © 2015 Craig Hamilton-Parker

All rights reserved.

ISBN-13: 978-1517568887
ISBN-10: 1517568889

TESTIMONALS

"I don't normally buy this stuff. I think it's odd and peculiar and you can't really put your finger on this kind of thing, however both these people everything they said about the stuff they talked about, they were accurate. They are the real deal and it kinda blew my mind a little bit. I'm not a mind blower by nature but you know it was real and all crap aside, it was real."

ERIC ROBERTS
(Talking to camera about his reading with Craig & Jane)

Eric Anthony Roberts is an American actor. His career began with King of the Gypsies, earning a Golden Globe Award nomination for Best Actor Debut. He earned both a Golden Globe and Academy Award nomination for his supporting role in Runaway Train.

"That was remarkable...In the World's Most Skeptical Person's Award in 2001 I was a runner up but I just don't know what to make of what I've just seen. I think he did remarkably well!"

CHRIS PACKHAM
(Talking on BBC 'Inside Out' about Craig's psychic demonstration)

Christopher Gary "Chris" Packham is an English television presenter.

CONTENTS

1	Introduction	1
2	**Messages from the Universe** The Secrets of the Naadi Palm Leaf Oracle	5
3	**Why Are You Here?** Sathya Sai Baba guides Craig to the Lost Oracle	9
4	**The Naadi Finds Me** About Naadi Astrology and how it works	13
5	**A Rishi with a Temper** The Oracle gives proof of Reincarnation	17
6	**Messages to the People** The oracle spots that we are Spiritualist mediums	19
7	**Beverly Hills Mediums** Craig and Jane give messages to celebrities	23
8	**America** Sneaking inside the Magic Circle	28
9	**The Destiny of the World** What does the oracle say about the our future?	32
10	**The Yugas** The Dark Age and the Golden Age	36
11	**Megaliths and Nazis** Ancient Magicians and Black Magicians	44
12	**Hare Krishna!** Chanting for liberation	53
13	**Testing the Oracle** Making sure it's all true	60
14	**Sadguru Sri Sharavana Baba** The Telepathic Guru	65

15	**More Messages from the Naadi** Toxic Clouds and Tsunamis	73
16	**The Spirits See My Future** Messages from Doris Stokes	77
17	**Seeing History** Entranced Police and Psychometry Powers	80
18	**Destined to Marry Jane** The Dead Grandmother Matchmaker	87
19	**Giving up the Fruits** The Corporate Bluff	91
20	**Next Week's News Today** Our First TV Show	95
21	**Paris** Contacting the Spirit of Princess Diana	100
22	**Opening the Third Eye** Psychic School	109
23	**Sathya Sai Baba Darshan** Clues about the next incarnation	117
24	**Sathya Sai Baba's Naadi** What Next?	122
25	**Bhavishya Purana & Bhrigu** More Mysteries of Tomorrow	130
26	**Richard Dawkins** A Chat with Darwin's Rottweiler	134
27	**Dreams** Trolls in Iceland and a detour to Serbia	141
28	**A Hug from Amma** Fixing a Curse from a Past Life	148
29	**Neem Karoli Baba of Rishikesh** LSD Enlightenment	153

30	**Arty Hippies in Marrakesh** A Stroll in the Desert	163
31	**Swami Sivananda Saraswati** A Yogi Encounters Spiritualism	170
32	**Ghost Hunting at Stratford-Upon-Avon** Crazy Spooks and Spirits	175
33	**Meeting Mataji Vanamali** The Death of the Personality?	180
34	**Maharishi's Abandoned Ashram** Where Have All the Flowers Gone?	186
35	**The Arundhati Guha Caves** Where Saints Have Sat	190
36	**Catacombs and Rome** Editing Christianity	195
37	**Temple Mount Jerusalem** Mysteries of the Netherworld	206
38	**Yoga in the Himalayas** Mediums in a Twist	210
39	**Sri Aurobindo's Ashram in Delhi** Five Subtle Bodies	219
40	**Mahatma Gandhi** His Naadi Destiny	223
41	**Varanasi** A Spiritual and Culinary Guide	226
42	**Paradise on Earth** What Is Heaven Like?	232
43	**Buddha's Deer Park** Spaced out by the Dalai Lama	236
44	**Paramahansa Yogananda in Calcutta** Trailanga Swami by the Bucket Load	240

45	**Thailand** Stuffed Monks & Buddha Emporium	244
46	**Calcutta** Ramakrishna and God Realization	249
47	**Assisi Miracles** Messages from the Tâmrapothi Oracle	254
48	**The Cosmic Boomerang** Clearing the Karma from Past Lives	259
49	**Commune and Kibbutz** Seeking an Alternative Lifestyle	268
50	**The Foundation** Help Ever, Hurt Never	273
51	**Will the Naadi Predictions Come True?**	280
52	**Naadi Readings and Remedies**	284
53	**Appendix and Transcripts**	286
54	**Naadi Reading 1**	289
55	**Remedies and Puja for Naadi Reading 1**	399
56	**Naadi Reading 2**	300
57	**Epilogue**	315
58	**Glossary**	317
59	**Mantras**	320

CRAIG & JANE HAMILTON-PARKER

Craig and Jane Hamilton-Parker
Psychic Mediums

INTRODUCTION

In this book I reveal the secrets of the Indian Naadi Oracle that tells me that new spiritual knowledge will be revealed to me by the gods—which I initially interpreted as my mediumship—and from studying the Naadis, learning astrology, and knowledge given directly by meeting living *rishis*. In the chapters that follow, I will share with you my work as a medium and how, together with my wife Jane, we took on the media. Together, we will travel to mystical places, share colorful adventures, meet some extraordinary enlightened people and join our relentless search for universal knowledge.

My task, I am told by the oracle, is to bring the message to the people. The oracle went into extraordinary personal detail about my life and my past before revealing the core messages as to why I am here—the question I had asked Sathya Sai Baba to answer.

How would you feel if a complete stranger told you the exact history of your life and everything that would happen to you in the future? You'd be skeptical, of course, and you would need to be sure there was no cheating going on. But suppose it really were possible to know the past, present, and future with complete accuracy? This would be life-changing information, and it would be particularly helpful if it showed you ways to steer destiny toward a happy outcome.

At the age of sixty, I consulted a 5,000-year-old Indian oracle with my name on it. It told me all about my life and what would happen next. It also "saw" my past work as a well-known Spiritualist medium, and how I could help people in the future to address some of the terrible—and wonderful—things that are about to happen to the world.

In this book, I tell the story of my encounter with the oracle, and how it revealed my future and hinted at the future of the world. I explain how the oracle knew all about my life working as an artist and writer, how it knew about my childhood and meeting my wife, and about the work we would do together with the media. It knew all about my life-long efforts as a yogi and psychic medium, and how I would meet rich and famous people, who would help fulfill the oracle's remit.

Using the oracle as a template for my narrative, I tell the tale of my quest for higher consciousness through LSD, meditation, yoga, and mediumship. I show how the silver thread of destiny has wound its way through my life and pulled me back to the right path whenever I have gone astray. The oracle reveals how providence has brought me to meet holy people, who are helping me to fulfill the spiritual plans designed in a former incarnation and as a *rishi*. The oracle explains why my work as a medium and Spiritualist is influenced by many of the great Indian holy men from the past and, in particular, the modern-day *avatar* Sathya Sai Baba, who, according to the oracle, will return after his death to initiate the Golden Age.

This book also takes you on a mystic journey to divinely charged places that reflect the spiritual message of the oracle—places where sensitives can connect with the other side of reality, places where gods and spirits guide our path. Together we will meet holy people, learn of their secret teachings, and wonder at the implications for the world and ourselves. Those who know my work as a psychic medium will understand my concerns about modern-day, mundane psychism and the limitations of the Spiritualist philosophy. You will know about my worries for the path mankind is taking, and how we must change our ways if we are to herald in a Golden Age. I hope that this book will give you useful philosophical insights and, for mediums and psychics, help reveal the bigger picture that Spiritualism may have missed. Yes, we do live after death—but that's not the end of the story. There's much, much more!

Guided by messages from my spirit helpers, and by other influences that resonate through my mediumship, I have included in this book some of my thoughts about the future of the world. The oracle told me that I, too, would become an oracle, and that my "big book"—perhaps the one you are reading now—would predict the future of the world. In its text, the oracle says: "In the olden times, all the *rishis*, all the spiritual people, they write all the things in the palm leaves. But since ancient time, you are going to write everything in the notebook. This is the difference." It tells of how these messages will help guide people, both now and in the far future. The oracle predicts toxic gas clouds and tidal surges that will cause panic in the world, but that we can—though spiritual practice—predict and negate some of the worst effects. This book is the first insight from the leaves. As I gain access to the rest of the oracle, I am sure even more will be revealed.

Sometimes, as I write, I am conscious of the spirit people influencing me to include a prediction, but at other times I am completely unaware of what's going on, and messages get entwined in the words I type. I find this unconscious clairvoyance happens in general life and in my interactions with people. Sometimes I am aware I am doing mediumship or making a psychic observation, but at other times it just happens, like an ongoing synchronicity. The oracle predicted that the gods would work through me to give messages from the universe. I understood this at the time to mean mediumship—messages from the spirit world—but the gods also have things to say about the future of mankind and the quest for enlightenment.

I am hoping that some of the ideas here will help intelligent mediums to drive forward the message of mediumship to a new level, which includes the expansion of consciousness and new forms of spiritual insight. For those of you who do not like me, hate Spiritualism, and wish to pour skeptical scorn on my work as a medium, I provide you with plenty of extra ammunition that you will enjoy. This book is "warts and all," so you can read about some of the mistakes I've made, jokes I've played, impossible situations I've gotten into, and about my self-evident stupidity.

Our multiple incarnations are journeys across this material world that eventually lead to the next stage of human consciousness. The journey is full of suffering and loss and, for most of us, it feels that we have been set loose in a terrible land, without a map, and with no knowledge of the direction we should take. We are usually fairly happy as children, but soon we encounter disappointments, boredom, rejections, unexpected misfortune, and terrible things such as illness or the death of a loved one. Can there be any happiness in a world like this? Is there anything we can do to find the true path of our soul so that we can travel these roads valiantly, quickly, and with a happy heart?

Many of the obstacles we meet in life are caused by our own actions—what we know as "karma," generated in this life and in previous incarnations. Our hearts know what is right, but our heads mess things up. We make choices based on self-interest, greed, jealousy, and so on, always selfishly taking, but never giving or forgiving. These are terrible energies that ruin our lives and collectively disrupt the harmony of the planet.

Our past-life actions determine the body we will be born with, our path through life, and the people and situations we will encounter. Our present consciousness and spiritual memory is creating the world around us. We create our problems, but we can also mitigate problems with remedies to counter our foolishness.

Through the oracle and mediumship, the universe can help us to find ways to overcome our problems. We can use techniques such as yoga, mantra, meditation, ritual, prayer, *archana*, and so on to free ourselves from the clutches of negative karma. We can acquire knowledge to help us transcend our petty ego and discover ways to immerse ourselves in the blissful river of becoming. When we engage our hearts and let our whole being melt into the great work of life, without expectation or a desire to reap reward, then problems evaporate. With fortitude, we accept all as part of the bliss of life; we give everything; and we soon achieve the consciousness, being, and bliss that is our true nature. The destination of life is love, which is the bedrock of all existence. Love is the power that guides the fates, moving us from love, through love, and to love.

MESSAGES FROM THE UNIVERSE

Five thousand years ago, a *maharishi* in ancient India wrote my first name and last name—in Sanskrit—on a palm leaf. He also wrote down the names of my father, mother, family members, ex-wife, and present wife, as well as all the significant things that have happened to me in the past and will happen in the future.

Your name may be on the leaves, too.

I had known about the ancient Indian Naadi oracle for a long time, but it took me many years to track down a reliable person who could introduce me to a true custodian of the palm-leaf manuscripts. They say that the Naadi oracle can reveal everything of significance that will happen in a person's life. It will talk of opportunities, pitfalls, marriages, careers, and a person's spiritual life, and sometimes it will foretell the exact time they will die.

If this oracle is real, then it can be a great force for good and can lead a seeker to a better material path or to great spiritual heights. It can reveal the meaning and purpose of your life on earth and, in the hands of the right interpreter, be a spiritual map to guide your life. In the wrong hands, it can become a way to trick and manipulate people. Just as there are many fakes who work in my own calling as a psychic medium, so too the reputation of the Naadi oracle is sometimes sabotaged by charlatans.

You can find some questionable readers on the Internet, and everything I had discovered up to this point was clearly a con-trick. Bogus readers will fish for information when doing the consultation and use search engines to give what appear to be startling insights into your life. The fake oracles contain only generalities about the person asking the question and lack any startlingly detailed information, such as knowing in advance the name of the person making the enquiry, and revealing their family names and personal histories during the reading.

Once these false oracles have you hooked, the readers will offer you expensive remedies to rectify the dreadful fate that awaits you. Many practitioners of Voodoo use similar tactics to extort money from their clients. I have heard of psychics in the West—and particularly in New Orleans—who will charge you thousands of dollars just to burn candles to lift a jinx or resolve a problem in your love life.

The bogus Naadi readers possess counterfeit palm leaves and can only give you guessed generalities and vague astrological information. Their insights do not contain mind-blowing information such as your name, your date of birth, and the names of your relatives, or astonishing revelations about your life and past. I had heard some wonderful stories about the oracle, but also many horror stories of people who have been well and truly ripped off. To enter this territory, you really need an informed and trustworthy guide.

I had made numerous direct attempts to find a real Naadi reader during my travels in India and was beginning to give up my search. In fact, one of the multiple meanings of the word naadi is "to seek," and it is believed that only a true seeker of truth will find a real reader.

Just as I began to suspect that the oracle was simply a legend, a friend told me about her remarkable reading in Bangalore as she was traveling to meet our mutual guru, Sathya Sai Baba. Sadly, she did not recall the address of the Naadi reader, and nor could she remember enough detail for me to track him down. The whole encounter with the Naadi oracle had taken her by surprise, and soon afterward she was overtaken by even more momentous events when Sathya Sai Baba tapped her forehead and flipped her into a whirlwind of super-consciousness.

A retired Wing Commander in India put me on track for a while, but this trail, too, eventually went cold. He had done considerable research and listed many of the Naadi centers, but he also warned about bogus readers, the false propaganda being spread about Naadi predictions, and the potential pitfalls associated with paying excessive fees for rituals to remove negative past karma. In addition, these were the early days of the Internet, so contact with the potential readers I discovered had to be made by letter or personal introduction—not easy when you are trying to connect with a Tamil-speaking person from an obscure village in India.

It is said that the oracle reveals itself to the seeker only when the time is right, and it will give you exactly what you need to know at that point in time. When one is on the right path to finding the true oracle, strange coincidences and odd synchronicities start to happen. But my path was blocked. It was not going to reveal its secrets; it was not the right time.

I made one last attempt to find a reader when I was traveling in India and studying yoga. I found nothing in Rishikesh, Calcutta, or Delhi, but had very limited time—just an overnight stay in the Delhi-based ashram of Sri Aurobindo, for example—so again, I missed my chance.

I had been looking to find the oracle at a time in my life when things were going exceptionally well. Over the previous fifteen years, I had been building my website, which had grown to become one of the most popular psychic communities on the Internet with hundreds of thousands of visitors a day. My health was good, I had lots of exciting books and media projects on the boil, and my wife, Jane, and I were happy and financially sound. We could even afford a new car and a luxury vacation in the Seychelles.

But the fates had other plans. I noticed from my horoscope that Saturn had moved into a particularly bad position in my sun sign, Aquarius. It was an ominous portent, one which I feared would bring difficulties into my life. Soon, everything started to go wrong. The god Saturn had clipped Cupid's wings with his terrible scythe, and I felt that I was no longer the master of my fate. Astrology teaches that Saturn is the great taskmaster. When its shadow crosses your sign in an inauspicious way, it usually means that times will get tough, but you—as a person—will get stronger.

In the space of a few months, our comfortable life was flipped on its head. A few days before we were due to fly to Walt Disney World in Florida with our daughter Danielle and little granddaughter Willow, while we prepared for our happy holiday, Google decided to launch a new algorithm that determines which websites will be listed on the first page of its search results. My site had always ranked well for years before Google even existed. It had a huge following, but overnight it crashed from the listings, and now you could hardly find it on Google.

The traffic fell from hundreds of thousands of visitors a day to just a trickle. Overnight my career, opportunities, and finances were in crisis. The two algorithm changes that did the most damage were called "Panda" and "Penguin." Far from being the cuddly toys their names implied, these were a couple of evil monsters that destroyed many mom-and-pop businesses like ours. So instead of enjoying Mickey Mouse, I was now pulled into a ghastly world of search-engine optimization and wrestling with strange, black-and-white cyber-creatures.

The algorithm was allegedly designed to stop web spam and punish websites that "farmed" content and claimed it as their own. I had been writing my site for fifteen years and, unfortunately, thousands of other sites had simply lifted my content and, with a simple click of the mouse, called it their own. Not only was I finding my original work on pseudo-psychics' websites, but my astrology articles were being used by sites to redirect searches to gross content. It was deflating to think that all the love and effort I had put into my work was now hijacked by wannabe psychics and porno spammers.

The new search algorithm saw my site as duplicate spam, since you could find the same content elsewhere. I tried everything—even getting Vince Cable, the UK Secretary of State for Business, to write to Google on my behalf—but I could not rescue my business. Google didn't care a hoot about who owned what content, as the changes had stirred things up so much that now more people than ever were clicking on the Google ads to find what they wanted—and Google profits were soaring! To Google, spiritually themed websites and forums that took a hit were simply "collateral damage." Evil had triumphed.

The loss of most of my business was the start of a series of difficulties. "Friends" walked out of my life when the money and opportunities evaporated, some of my real friends and family members died, both of my daughters' marriages failed, and everything you could think could go wrong, did go wrong. Perhaps the worst of all was that my guru in India—Sathya Sai Baba—died.

I felt that these were dark times for my family and me, but also for a great many spiritual people in the world.

WHY ARE YOU HERE?

In the midst of our difficulties, I had a dream about Sathya Sai Baba. For those of you who have never heard of Sathya Sai Baba, he was an Indian holy man who looked a bit like Jimi Hendrix, with his huge Afro haircut. He was born on November 23, 1926, and at the age of fourteen, after a two-month period of illness and unconsciousness, he announced to the startled villagers that he was an *avatar*—a teacher sent directly from God. This, he said, was his second incarnation, the previous being as Sai Baba of Shirdi, a Muslim fakir who had died in 1918. There would be a third to come, Prema Baba.

Over the course of these three lifetimes, he intended to bring the religions of the world together as one brotherhood, with universal love as their foundation stone.

Jane and I had been to his ashram in Puttaparthi, India, fifteen years ago and had come to understand that this was no ordinary man. He had the power of omnipresence, which is the ability—just like St. Francis of Assisi—to appear in multiple places at the same time. If Sai Baba appeared in a dream, it was a real communication—something that had been proved to me many times before and has been verified by many other people. Sathya Sai Baba says that you can only dream of him if he wills it.

My dream was set in the sacred Indian city of Varanasi on the river Ganges. It is a place I had visited, and it is one of the most sacred places in India, where many Hindus go to die or be cremated. From here, their ashes are cast upon the sacred waters of the river so that the soul can quickly make its journey into the next life.

In the dream, I am sitting on my yoga mat beside the funeral pyre of the Cindy Ghat. Through the smoky air, I watch the children playing in the murky waters and am startled to see the dead Sathya Sai Baba standing before me in his bright orange robe. His eyes glint mischievously, and he flashes a bright, child-like smile.

"Why are you here?" he asks.

"Swami, I am here to seek direction," I reply.

"Why are you here? Why are you here?" he repeats as I awaken from my sleep.

I was, of course, hoping that Sathya Sai Baba would tell me what I should do about my material problems, but the dream was clearly pushing me to look at the bigger picture of life. The direction I was hoping to know about was whether to continue with my website, write more books, or throw myself into my mediumship. But Baba had posed an even bigger question.

At first I thought that, because the dream was set in Varanasi, it could mean that I would die soon. Perhaps I was at Shiva's sacred city because my journey through life was complete. If this was the case, then all these worries about livelihood, friends, family, and health were insignificant worries compared with the prospect of my imminent death.

Of course, I didn't die, but for a long time I grappled with the ultimate question my guru had given me. There is the big question as to why any of us is here at all. I call this the "to be or not to be" question, the one that asks if there is any purpose to life, the universe, and everything.

Perhaps existence cannot have a direction because everything is already perfect, so all my belly-aching to my guru about wanting to find a "direction" had been an illusion. But this begs the question as to why we are here at all.

Earthly life does at least *appear* to have a direction. This is evident if we look at the history of the universe, the birth of the solar system, and the evolution of life on Earth. But all this may simply be a comic joke that we just don't get. The Vedas (ancient Indian scriptures) say that from the "Big Bang" to the "Big Crunch," when the universe ends or returns to a singularity, is just one heartbeat of Brahman (God). So it is all perfect after all! The snag is that our limited minds just cannot comprehend the scale of it all.

We can also ask the "Why am I here?" question on a personal level. We are thrown into this world without a manual or map, nor with any clue as to why we are here or what we should be doing with our life. Most people quickly succumb to the conformity of the world around them and fall into a living sleep. They become drowsy zombies, hungry to consume the poisoned honey of money, sex, comfort, family security, a pension, and an easy-to-afford burial plan.

Our heart knows that life is hollow when all our attention is focused on having the billions of worldly things. Sai Baba says of this: "Life is lost in dreaming.... Being is lost in becoming."

Occasionally we may stir for a short while from our somnambulism: "Hey! I'm awake! Now why am I ... zzzzzzz." Our attention is just not trained to sustain spiritual awakening for any length of time, and soon we fall back into the illusion. And, of course, religions of all flavors do not help us awaken. Beliefs are poison in that they block our access to the direct experience of Truth.

But we can awaken, and often many of us do rouse from the dreamy slumber of life to get a glimpse of the greater reality. If you are reading these words, this has happened to you too, for just like the magical synchronicity of the true Naadi oracle, only a person who is aware that we can awaken, is in the process of awakening, or has awakened will read these words. You would not be reading about Sai Baba or the Naadi if the possibility of awakening were not alive in you right now. You stumble upon books like this for a reason: you are also on the mystic journey.

You may have had only a flash of insight or sustained awareness, but you know it is there, and you can feel the call to wake up. In fact, your soul aches to know it. The call is like a half-remembered melody that dances just out of earshot. Its music is pulling you to awaken and join the mystical journey with me and others already around you who are awake right now.

The Sathya Sai Baba dream was an inspiration to the heart, and it fired up my desire to find out who I was and why I am here—not just in a cosmic sense, but personally, too. I wanted to know about my personal mission on earth. It's something everyone has, but most people are just too distracted by the game of their lives to even consider the possibility that there could be more.

After a considerable time of struggle—nearly two years wrestling with the "Why am I here?" question—I was running short of patience with Swami. I had clues from my meditations, but the messages I was getting from the spirit world were unclear, as my own hopes and fears were in my way. I'd had a number of readings with other mediums (since mediums cannot see clearly for themselves), but their insights were very shallow, and the mediumship was sincere but of shockingly poor quality.

A Sai Baba devotee friend suggested that the way to get an answer from him was to meditate on his photograph for twenty minutes and then write a question as a letter to him. So what's twenty minutes? I gave it a try, sat in sincere meditation, and wrote my question. Actually, there were a few, and all of them were answered within days.

The most important one, and the one that we are concerned with here, was the question I asked about my destiny and my life's mission. I had actually asked Sai Baba not to just give me hints. I was fed up with auguries, signs, portents, and symbols. I'd had too much of this already from fork-tongued psychics. I more or less demanded that I get a direct and clear message that would completely clarify what I needed to know. I didn't even care if it meant the death of me—I needed to know the new direction of my spiritual journey now that so much of my previous life had been swept away.

Sri Sathya Sai Baba

THE NAADI FINDS ME

I was glad to get a "friend request" and a private message on Facebook from Vivek, a long-time, Indian school-teacher friend whom I hadn't heard from in some years. When the Internet was in its infancy and I was first building my website, I had long email conversations with Vivek about Sathya Sai Baba, Indian philosophy, and spiritual values. I respected his ideas and sincere insights, and knew him to be an extremely trustworthy and spiritual person.

With long-standing spiritual friends, there is a deep connection, and you can pick up a conversation after years as if it was only yesterday.

"Last time we spoke, you said you were interested in tracking down the Naadi readers," messaged Vivek through Facebook. "Well, you may be interested to know that one of them is visiting me soon, and it may be possible to arrange a reading for you."

Vivek explained that he was hoping to introduce the West to this wonder of India and asked whether I would consider testing some of the readers for him. He had astonishingly accurate messages himself, but he needed someone to test things whom the readers couldn't possibly know anything about. I was the perfect choice, because they could never connect me to Vivek and, of course, I had tested and vetoed psychics and mediums working or training through my website. I could spot someone fishing for information, feeding back known information, giving generalized "Barnham" readings—generalities that could fit anyone—or giving what some call "cold readings."

If these guys were up to no good, I would know. And, of course, I was very keen to eventually get a reading. How wonderful that it was being arranged by someone I could trust.

It was a simple process to get started. All that was sent to the Naadi reader was a scan of my right-hand thumbprint, in a PDF file, together with the time I made the scan. This I emailed to Vivek, who then independently re-emailed (not forwarded) the file to the reader, making sure that there were no references to my email address, website, or identity. From the thumbprint, the Naadi reader could identify a group of leaves that might contain my reading, and from these he would later ask me a series of questions to get to exactly the right one.

We arranged the reading by Skype, again ensuring that there was absolutely no opportunity for the reader to know my identity.

It is easy to find quite a lot about me on the web. I have an extensive website and have published fifteen books, and there is a page about me on Wikipedia. We ensured that there was no way he could access this information, though, as it turned out, the great majority of what he told me could not be discovered through the Internet anyway.

Doing one of these readings over Skype was a new idea. Since having my readings, I have researched many mind-boggling accounts of Naadi readings that were just as accurate as mine, but done at a time before the Internet was invented.

The origin of the Naadi leaves is unknown. The palm leaves have been copied and recopied over generations, with each batch of leaves lasting perhaps 300 years before being copied again and again and again. Carbon-dating of some of the leaves shows them to be between 300 and 400 years old.

Vedic astrological teachings deal in vast tracts of cosmic time (*manvantaras*) and tell us that some of the first men lived billions of years ago and had superhuman powers. The first visionaries were decedents of the Aryan race and called the "Dravid"—a word from Sanskrit meaning "learned seer." These people had extraordinary prophetic powers that foresaw the lives of every person who will walk this earth until the end of humanity. Their omniscient visions saw me writing these words and you reading them. These superhuman visionaries—guided by the god Shiva—are believed to be the authors of the leaves. Perhaps these people have insight into the world of quantum physics that we are only now uncovering. They "saw" the vastness of the quantum world, where everything can happen simultaneously, and where past, present, and future are one.

Many of the leaves had been destroyed by the British during the times of the Raj, but originally they were said to contain the lives of everyone who lived, had lived, or would ever live on Earth. Impossible?

Would my leaf be there, waiting for me for millennia? When I connected with the Naadi reader by Skype, he was sitting in blue robes, with a picture of Shiva hanging on the wall behind him. He was a cheerful man who could speak reasonably good English. He explained that our task was to find the correct leaf, and that I was only to answer "Yes" or "No" to the series of questions that he would ask.

The thought crossed my mind that perhaps he was going to be using a method called "lateral thinking," pioneered in the 60s by Edward de Bono. This is a sort of game that allows you to find out what someone is thinking using a series of logical, sequential questions that quickly get to an answer. Fortunately, the questions he asked were very odd, such as whether I was a miner, if I imported foreign goods, and so on. These were the messages on other people's leaves, which he discarded every time I answered "No."

First he would chant the words on the leaves in Tamil and then ask me a question in English. Eventually a leaf was found that could be only for me. After a long string of what seemed to be hopeless questions, he looked up and said, "Your ex-wife's name is Tina."

I nearly fell off my seat! This is not something most people would know, and it is not mentioned in my books or on the web.

"Your mother's name is Ethel?" Again this was a huge shock, as my mother's name, Ethel, is not a modern name and not that common. It is also a birth name she hates, and so she goes by the name of Vicky. Only a few people know that her real name is Ethel.

"Mother is living. Your father is dead. His name was Donald?" I was beginning to freak out. This was not clairvoyance—he was reading this directly off the leaf!

"Your present wife's name is Jane?" This man was not throwing out names and initials. He was going straight to the mark, without any mistakes. He then spoke about my life and how I had been an artist for many years, and that now I have a spiritual business—an

Internet-based spiritual business—and that I write spiritual books and give people "messages from the universe" (I interpreted this as mediumship). "Your wife, Jane, also has a spiritual business, but she works independently from you."

There was much more, but all of it was fact after fact that could relate only to me. He gave details about my life that nobody could ever have known, even with the Internet at their command. He told me about my education, my jobs and profession, the type of house I owned, my hopes, ambitions, and relationships, as well as my children and grandchildren. He then revealed the exact time and date of my birth, and that I was born on a Sunday.

"Your name is Craig," he said.

Clearly he had found my centuries' old leaf, and in the next session he would tell me what it says about my life and future.

The moment my Palm Leaf is found

A RISHI WITH A TEMPER

The leaves revealed all sorts of things about my life, but the one I found most shocking was that it claimed I had been an Indian *rishi* (saint) in my past life. In some ways, this could explain why I was born with mediumistic abilities and started doing yoga and meditation from the age of twelve, but I certainly do not consider myself spiritually at the level of a *rishi*.

A *rishi* is usually defined as a Hindu sage or saint, but in Sanskrit the word comes from the word *drish*, meaning "to see." One definition calls the *rishis* the "seers of thought," which in some ways perfectly expresses my work as a medium and psychic. We "see" the thoughts of people in this world and, in a similar way, we "see" the thoughts of people communicating from the next life. Jane and I also attempt to live moral lives that adhere to good human values and endeavor to see good, do good, and be good. But I am certainly riddled with many faults, and I am sure Jane, my family, and my friends would be extremely pleased to explain them in great detail if you cared to ask them.

According to this first reading with the Naadi, my name in this former birth was Kala Bhairava. This is a god's name, and I presume people in India took the name of gods, particularly when they followed the life of a *sannyasin*. Kala Bhairava is a Hindu deity, a fierce manifestation of Shiva associated with annihilation, so someone taking a name like this, I would presume, would be very determined to progress quickly. In this life I have a tremendous drive and energy at times, and have always felt that something pushes me onward at times when I would rather put my feet up. Perhaps Kala

Bhairava, the Lord that drives forward time, still relentlessly motivates me in this life, too, and gives me this impulsive desire not to waste a moment of this precious human life.

Kala Bhairava is a deadly form of Shiva, when he changed into a destructive mode to destroy time. All material reality exists within the flow of time, but Kala Bhairava is the aspect of Shiva between time and timelessness—like the intense moment at death when everything plays out in an instant. With Kala Bhairava's influence, the pleasures and pains of many lifetimes happen in a moment, but with such power that mortals cannot hold or retain it. It is like the ultimate suffering of Hell.

Shiva in the form of Kala Bhairava creates impossible pain, but just for a moment, so that after that, nothing of the past remains in us. According to Hinduism, this happens at the moment of death, when we can't run. At this time, and in this terrible-looking form, Shiva makes suffering as brief as possible. With this super-intensity, suffering ends quickly and does not linger forever. Kala Bhairava is a blessing in disguise, a liberator from the karma of the past.

As a personal symbol, Kala Bhairava can represent the world of a medium. Although not a life of suffering, we do often shift our consciousness to the threshold of life and death. As part of my mediumistic evidence, I always give the illness and passing conditions of the communicating spirit which, for a brief moment, I painlessly sense in my own body.

According to the leaves, in this past life I came close to liberation, but my flaw was my bad temper. My temper caused everyone a great deal of trouble, and because of this intolerance, I rejected many common people from entering the temple. The hatred and resentment felt toward me at this time have now reverberated into my present life and often prevent my getting the recognition I deserve.

Do I have a bad temper in this life? Would I empty a pot of hot tea on the floor in the restaurant of the garden center when they refused to give a refund and say, "Here, have your bloody tea back"? Would I tell my neighbor to shove it up the place where the sun never shines? Do I ever lose my rag at people who drive at 15 mph in a 50 mph speed zone? Do I ever fire a torrent of abuse at power-mad, stupid people in positions of authority or snooty old ladies who jump the queue? Not me, Your Honor!

The truth is that if someone pushes me too far, I can and do lose my temper sometimes, but this happens only when someone pushes me very hard into a corner. Intractable people who will not be reasonable or flexible get me going, as do secretive people who lie, scheme, and plot. I abhor disloyal people. I never break my word, lie, cheat, or steal, and I have very little tolerance for people who do.

At the end of this book, in the appendix, you can read the full transcript of my Naadi reading, as well as the readings I had to get confirmation or otherwise. In my second Naadi reading (Maha Sukshma Naadi), it too said I was a *rishi*, but not male as in this first one: "In his past birth, the native lived in a place named Kucherum, which is nowadays called Gujarat. The native was born in a cast named Yarava. In the previous birth, the native was born as a girl. The girl was very beautiful and was living with her parents. She was very beautiful and also very talented. The birth which is explained now is the native's fifth birth."

According to the oracle, I left my family to seek a spiritual life and nearly became a saint, but incurred the wrath of my husband and children, whose curses follow me into this life. The anger in my current life was also shown in the leaves, but as something that only affected me in early childhood.

So as you can see—and will see in more detail, if you want to read the appendix—the themes of the past-life part of the reading are similar, but also have striking differences. In other parts, the leaves were word-for-word the same and mind-bogglingly similar. Other people who have had multiple readings say that the past-life aspect of the leaves can often vary, though the details about their current life remain the same.

One of the aspects of the Indian way I like is that, despite the fact we may accumulate past karma, none of us is actually a sinner. There is no damnation or fire and brimstone in the Indian way, for rather than be told, "You're a sinner!" wouldn't it be better to be told, "You're a saint!" since one day we may give in and actually become one!

MESSAGES TO THE PEOPLE

Within Spiritualism, there have often been debates about whether mediums are born or made. I believe that it is a latent gift you have from birth, but which at some stage in your life has to be trained and disciplined to become full-blown mediumship. Unlike many Spiritualists, I believe that these spiritual skills are brought with us from former lives and are the result of intensive spiritual work. It is puzzling, however, that some mediums I have met have mediumistic skills but lack any moral compass, and some will sneer at yoga and meditation. I will often warn people that spiritual powers are not necessarily a sign of spirituality.

I have always felt that my mediumship is something that is an echo from past lives. Initially I resisted the gift and at times tried to suppress it, but it burst into my life whether I liked it or not.

The Naadi oracle tells me that new spiritual knowledge will be revealed to me by the gods—which I initially interpreted as my mediumship—and from studying the Naadis, learning astrology, and from knowledge given directly by meeting living *rishis*. My task, I am told, is to bring the message to the people. This is my purpose in life and the reason I am here. The oracle went into extraordinary personal detail about my life and my past before revealing the core messages as to why I am here—the question I had asked Sathya Sai Baba to answer. This powerful verification of the past and the future gave me faith in the fact that the future prophecies are also true.

According to my palm leaf, I have six distinct dots on the thumbprint, which reveal that my life cannot follow an ordinary path. My leaf (*patti*) is named Iru Sali Meru Reka, my guiding star is

Hastam, and I am destined—like it or not—to fulfill a spiritual fate. I am to give "messages from the universe"—which I interpret as mediumship, but which may also point to what the Vedas call *sruti*, meaning "what is heard" or "revealed knowledge." The holy texts of the Vedas are *apauruseya*, meaning "not of human agency," and are divinely revealed. So, too, are the true Naadis, which reveal God's plan on a very personal and human level.

As a medium, I am used to having the spirit world guide and influence the flow of my books, but the Naadi prophesizes that a divine influence will come into play. This will become more apparent as I begin more research into the oracle itself, complete my psychic travelogue television shows, and eventually meet a number of Himalayan masters, who will help me to complete the great work that is the purpose of my present life and the reason I have been put on Earth.

I am to share this journey with others who are open and willing to join me as fellow travelers. Sometimes this will be a literal journey with me to the places named in the oracle, and also many will join me on the inner journey that I hope this book and others will reveal to you personally. Some of this teaching is already being revealed by the spirit world through the course of my life, and more is to follow as I work with the leaves.

We had been able to arrange the reading via Skype with an English-speaking reader, so there was no need for the usual translator. When I stepped out of my home office to tell Jane how the reading went, I was unsteady on my feet and could hardly speak. I was dumbfounded by the matter-of-fact detail he was able to tell me about my life. I am no stranger to miracles and have seen amazing mediumship, and of course I spend a great deal of my life giving evidential messages from the spirit world. But this was beyond any form of clairvoyance I had seen. The reader clearly did not have "special powers." He was a nice and amicable man, but all he was doing was simply reading off the messages written on the leaves and telling me fact after fact about my life that nobody could possibly know.

To add to my bafflement, I had my life-purpose revealed, being told more or less when I would die, and given momentous tasks to perform—most of which I have not included here, for fear you will think me a spiritual megalomaniac. To clear any bad karma from the past, I am also to undertake various "remedies," consisting of various rituals, chants, and charitable acts that I am to perform at various holy sites in India or comparable sites around the world.

I stuttered out what I had been told and was pleased to see Jane's astonishment when I played her the recording. Like most people, she assumed that this had been all looked up on the Internet, but she could not explain how the reader knew very personal things about her and the family as well. I assured her that we had put extensive safeguards in place to guarantee the accuracy of the reading.

The predictions of the oracle started immediately. The oracle had correctly stated that Jane and I own a television production company. (In the original Sanskrit and ancient Tamil, phrases like this are written in odd ways, such as "business using modern means of visual communication to the masses." It is interesting that the oracle foresaw television 5,000 years ago!) A trip to Los Angeles had already been planned to make a pilot for a new TV show we were pitching to U.S. channels via some of our media contacts.

The oracle said that we should do this from June 19 onward, as this was when the astrology for this venture was most auspicious. We were, of course, hoping for success, but what we hadn't anticipated was the oracle's message that we would meet famous people who would help us with our quest. These people would eventually fund our activities, which would enable us to set up a charitable foundation that would give us a platform to demonstrate mediumship and help people to spiritually advance, as well as feeding the poor, aiding with disasters, and doing good, charitable work.

BEVERLY HILLS MEDIUMS

At the time of my first consultation with the Naadi oracle, Jane and I had a trip to the U.S. already planned and flights in place. Marina, our U.S. manager, had set up some meetings to present a program idea based around a UK TV series that we had made a few years ago titled "Our Psychic Family." In addition, we had a second idea to present, in which we set up a psychic school in the U.S. and film this as a reality-television show.

We had a loose idea of what to film and some good contacts in place. The flavor of the month at the time of pitching was a dreadful show called "Duck Dynasty," which, for British readers who have not seen it, is a pretty funny show about a Louisiana family who live for duck-hunting season. What makes the show compelling is the larger-than-life personalities and their outrageous antics. What I would call "making an ass of yourself," producers prefer to call "levity."

Anyone who knows Jane and me, or has seen us on TV, will realize that we are naturally quite outrageous and don't give a hoot about social norms and right behavior. We are natural nonconformists, even on a spiritual level, but this can cause a problem when you are trying to make a serious point on TV, since editors lap up "levity" and don't give a hoot about spiritual messages. TV is all about entertainment. The bottom line is, does it make bucks? What they wanted was another "Duck Dynasty," but this time with a psychic twist. It was clear from the start that we would have a lot of trouble convincing anyone that there was room for a thoughtful show about mediumship and clairvoyance.

A few years ago, I had hosted a popular television show about dream interpretation with a New York–based company. This show, titled "Nightmares Decoded," had me interpreting dreams, but also added a little clairvoyance, so that people would be caught off-guard and fall off their chair with surprise when I came out with things that nobody could possibly know. It was a sort of guerrilla clairvoyance. One of my favorite moments was a nightmare the subject had experienced, which I interpreted as a symbolic attempt to deal with the loss of his dead son. I made my interpretation but also added, "Was the boy's name Bailey, and have you had his name tattooed on your thigh?" The poor man nearly dropped dead on the spot, as this was information he had not told the researchers and was something I had identified by making a mediumistic connection with the spirit of Bailey.

The program makers we met in L.A. were not interested in a serious show; they wanted to see Craig and Jane acting the fool. This was the "Pope on a Skateboard" type of show that was never going to get any serious spiritual message across. We shot some excellent footage of a demonstration we did at a venue in Venice, California, which included lots of highly evidential messages and testimonials from people who were nearly wetting themselves with excitement and enthusiasm. But, again, the networks were not at that time looking for the mediumship demonstration show, as the network buyers had grown weary of worthy shows like "Crossing Over with John Edward" and "Beyond with James Van Praagh." The new mediums I'd seen on the most recent U.S. networks had brought the quality of mediumship and its presentation down very low. In my opinion, the mediums we see on today's TV are mostly interested in becoming famous, making money, and hiding behind their work.

Film and TV buyers never actually say "No" in Hollywood, just in case you come up with something hugely popular, so they can keep their options open. The bleak reality was that the uplifting and inspiring content we wanted to offer was yet again going to be sacrificed at the altar of entertainment. It never ceases to amaze me that the regulators in both the UK and the U.S. insist that the channels provide a certain amount of news and documentary, so they use "fly on the wall" and "human interest" stories to fill these slots. And as TV content is determined by how much advertising it can sell, and also costs a fortune to make, the networks are rarely willing to take risks on anything new. They just take previously successful shows and repackage them, but next time stuff in more of what they think works. It's like saying: "Sugar tastes nice in a cake. Let's stuff it with tons more sugar, and it's bound to be better."

Pitching a new show and making the sizzle reels are really expensive but also great fun. It reminded me of my days when I was the managing director and creative director of a UK advertising agency, and we had to pitch ideas to my clients—British Airways, Esso, and HSBC. Getting a great idea into production is never easy. Few people have the vision to commit to something revolutionary. They always want tried and tested and, of course, get middle-of-the-road results.

As part of the filming, Marina's contact, Jon, invited us to film some of his celebrity friends so that we could use it as part of our presentation. We were soon filming in Beverly Hills and Hollywood Hills. It struck me that this sudden opportunity had been mentioned in the oracle, which had said: "The native will get unforeseen friendship with good people and great people. The native will also get the blessings of Saint Siva Vakiya Maharishi and also the blessings of the Naadi Shashtris. By getting the blessings of Siva Vakiya Maharishi, there are a few turning points in the native's life."

Arrangements were made to film Jane and me doing one-on-one psychic consultations with Eric Roberts, the brother of Julia Roberts, star of *Pretty Woman*, *Ocean's Eleven*, *Notting Hill*, and so on. Eric, of course, is known for *King of the Gypsies*, which earned him a Golden Globe Award nomination for Best Actor Debut, and his nomination for his supporting role in *Runaway Train*. He made an incredible 150 films between 2013 and 2015, but the ones I knew and enjoyed the most were his gangster roles, such as in the Batman movie *Dark Knight*, and his various roles as a tough cop or vigilante.

The filming was done at Jon's house in Hollywood Hills. I was to give Eric a reading, and then Jane would take a turn. I'm generally pretty bad with remembering people's names or recognizing people. In the past, I'd felt a bit of a fool after chatting for ages with Patrick Swayze on the set of the "Big Breakfast" TV show and not realizing until way into our conversation that he was a film star. I really do struggle sometimes with names and faces, and I often come across as a bit of a twit when introduced to famous people.

Fortunately I knew who Eric was, but prior to the psychic sitting I didn't know anything about his off-stage life. As I opened the reading, I could feel a man draw close who had trouble breathing and swallowing, and whom I described and correctly identified as Eric's father. My feeling, though, was that there was very little love between them, but that his father's spirit desperately wanted to try and make amends.

I told Eric how his father's spirit was telling me about how he had struggled a lot in life and came from abject poverty. I explained, to verify it was him, that he was telling me how he loved the old-style movies, and in particular he was an admirer of the early film director D. W. Griffith. An important, fond memory was that they had watched *Ben-Hur* together when Eric was a child. This was a time when something important had happened, and his father at this time felt very proud of Eric. This was information that could not be researched on the Internet.

Eric confirmed that all I had said was absolutely correct. The reading continued, and I felt his father talk about the time of his death and communicate that there were many words that needed to be said but weren't. There was so much he wanted to say, and he could hardly speak, but Eric and his family held his father's hand, and he communicated by opening and closing his eyes in response to questions. In this way, he got the messages across.

To conclude, I explained that his father had read the note that Eric had put into the coffin at the end, and that it was a four-line stanza from a verse that was emotionally significant to both of them, and with it was something else. Eric explained that the note was rolled up in a ring.

Eric was very happy with the reading, though I would have liked to have told him the exact words on the note. A number of accounts, verified by newspaper articles, have included the messages I gave about things put into coffin, such as the poem "The Owl and Pussycat," a blue teddy-bear with only one eye, a china doll, and a set of false teeth because the undertaker had lost them. I was glad Eric was so pleased. "Craig hit some real accuracies about my father and our relationship," said Eric afterward. "My father came to him, and everything he said was accurate. He didn't miss a trick. And we don't know each other, and he knows nothing about me. Unless he knows an old friend, there's no way he could know the things he knew. It was very satisfying and very accurate."

Jane used a combination of the tarot cards and her clairvoyance to give her reading to Eric. Part way through, she broke off the tarot and said that she felt someone around Eric who was hesitating to come, since they needed to be healed. This was a young person who needed to say, "Sorry, please forgive me." Eric identified that as his half-sister, who had passed just recently, and who was in her mid-thirties. Jane explained that it was hard for her to communicate, as she had not been over that long, and healing needed to happen in the spirit world. Eric agreed that she would have needed a lot of healing to be done. Jane explained that there had been a lot of problems around her at the end and, in particular, jealously. Eric nodded, and he said that there was indeed a lot of jealousy surrounding her. He described a few private, family issues, which Jane had also identified. Jane picked up on self-harm, too, but explained his half-sister was happy and in a better place.

In the tarot cards, Jane "saw" that Eric's wife was a lover of the piano and very creative. Eric explained that his wife is an incredibly gifted pianist, and that her son is also an incredible musician. Jane felt that Eric and his wife had been together in a past incarnation, and that it was love at first sight when they met. Eric agreed. They are around each other 24/7, and that's how it's meant to be. "I love it!" exclaimed Eric.

Eric loved his reading with Jane, too. He said: "Jane's reading was more about me. It's about what I have or have not gone through, and what I'm like. And it was pretty accurate—not altogether positive, but accurate. I was impressed with that, and what you see here"—Eric put his hands around his face—"is not necessarily what you get. And she got that."

Eric said of our collective work: "I don't normally buy this stuff. I think it's odd and peculiar, and you can't really put your finger on this kind of thing. However, both these people, in everything they said and the stuff they talked about, were accurate. They are the real deal, and it kind of blew my mind a little bit. I'm not a mind-blower by nature, but you know it was real, and—all crap aside—it was real!"

AMERICA

Apart from family holidays, the last major media event Jane and I had done in the U.S. was in 2003 for the program we made titled "Spirit of Diana," in which we were asked to conduct a live TV séance to get messages from the spirit of Princess Diana, which you will read more about later. The show had caused an international media storm, and the producers called us to New York to promote the upcoming show.

We were a bit naive at the time and completely underestimated the media impact of the show. We had already refused a fee, as we wanted to do this for its own sake in order to prove to a wide audience that we all survive death, and that spirits can give evidential proof of survival. Of course, everyone assumed we were doing this to make loads of money. As a benefit in kind, the producers did put us up in the luxurious Plaza Hotel, with a room overlooking the snow-covered Central Park and all the steak and lobster we could eat. When we got back to the UK, it would be back to scraping around to find money for the basics.

We did a tour of the main news channels, and we were astonished at the scale of their operations. At places like the BBC in London, the studios we'd seen were comparatively small, but in New York the studio is a huge arena, with computers all around, and the host and ourselves perched in the middle. It was like entering the Roman Colosseum—and felt like it, too, when we faced the assaults from the hosts. In retrospect, perhaps we should have kicked our morals into touch and taken the money for the show.

The media tour to promote our ideas in L.A. was far more fun.

We filmed Jane and me interacting with America on Hollywood Boulevard and Muscle Beach, and we caught on camera how people reacted to our surreal humor and psychic gifts. We filmed some footage at the Beverly Hills Hotel and gave our manager, Marina, a reading in which we contacted her dead ex-husband, David Carradine—the American actor and martial artist, best known for his leading role as a Shaolin monk, Kwai Chang Caine, in the 1970s television series "Kung Fu" and in Quentin Tarantino's movie *Kill Bill*. As well as some very personal messages, which I will not quote here, Marina was given some specific personal proofs that nobody would know about, such as the fact that David gave her a unique, custom-made ring to mark their love, and that it was made from two separate rings intertwined.

Again in Hollywood Hills, we filmed us running a psychic development workshop and gave some mind-blowing demonstrations of psychometry, which saw some of the people present crying at the very deep and personal revelations about their lives and the people they knew in the spirit world.

I demonstrated how to get started with learning the art of psychometry (reading the history of a person from the vibrations embedded in objects they've owned), while Jane demonstrated how to use clairvoyance with pets. Jon and his friends owned many rescued dogs, and they were amazed at how much accurate information Jane could tell about their dogs' backgrounds and natures. She gave a few remedial measures that could be used to help sort out their feeding or behavioral problems.

To show the broad remit of our skills, Rachelle Carson and her husband, Ed Begley, Jr., invited us to their new house, which was under construction, so that we could clear the negative energy that Rachelle felt was hampering the project. Ed Begley has appeared in hundreds of films, television shows, and stage performances. He is best known for his role as Dr. Victor Ehrlich on the television series "St. Elsewhere," for which he received six consecutive Emmy Award nominations, and his most recent reality show about green living called "Living With Ed on Planet Green," which he made with Rachelle.

Ed is a dedicated environmentalist and is probably the only person in L.A. who travels everywhere on his bike—even to the Oscars. Ed and Rachelle's new house is being built as an example of how technology and specialized materials can be used to build high quality houses with a near-zero environmental footprint. Ed, of course, is also a comedian, so our attempts at the "clearance" were interspersed with banter and hilarious quips. Ed explained to Rachelle what a kitchen was and joked about her wardrobe requirements. In the end, Jane decided that it was Ed who needed clearing and, with bells and incense, chased him from the room. It all made for a amusing clip that we could use on our sizzle reels, and it was also screened on Ed and Rachelle's own show about the house.

The Naadi leaves spoke about "unexpected meetings." Perhaps one of the most startling was finding ourselves invited to the Magic Castle for a personal tour and demonstration of magic by Brooks Watchel, who does card tricks for a pastime, but in real life is an Emmy Award–winning writer. Brooks made for interesting company, particularly as he has a superb knowledge of history, and we had a mutual interest in the Fleet Air Arm, as both of our fathers had been wartime pilots.

The Magic Castle, located in the Hollywood district of Los Angeles, is a nightclub for magicians and magic enthusiasts, as well as being the clubhouse for the Academy of Magical Arts. It bills itself as "the most unusual private club in the world." You can only visit by personal invitation, and of course I made an ass of myself before we even stepped through the door. Jane was fine in her yellow, diamond-studded cocktail dress, but they have a no-jeans policy, and my trousers looked a bit "jeanish." After a frantic dash around Hollywood to find a late-night clothing store, I eventually entered red-faced, sporting cheap and impossibly tight rupture trousers. A slight saving grace was that we were soon recognized by some film producers from the UK, which restored a little of our status with our celebrity chaperones.

The castle itself is a chateauesque mansion, filled with trap doors, two-way mirrors, and secret corridors. Just about everywhere you look, there is something odd or out of place. It has a surreal, dream-like ambience. Our favorite room was the séance room, which was set up, of course, to mimic every paranormal trick you can imagine.

The Magic Castle is one of the favorite haunts of the magician and arch-skeptic James Randi. Here we were, right in the heart of the lion's den! I was surprised to discover that most of the magicians we met that night were far from skeptical about the possibility of psychic powers being real. Most felt that Randi had taken his hatred of all things paranormal far too far, and I suspect that—like his lookalike, Sigmund Freud—his debunking was more about his own emotional issues than simply a quest for the truth.

Within a week of consulting the Naadi oracle, we were mixing with and giving readings to A-list celebrities in Beverly Hills and Hollywood Hills. To our astonishment, the prophecies of the oracle were coming to pass, and many more were to follow.

THE DESTINY OF THE WORLD

The Naadi oracles also have a lot to say about the future of the world, and they foresee events that will affect all of us. Some Naadi readers are saying that recently revealed texts foresee calamitous changes, which will begin with the election of the new Indian Prime Minister, Narendra Modi, who will be the catalyst for huge economic and political change. In the near future, the Indian economy will accelerate and overtake China and other emerging powers.

They predict that in the near future India will gain political and military power and expand its borders, perhaps though the intervention in a major war in the Middle East or by invading Pakistan, Bangladesh, or Nepal. It seems unlikely that modern India—which was founded on the non-violent (*ahimsa*) teachings of Gandhi—could ever engage in a traditional war. But perhaps this will unfold in ways we cannot yet foresee, maybe by annexing failed nation-states for their own good. The oracle certainly predicts that India will become the second-most powerful nation in the world.

Recent revelations from the texts claim that following many world problems and calamitous events in the U.S. and Europe, the New Age will arise. These events are imminent, and this is the reason that the oracle is revealing its hidden truths today. The leaves are telling us that we stand at the threshold of the turning of the eons, moving from the dark times of the *Kali Yuga* to a Golden Age for mankind. Also, among the ancient Hindu scriptures, the epic *Jaimini Mahabharata* contains a detailed and complete account of Bhagavan Sri Sathya Sai Baba. It mentions the name of the *avatar*, and it contains a full account of his dynasty and descriptions of several wonderful miracles performed by him. It describes how he will reform religion along the lines of the *Satya Yuga*. The Upanishads also speak of a Golden Age that will be initiated by the descent of God in three consecutive incarnations over a period of 250 years.

If everything in our lives remained the same and nothing ever changed, it would soon become suffocating and boring. Some think they are safe by having little or no change in their lives, but this sort of person invariably becomes psychologically and spiritually weak. Simply grazing through life, like sheep moving from one patch of grass to another, is the lot of many uninspired souls. But their sense of security is misguided, since illness, misfortune, and death stalk even the most placid of beings. They know this, of course, and this is why, behind the comfy world in which they live, there resonates fear.

We often feel fear in our lives when our spiritual energy is not flowing, or life situations have become inert. From a spiritual standpoint, fear is a concentration of negative thoughts, just as worry is unfocused and scattered thoughts. Both inhibit our life-force and can stop us achieving our potential, or they may even attract misfortune and destroy our body through illness.

What we fear the most is time, for time brings change and eventually death. It is time that creates and destroys the material world. There is no security in the world, for at any point we may be forced to give up everything and exit the physical body. Only the soul is everlasting, but few people today know this as an absolute certainty.

When we consider the vastness of time and space, our human condition appears even more vulnerable. It makes you dizzy to think that it is 13.8 billion years since the Big Bang, and that the universe may continue to expand forever into a thin, freezing wasteland, or it may be pulled back by gravity into a singularity for a "Big Crunch," followed by another "Big Bang," expanding and contracting like a cosmic heartbeat for eternity.

As yet, science does not have an answer to how long the universe will continue, since there are still many things to discover about material reality before we can agree on a definitive model. Theories propose that the universe may bang, crunch, rip, or bounce, or that it may even be part of an infinite number of expanding regions called the multiverse.

Compared to the vastness of material reality, our worries about change, time, and death are miniscule. Einstein recognized our place in this cosmic order when he said, "The most important decision we make is whether we believe we live in a friendly or hostile universe." In other words, if we live in fear of reality, we will have a miserable life, but if we believe the universe is benign, then we will move forward.

Our existence is a mystery that we cannot understand, so it is best to accept this and simply move with time. Death, too, throws up questions that cannot be answered—at least from a material standpoint—but it does prompt us to grapple with the big questions and thereby become more self-aware. If it turns out that we live in a heartless, material universe, it is nonetheless psychologically healthy to simply accept this fact and move forward without fear.

The mystics—and particularly the yogis of India—approached the cosmic questions from a completely different standpoint. To the mystic, everything—including matter and the whole of existence—is consciousness. Consciousness alone exists. If we come to the center of our being, say the mystics, we discover that we are the *atman*—pure, infinite consciousness.

Our very nature is sublimely blissful and boundless, and it is the ultimate reality. All is One. Everything is consciousness and can be accessed by our own, individual awareness. Armed with this knowledge, the ancient seers looked within to discover the secrets of the universe and found things that science is only now beginning to uncover.

The Vedic holy books contain many ideas that are very close to modern quantum science. Some have claimed that the Vedas contain lost scientific knowledge, as there are many concepts within them that are strikingly similar to the theories we have about dark matter, parallel universes, string theory, and the Higgs boson. In fact, J. R. Oppenheimer—the theoretical physicist who is often referred to as the father of the atomic bomb—quoted the *Bhagavad Gita* soon after he saw the first bomb detonate at the Trinity test in New Mexico on July 16, 1945: "Now I am become Death, the destroyer of worlds."

Although born a Jew, he was inspired by Vedic philosophy. While giving a lecture at Rochester University, he was asked by a student if the bomb that exploded at Alamogordo was the first one to be detonated. Oppenheimer replied: "Well—yes, in modern times, of course."

It has been suggested that Oppenheimer was making reference to the Brahma Astra weapon mentioned in the *Mahabharata* and a number of Puranas. Legends say that this weapon never missed its mark and would completely annihilate an enemy, causing vast environmental damage. The land would become barren and cracked, as in times of drought, and men and women from the affected area would become infertile. It was considered a weapon of last resort.

Oppenheimer may have noticed that what he read in the India holy texts corresponded to an atomic explosion. These "mythological" events happened in eons gone by, at a time when mankind had access to extraordinary spiritual powers. The Sanskrit text says that the Brahma Astra is obtained by meditation on the infinite creation (Brahma) and is invoked by using a key phrase (probably a mantra). The texts may be telling us about a spiritual power that mankind once had, which had power akin to that of the atomic bomb.

The American seer Edgar Cayce had similar visions of a past age that could alter the world by the power of the mind, and in 1871 the mystical writer Edward Bulwer-Lytton, in his book *The Coming Race*, claimed that the ancients harnessed a mysterious power called "Vril," which had the power to make aircraft fly.

If all is consciousness, as the mystics say, then maybe our own personal consciousness has the key to unlock greater power than we have ever imagined. The lost knowledge of the ancients may be their ability to manipulate the level of conscious we call matter with their transcendental awareness. Perhaps also—as the Naadi oracle proved to me—they also had the power to see through time.

The Vedic science made its discoveries by looking within rather than by the repeatable experimentation of Western science. In ancient times, just as we may have had miraculous spiritual powers, so too did the ancients have access through their meditations to the secrets of the universe.

THE YUGAS

Written in my Naadi leaves, it says that these messages are sent to me from 5,000 years ago, which in the Hindu tradition is the time of the *Dvapara Yuga*. Hindu teachings tell us that civilization has been around far longer than the archeologists tell us, and that in ancient times there existed a spiritual value system called the *sanatana dharma*—the eternal knowledge. In one talk by Sathya Sai Baba, he says that the stories about the god Rama took place 30,000 years ago—suggesting that human civilization and the Hindu teachings are far older than we can imagine, and perhaps confirming the theories of archaeologist Graham Hancock, who claims that a great civilization existed in the Indus valley that pre-dated the last Ice Age.

Hindu cosmology takes its teachings from these ancient insights, which were intuitively received, deal with events over vast tracts of time and have many correspondences with modern cosmology. From the ancient teachings, we can learn about the spiritual knowledge of the past and gain an understanding of the way the future of the world will unfold.

In Hindu cosmology, vast tracts of time are measured in huge cycles called *kalpas* (cosmic rounds), *mahayugas* (great ages) and *yugas* (ages). Each great age is divided into four smaller periods: *Satya Yuga* (Golden Age), *Treta Yuga* (Silver Age), *Dvapara Yuga* (Bronze Age), and *Kali Yuga* (Dark Age). As you may surmise from the calamities of history, we are currently living in the *Kali Yuga*, but as time in the universe is like a great wheel, each age returns in an eternal cycle. In traditional Hindu beliefs, the Dark Age of *Kali Yuga* will eventually transform into the Golden Age of *Satya Yuga*. The names of the four *yugas* of time are named after "dice throws" from a game of dice popular during the Vedic period. Their order coincides with the favorability of each throw: Satya is the best throw, whereas Kali is the worst.

In each *yuga*, *dharma* (or "righteousness") is either dominant or weak. Righteousness is symbolized by a bull that stands on all four legs through the Golden Age of *Satya Yuga*, three in *Treta Yuga*, two in *Dvapara Yuga*, and, in our age of *Kali Yuga*, righteousness stands with just one leg. Righteousness was so well established in the last Golden and Silver Ages that there was no need to build temples, wage wars, or write religious scriptures. In those times, people lived differently, had no need of cities, and because they left such a light footprint on the Earth, this may account for why archeologists find it hard to discover evidence for advanced prehistoric civilizations except through legends, verbal traditions, and holy texts. Legend has it that mankind only began building and writing things down in the *Dvapara* and *Kali Yugas*.

In the *Satya Yuga*, mankind cherished meditation and was without wickedness and deceit. The people of this age experienced spirituality by direct realization of truth, and there was very little distinction between the material and spiritual worlds. The nature of reality was different. There was no need to write ideas in books, as people were God-conscious, had direct access to the Akashic Records, and could communicate with one another by telepathy. When times deteriorated into the *Treta Yuga*, mankind lost some of their spiritual gifts but still retained great mental powers and inventiveness. With the coming of the *Dvapara Yuga*, there was a dramatic decline in righteousness, and divine intellect ceased to exist. People became deceitful, while living standards increased. Instead of living for thousands of years, people's lifespans were now shorter, as people were filled with cravings and diseases. Despite these problems, inventiveness still flourished, and people continued to understand and harness subtle energies. This was the time of the events described in the great *Mahabharata* epic, when Krishna walked the earth.

The *Kali Yuga* in which we now live is said to have begun on January 23, 3102 B.C., and is known as the "Age of Darkness" because ignorance and evil are the dominant conditions. Most people in this *yuga* are materialistic and only interested in worldly things, sexual lust, and survival. Society's spiritual life is dogged by superstition and the misguided authority of religion. In the *Bhagavata* and *Vishnu Puranas*, it is described how the world's leaders will become unreasonable and no longer consider it their duty to promote spirituality and good values. They will not protect their subjects, will feud with others, and will levy unfair taxes. In *Kali Yuga*, desperate and starving people will migrate from the lands of their birth to countries where wheat and barley form the staple food source. In these times, most real gurus will be overlooked, and many spiritual imposters will claim to teach the truth.

In this book, I will be telling you more about my life and work as a medium, as well as more about my interest in the Naadi readings. Hopefully I can help lead you from darkness into light, but I would also be horrified if people reading this book rush off and consult Indian Naadi holders who may misguide them. The true Naadi readers are aware that in the age of Kali, even these sacred texts can be influenced by the negative influences of this *yuga*. The Naadi reader himself can fall under the spell of this Dark Age and miss the true purpose of the oracle, which is to discover the divinity within. They are usually spiritually inclined people but are not enlightened beings, so are susceptible. Readings cannot be 100% accurate, as we live in the world of *maya*—illusion.

Your own mindset can also influence the reading. If you seek answers to questions through the Naadi with a cynical heart and bad intent, then the Naadi will lead you on a road to disappointment and trouble. You have been warned!

The good news is that today *Kali Yuga* is on the wane, and the Golden Age is gradually dawning. The movement of the great wheel of the *yugas* brings about many radical changes in the world, and with them will come a fundamental change in human consciousness. Many cosmically aware people are already noticing the changes in the energy. One apparent change is the fact that clandestine and hidden evils are beginning to be revealed as the light of consciousness re-enters the world.

In recent times, we see corrupt financial and political institutions uncovered for their fraud and deceptions, we see celebrities revealed for their rotten values, and we see pedophiles exposed in the Catholic Church, within our most cherished charities, and in the media world. There will be much more to come, as the turning of the age will reveal all that is corrupt and clandestine. Sathya Sai Baba describes the coming new time as one when "falsehood will fail, truth will triumph, and virtue will reign. Character will confer power, then—not knowledge, nor inventive skill, nor wealth. Wisdom will be enthroned in the councils of the nations."

When the tides of the *yugas* turn, there will inevitably be some adjustments that could cause problems in the world. The outgoing and incoming tides move against each other, but inevitably the new, incoming tide will predominate. Nostradamus and others have seen this as a series of cataclysmic events, but perhaps the world has already experienced some of the worst events and—as other prophets foretell—we are soon to enter a much happier epoch of history.

It is my belief that the conscious universe does not necessarily reveal to prophets all that will happen, but only what we need to know right now, just as the Naadi oracle on a personal level told me only what I needed to know about my life path and destiny. I have to make my destiny happen, just as we collectively have to bring about a better future for the world. The tide is turning, but we can hasten its arrival by our own efforts.

The timing for the coming of the Golden Age is a puzzle. The traditional Hindu cycle says that *Satya Yuga* lasts 1,728,000 years, the *Treta Yuga* 1,296,000 years, the *Dvapara Yuga* 864,000 years, and the *Kali Yuga* 432,000 years. A complete cycle lasts 4,320,000 years, a period of time which is known as a *mahayuga* or "great eon." One thousand *mahayugas* are said to constitute a day in the life of the creator god Brahma, also known as a *kalpa*, which is the fundamental cosmic cycle in Hinduism. Some people's Naadi leaves, and a Vedic scripture titled the *Bhavishya Purana*, say that there will be a 10,000-year respite during the time of *Kali Yuga*—that a temporary Golden Age, which appears like a flower in the desert, will bloom very soon. This period is called the *Golokarohanam* in the *Brahmavaivarta Purana*, and it is described as the time in which Krishna returns to his abode. After this period of respite, the *Kali Yuga* will return with full force.

Swami Sri Yukteswar has proposed a different model for the cycle of the *yugas* and says that we are in the process of entering not the *Satya Yuga*, but a second age of *Dvapara Yuga*, which will be a time of less materialism, greater spiritual awareness, expanding consciousness, and harmony between peoples. This will also be an age of "energy and nature"—a time when we harness unlimited energy from a source such as cold fusion, zero-point energy, or a hitherto undiscovered form of quantum energy. Some call the *Dvapara* the "Electrical Age" and say that advances in modern computing technology are just the first baby-steps toward huge leaps in our capabilities. We are—right now—close to cracking quantum computing, which makes direct use of quantum-mechanical phenomena, such as superposition and entanglement, to perform operations on data. This could completely revolutionize computing and make some technology, such as password encryption, obsolete. On a spiritual level, we will understand the subtle energy of consciousness.

Swami Sri Yukteswar was considered one of the greatest astrologers of his time, and in 1894 he spotted a flaw in the traditional Hindi almanacs. With this knowledge, was able to recalculate the exact dating of the changes of the *yugas*. He considered it ironic that in *Kali Yuga*—the age of ignorance—even the knowledge of the ending of ignorance should be lost to mankind. Swami Sri Yukteswar suggests that since no one at the time wanted to announce the bad news of the ascent of *Kali Yuga*, the astrologers fixed the charts to postpone the date of the ending of *Dvapara*. The move out of the Iron/Kali Age of ignorance began during the period between A.D. 1600 and 1900, and we now move ever into the next age. As this happens, serfdom and slavery fall, and there is a rise in democracy and humanitarianism, as well as a flowering of our inventiveness. We will become free from the bondage of religious beliefs and gain direct spiritual experience of the divine within us.

Many great cultures share the idea that there are ages of man, and similar ideas to the *yugas* can be found in the cultures of the ancient Egyptians, ancient Greeks, Aztecs, Sumerians, Persians, and the Norse people. Many of these ancient traditions may have a common source, passed down by the *rishis* (illuminated sages) from the previous Golden Age (*Satya Yuga*) through the traditions of Hinduism, the architecture of places such as Stonehenge and the pyramids of Giza, and through oracles such as the Naadis.

Sri Yukteswar's disciple Paramhansa Yogananda tells us that we will think differently in the coming age. Rather than creating ideas though effort, great minds will simply tune in to the universe, and the concept of "received knowledge" will again become the norm. In the future, there will be super-savants who simply know the answers to what we need to know, without having to calculate or reason to get to the answers.

This new knowledge will come through freedom of thought, making democratic countries such as India, Europe, and the United States the driving forces for material and—more importantly—spiritual change. Yogananda goes on to tell us that the present-day material success of the United States is a karmic blessing of its religious founders. It could be argued that the colonial and empire-building nations of Europe may today be paying for their exploitation of other races through excessive immigration, cultural break-down, and seeing manufacturing and wealth move to the countries they once exploited.

Many great astrologers and philosophers have been preparing mankind for the next great turn of the *yuga* wheel. Known better for his political values and less for his keen interest in astrology, Benjamin Franklin was one of these, and he may also have been aware of America's spiritual destiny. He devoted much of his life to astrology and, in 1733, at the age of twenty-seven, and for the next twenty-six years, he published an astrological almanac. It has been argued that the Declaration of Independence on the Fourth of July, 1776, was chosen because it was a particularly auspicious alignment of the then-known planets (excluding Uranus and Neptune). The quadruple parallels of the sun, Jupiter, Mars, and Venus are taken by some astrologers to represent victory in war. The grand trine in the traditional horoscope for this date shows that the country will be stable and—without my going into great planetary detail—it was all, basically, pretty bad for the British. Similarly, the ratification of the United States constitution on June 21, 1788, has a triple parallel of the sun, Jupiter, and Mercury, which some astrologers interpret to symbolize "laws that are equitable and just."

As a follower of Sathya Sai Baba, I am inspired by what he has to say about the upcoming Golden Age: "So, in your lives, by your examples, live and practice my message, knowing that some will understand, and others will not. Have no concern with the outcome of your efforts, for some people are ready, and others are not. Each one is free to go his own way, in his own time. Many will choose to remain in darkness with all the attachments that hold them back from the true path. But, eventually, their time will come and, one day, all will be reunited in the Kingdom of God."

This suggests to me that the dawning of the New Age also has something to do with an inner transformation, and that some will realize *Satya Yuga* before others. People assume that the age of *Satya Yuga* is all about seeing our material world transformed into a utopian society, but this, I think, is only part of the answer. The external world is just *maya*—illusion. The only true reality is what is within us; the true reality is consciousness. It may be the case that the dawn of the New Age will come first from an inner transformation of the minds and hearts of people like you, who are reading this book and hoping for a better world. Sathya Sai Baba also said: "Today the seeds are still in the ground, slowly germinating, as the teachings of the Lord begin to spread throughout the world and infiltrate the mind of man. Soon, those seeds will begin to grow, and what emerges will brighten the world as the beauty of the absolute truth begins to reach so many people. It is a process which takes time, and the new Golden Age will evolve gradually."

I believe that the goal of human evolution is higher consciousness. We will attain a state that some call Divinity, and we will have control over the material world without the need for science and engineering. The *Satya Yuga* is not something that just happens "out there" in the world, but happens "in here"—inside our spirit, mind, and soul. Through the bridge of the inner "third eye," all the worlds can become one. Sathya Sai Baba explains to us how the new era will dawn through our own God-realization: "So you should live in hope. . . . Let the Divinity within shine forth and become one of the great beacons to light up the world and hasten the arrival of the new Golden Age. It is there now for some, those enlightened souls who have already reached the state of God-realization. It is that awakened state that will lead to the New Age."

If we think of the Golden Age as something that is going to happen to the world in, say, a hundred years' time, then it's not that important. If we feel it will arrive next year, then we will have a greater sense of urgency, and we will put tasks in place and start doing spiritual work on ourselves in preparation for this change. If we knew for certain that the Golden Age starts tomorrow, there would be a huge mind-shift, and we'd probably be clamoring to make immediate changes to ourselves. But what if we discovered that the Golden Age is already here and has been here for some time? You'd open your eyes to recognize it!

There has never been a better time to attain Self-realization. The important thing is that we all start to practice spirituality, and those with a spiritual mindset should actively start to lead the world toward awakening—to embody love and live in love. If we find our spiritual path, then everything else we are looking for will fall into place. This is when the Golden Age has dawned within you.

MEGALITHS AND NAZIS

The *Kali Yuga* times have been an oppressive period in history in which powerful and evil forces have cast their shadow over the world. According to Sathya Sai Baba, the *Kali Yuga* began December 20, 3102 B.C., which was the date of the death of Krishna, the eighth *avatar* of Vishnu.

The Naadi leaves are claimed to have been written in the era before *Kali Yuga*, and in my leaves it says: "His birth star is Hastam. His moon sign is Kanya, that is Virgo. Palm leaf manuscript was not written in the current *yuga*—that is *Kali Yuga*—but it was written in *Dvapara Yuga*—that is the previous *yuga*. Saint Shiva Vakiyam Maharishi, being in the state of meditation, and through intuition, and when Goddess Parvathi and Lord Shiva conversed, the saint got the *gnaynum*—that is divine spiritual knowledge—and wrote this manuscript."

If the Naadi tradition really does date back to before 3102 B.C., and if some of the people of these times had these incredible powers of clairvoyance, then surely we must look at these times in awe and wonder what other powers the people of these times possessed. When Jane and I recently visited the Ggantija megalithic temple complex on the island of Gozo, Malta, I sat on one of the large standing stones, immersed in the wonder of what had once been. The megaliths are the world's oldest extant, unburied, free-standing structure and the world's oldest religious structure. Theses temples are older than the pyramids of Egypt, erected during the Neolithic Age (c. 3600–2500 B.C.), making them 5,500 years old and the world's second-oldest manmade religious structures, after Gobekli

Tepe in Turkey. And yet unlike my local megaliths at Stonehenge, you can still touch the stones at Ggantija and, for a moment, as I sat looking out across the big landscape beneath the glorious blue Mediterranean sky, I felt connected to the residual energies of these ancient times. In your bones, you can tell that these were spiritually awake times—not just times of savagery and hardship, but times when people had the space to experiment with "divine spiritual knowledge" through meditation, and I suspect also the hallucinogenic mushrooms that may have grown there when the climate was wetter. I had visions of rituals from the *Dvapara Yuga* involving fire and water under a clear night sky, similar perhaps to the ancient Vedic fire rituals of *agnihotra* (also known as *yagya*, *havan*, and *homa*) that have been used to transform energies and attract good fortune since the times of the *rishis*.

A few days before, we'd also visited the Hagar Qim and Mnajdra temples atop a hill on the southern edge of the island of Malta, on a ridge capped in soft globigerina limestone. The temples stand on what is now a stark Mediterranean garrigue of low, soft-leaved scrubland, but may once have been a far lusher environment. From our visit to the 500,000-year-old Ghar Dalam caves earlier that day, and its adjoining museum full of fossil bones of dwarf elephants, hippopotami, micro-mammals, and birds, we saw that this area had been very different in ancient times, and had been populated by humans for 10,000 years. Perhaps this place, and the Naadi oracles too, were part of the "mother culture" from which the archeologist

Graham Hancock believes all ancient historical civilizations sprang.

If the Naadi writers of India had insight into past, present, and future, these people too must have shared similar knowledge and, in particular, a knowledge of astrology. At the Mnajdra temple, there is evidence of astrological alignment with equinoxal sunrises, and square holes in the stones allow the sunlight to mark the position of the rising sun on the first day of spring and autumn (the equinoxes) and the first day of summer and winter (the solstices).

Why was it that, in the times before *Kali Yuga*, people expended so much time and resources to know about the equinoxes, solstices, and the positions of the moon, sun, and planets? I can understand that it would be very useful to know the seasons for planning crops, predicting animal migrations, foreseeing annual floods, or seasonal activities, and that someone who knew the exact timing of an eclipse would have tremendous power over people's imaginations. But did the ancients discover something real in astrology that was far more potent than anything we have ever imagined? If an ancient seer could look thousands of years ahead, identify my thumbprint and name, and describe with pinpoint accuracy the story of my life, then what other things could the magicians and astrologers of these times have seen? Just as the Naadis offered remedies in the form of rituals for my personal troubles, so also these temples, I believe, were designed for ritualistic remedies to mitigate the troubles of their age, and they may have the power to help our times, too.

Echoes of our fall from the Golden Ages of spirituality reverberate in myths such as Biblical story of the Fall from the garden of Eden. According to the maverick archeologist, Graham Hancock, there existed a civilization tens of thousands of years ago that was wiped out 12,800 years ago when the glaciers of Antarctica were hit by a fractured comet. The resulting floods washed away these civilizations and their unique knowledge. Could it be that these civilizations knew things about astrology that we can hardly imagine?

When I was a young man, touring Europe with no money and a rucksack on my back, I visited the Parthenon in Athens, with a whole day to spare, and was able to sit and meditate for a number of hours in a relatively quiet spot in the ruins. (Today the place is swarming with tourists.) In my meditations, I soaked in the vibrations and tried to attune myself to the vibrations of the place. This is the 2,500-year-old apotheosis of ancient Greek architecture, but it was also a spiritually charged place which, I strongly felt, had a connection with Indian lunar astrology and was oriented according to the heliacal rising of Venus. This could be just my own fantasy, of course, since there is no evidence to support this notion, but it's out there now, and maybe someone would like to investigate this idea. Historians say that Athenians set its orientation without any calculation by looking at the position of the sun as it rose behind the mountains on the day of the foundation of the temple. But I feel that the building has a special significance that is yet to be discovered. I had a similar feeling when, more recently, Jane and I visited the Valley of the Temples in Agrigento, Sicily.

The Greeks were certainly in contact with ancient India, and this link with the West was most firmly established when Alexander the Great marched the Macedonian army to an unsuccessful invasion of India. He brought back with him the yogi Kalyana (called "Kalanos" by the Greeks.) On a pre-stated day, at Susa in Persia, Kalanos gave up his aged body by entering into an open pyre in presence of the amazed Macedonian army. He had no fear of pain or death. Kalanos embraced his close friends before leaving for his cremation but apparently shunned Alexander, to whom he simply remarked: "I shall see you later in Babylon." A year later, Alexander left Persia and died in Babylon. The Indian guru's prophecy was his way of saying that he would be with Alexander in this life and the next.

There are other ancient oracles that reference times of superhuman intuition and astrological knowledge from great antiquity. Legends about the *I Ching* (or *Yijing*) oracle from China claim that it was designed by the first emperor, Fu Xi (or Fu Hsi), who is said to have had a miraculous birth as a divine being with a serpent's body, and lived in the twenty-ninth century B.C. I am struck how the knowledge of the *I Ching* is, like that of the Naadi, a "received" knowledge, which was discovered through the intuition, spirit communication, observing nature, and looking to the "symbols hanging down from Heaven." In the *Ta Chuan*, translated by Stephen Karcher, it says: "In antiquity, Fu Hsi ruled the world we live in. He looked up and saw the symbols hanging down from Heaven. He looked down and saw the patterns on the Earth. He saw markings on birds and animals, and the places where they lived on the Earth. He drew on what was near within his body. He drew on what was far. He spontaneously brought forth the Eight Diagrams to connect with the bright spirits and to categorize the natures of the myriad things. He was the first to use Change to help the people."

I have worked with the *I Ching* throughout my life, and I know that it can give startling insights in my life, and is a means of understanding and influencing future events.

We find other references to the same lost knowledge in Indian astrology. The earliest treatise on Jyotish astrology, the *Bhrigu Samhita*, dates from the Vedic era. The sage Bhrigu is one of the *saptarishi*, the seven sages who assisted in the creation of the universe. Written on pages of tree bark, the *Samhita* ("compilation") is said to contain five million horoscopes, comprising all who have lived in the past or will live in the future. My guess is that the ancient sages had omnipresent consciousness, which could see the future of individuals and mankind, and they coded these insights into ancient astrology so that we could find remedies to help us counter evil. Modern astrology has lost most of this knowledge, but there remain traces of these omniscient insights in the Naadis.

Just before the beginning of the *Kali Yuga*, and around the time of the building of the temples I was looking at in Malta, the sage Markandeya recorded a conversation he had with the god Vishnu. In the *Mahabharata* texts, it is recorded that Vishnu spoke of a time during the darkest period of the *Kali Yuga* when human values would deteriorate, violence and injustice would be widespread, falsehood would triumph over truth, and oppression and crime would be prevalent. Vishnu told us not to worry, for during these dark times he would take a human birth and help the world to a brighter future. The coming of this great redeemer of the world is also predicted in many holy books, including the book of Revelation, the prophecies of Nostradamus, and the ancient Persian manuscript of the prophet Zoroaster. The *Shuka Naadi Granthi* leaves also containing detailed prophecies of the Kalki *avatar*, written on hundreds of palm leaf manuscripts by the sage Shuka over 5,000 years ago. Sathya Sai Baba may be the *avatar* mentioned in these prophecies, and I will talk about this later in the book.

In this age of darkness, most pompous scientists consider astrology to be bunkum and dismiss it, but throughout history, and in recent times, astrology and occultism have been used to influence world events. Nostradamus predicted that there would be three Antichrists, which occultists generally agree were Napoleon

Bonaparte, Adolph Hitler, and the third—open to heated debate—was either Alexander the Great, Nero, Stalin, Pol Pot, or Osama Bin Laden. Some say the third Antichrist is yet to come.

(I interpret the word "Antichrist" as someone who is anti-spirit, an arch-materialist who is against all spirituality, including the religion of Christianity. There is a difference between the name Jesus and his honorific title "Christ." According to the teacher Paramahansa Yogananda, Jesus not only knew yoga, but he also taught God-realization to his closest disciples. The word "Christ" refers to the "vast Christ-consciousness, the omniscient intelligence of God, omnipresent in every part and particle of creation.")

It is alleged that a form of dark magic was used by Napoleon to push forward his rise to power and conquest of Europe. Coming from Corsica, he was deeply superstitious and believed in destiny, which, as his father recorded, was "written in the sky." His first wife, Josephine, was also interested in the occult and used the tarot to predict the outcome of battles. Before setting off for France and her first marriage, she had her fortune told, and it predicted that she would eventually "become more than the Queen of France."

On May 26, 1805, at Milan Cathedral, Napoleon crowned himself King of Italy by placing the Iron Crown of Lombardy on his own head. This was the iron crown that was once worn by Charlemagne, and it is said to be partly made from the nails of the crucifixion of Jesus. When Napoleon conquered Egypt, he took with him a large number of historians, astronomers, and archeologists, and he had a deep fascination for the Great Pyramid, which many believe is an oracle in the form of a monument, which foretells the future. Napoleon requested to be left alone in the King's Chamber, where he is reported to have had a vision that shocked him terribly—so terribly that he refused to discuss it and ordered that the incident never be spoken of again. On his deathbed, a friend asked him to tell him the secret of that day, and it seemed as if Napoleon was ready to confess but changed his mind, and he said: "No. What's the use? You'd never believe me."

Astrology and occultism also influenced the Second World War, and the Nazis wittingly summoned the satanic powers of *Kali Yuga* and used dark magic to shape history. Just as the ancient seers used their intuition, spiritual energies, and astrology to help mankind, in the age of *Kali Yuga*, evil people use magic and psychic insight to seek personal power. No group of people more aptly symbolize the "great evil" seen in the prophecies of the world, and actively engaged in black occult arts, than the Nazis.

The Nazis believed in a former Golden Age, when there existed an Arian civilization on the island of Thule, which legend claims once existed in the frozen wastes of the far North. They believed that here existed a utopian society in which blond, blue-eyed, vegetarian Nordics ruled over the first human civilizations. Could this have been the same lost civilization described by Graham Hancock, which was destroyed 12,800 years ago when the glaciers of Antarctica were hit by a comet?

The Nazis, however, were not looking to restore spirituality to mankind, but saw these ancient myths as an excuse to impose their racism and arrogant dictatorship on the world. They would restore the pure Arian genes from the times of Thule and exterminate anyone they believed was from inferior stock. The Thulists were a strange, occult group that used the powers generated by black magic, human sacrifice, and sexual perversions to gain power and influence.

Hitler, in a peyote-induced vision in 1911, experienced a past-life regression that revealed he was the black magician Klingsor from the story of Parsifal, and before that he had former births as the Roman emperor Tiberius and Bernard of Barcelona—another black magician and the betrayer of Christianity to the Arabs. Hitler was the Antichrist of the *Kali Yuga*, foreseen by Nostradamus as the person who would bring calamity to the world. Hitler immersed himself in occult teachings and sent out expeditions to find holy relics and twist their energy to a new purpose.

His first triumph was to take the Spear of Destiny from the Weltliches Schatzkammer Museum in Vienna after annexing Austria in 1938. This was the spear from the lance used by the Roman soldier Longinus to pierce the side of Jesus of Nazareth several hours into the crucifixion. Connected to the spear was a prophecy that "whoever claims it and solves its secrets holds the destiny of the world in his hands, for good or evil." After the war, it was retrieved by General Patton, together with two other lances that claimed to be the Spear of Destiny. Carbon-dating shows that the spear that now sits in the museum in Vienna is a fake, and some say that the true spear remains in the hands of the Americans, with some broken-off fragments in Saint Peter's Basilica in Vatican City.

Together with Himmler, who was equally fascinated by satanic arts, Hitler and the Nazis sent expeditions to find the Holy Grail and other artifacts in Tibet and India. They connected with the Tibetan black magicians of the oracle Agarthi to find the *lapis exillis*—a powerful magical stone once held in the lost city of Shambhala, which some claim was the Holy Grail. The oracle of Agarthi sought to create false leadership in all nations of the world and to keep men in ignorance.

The Second World War saw magic being used to influence the course of the events, with black masses conducted for an elite S.S. corps at the "Black Camelot" in Wewelsburg. Here a satanic coven of thirteen initiates, presided over by Himmler, tried to connect to the "Racial Soul" and evoke the help of satanic entities. All S.S. members had to participate in various magical ceremonies designed by Himmler, based on the old Teutonic worship of Woden. Himmler also substituted the summer solstice as the chief "holy day." For S.S. members, services of marriage, baptism, and burial were performed not by the clergy but by the local S.S. commander.

The Nazis are a good personification of the demon Kali and the *Kali Yuga*, but this age is also blighted with many other vile expressions of these corrupt values. The few examples I have given are just a few of the thousands of accounts of Nazi involvement with magic and the occult. The Allies, too, got involved, with Stalin and Churchill also employing psychic advisors—including talks with Aleister Crowley—to anticipate Hitler's likely plans and the advice he would most likely receive from astrologers, mediums, and occultists. At the same time, there was a continued interest in Spiritualism in the UK, with physical mediums such as Helen Duncan giving messages from the spirit world about the war. The most controversial was that she materialized the full form of a sailor, with the name "H.M.S. Barnham" on his cap—a ship which the English government denied had been sunk. She was arrested and jailed as a spy and a witch. One of the most famous proponents of Spiritualism at the time was Air Chief Marshal Lord Dowding, who oversaw Fighter Command for the Battle of Britain and was one of the key people to help defeat Hitler.

Kali Yuga is a time of world wars, famine, mad dictators, pedophile clergymen, nuclear arms, inequality, diseases, pollution, crime, violence, catastrophes, and a general rise in selfishness and decline in morality. It has been a time of war between the forces of light and dark; between human values and the powers of greed, egotism, and sadism. The battles have been fought in both the material world and the spiritual plane, and the world continues to fall under the shadow of Kali. But eventually the times will change and—as the oracles foresee—there will be a brighter and happier time ahead and, for some people, it may already be here.

But is there a quick way out from the trials of Kali Yuga? One group of people that may have the answer are the Hare Krishna Movement that we will look at in the next section.

HARE KRISHNA!

My first encounter with the Hare Krishna movement happened when I was a teenager in the 70s. I visited the first London temple at 7 Bury Place, near the British Museum. As part of their ritual before *satsang* (a meeting for discussion), they poured a little blessed milk into my palm and asked me to drink it. It was only afterwards that they said, "This milk has been used to wash the feet of our beloved guru."

"Ahhhgggghh!!!!!" my friends and I exclaimed in unison, as we spat it out and searched for a little water to rinse our mouths. "You could have bloody well told us before we drank it!" Not a good start, and we were deliberately exaggerating our reaction. The followers I've met usually are intelligent, certainly very devoted, and occasionally—it has to be said—a bit mixed up.

During a trip to India, we stayed briefly at the Hare Krishna ashram at Mayapur, eighty miles north of Calcutta. The Mayapur complex was certainly very impressive in its scale and architectural accomplishment, but this was not a place that touched my soul. During the early morning *aarati*, the Hare Krishna devotees danced around, waving their hands in the air, and chanting the Hare Krishna mantras. I joined in—when in Rome and all that—but with not quite the same enthusiasm as I enjoyed with the *bhajans* and mantras at other settings. Perhaps I was just too, too tired from so many days and nights of nail-biting travel; perhaps devotional singing was not for me; but here I felt like an alien. At the climax of the chanting, plush, red velvet curtains drew back to reveal a huge, brightly colored statue of Krishna, surrounded by eight *gopi* girls. It was all a bit "over the top" and in Disneyesque bad taste. I giggled at the surrealistic nature of this moment when it struck me that this was like worshiping super-dolls housed in a giant, glitzy Barbie House.

John Lennon had his doubts about the International Society for Krishna Consciousness (ISKCON) and certainly didn't hold his punches when he met A.C Bhaktivedanta Swami Prabhupada, the then leader of the movement. He did not easily accept the authority and "say so" of gurus, and the published transcripts of the meetings often show Lennon in what I read as a sarcastic tone of voice—particularly when he is advised that he should study the *Gita* in the original Sanskrit. "Study Sanskrit? Oh, now you're talking."

Swami Prabhupada did, however, make a deep impression on George Harrison, whose life and spiritual merits are a good example of the values he discovered through Krishna, so I clearly do not want to appear disparaging of what, to some, is an important spiritual path, but one I feel is not mine—even though I wear the same *shikha* ponytail haircut as a Krishna devotee. Tradition dictates that anyone who recites Vedic mantras should not have hair on face or head, and they are advised to remove their hair. Mine fell out anyway, so a cosmic ponytail seemed like a good idea (though Jane thinks otherwise, of course). The *shikha* ponytail is said to also protect the *bindu visarga* chakra at the back of the head, which is the source of the divine nectar, or *amrita*, which falls down to *vishuddha* chakra for distribution throughout the entire bodily system. In other words, it keeps me young and beautiful!

Most people associate the Hare Krishna movement with the music of George Harrison and the chanting of the mantra "Hare Krishna," and many also would consider the endless repetition of a mantra to be a complete waste of intellectual effort and time. How can this sort of repetition be of any use to the individual or the world?

Among my Naadi remedies is the charge to repeat the *Panchakshara* mantra to Shiva, which I commissioned from the Naadi reader and also perform myself as well. Apart from the karmic remedy from the Naadi, the repetition of a mantra can have spiritual benefits for the individual that can help them to raise their awareness and spiritual insight. As well as the *Panchakshara* mantra, I also like to chant the *Gayatri* mantra, which Sathya Sai Baba tells us is the royal road to Divinity. You can recite a mantra at any time, as Divinity is beyond time and space, but it is considered best to chant in the early morning and at twilight, so that you start and end the day with divine thoughts.

One of the big problems of the modern age is that we are constantly distracted by television, social media, news, shopping, and so on. Our lack of focused attention will cause us to lose energy, and with it happiness, for our mind is always elsewhere but never in the here and now. Worldly distractions are called *vikshepa*, and the remedy is *sadhana*, a Sanskrit word literally meaning "a means of accomplishing something," but used as a term for spiritual work upon oneself, which includes employing methods such as meditation, concentration, and performance of good deeds for achieving purity of mind. Mantra as a *sadhana* is used to stop the mind wandering, controlling and internalizing the attention, with the final objective being to bring the focus of our whole being to the divine Self.

As I explained in earlier chapters, we now live in the *Kali Yuga*—the Dark Age of ignorance which, according to Hindus, is the fourth of the *yugas* and started with the death of Krishna, the eighth *avatar* of Vishnu. Though the evil is thickest in this *Kali Yuga*, the remedy is the simplest, and that is the chanting of the divine name to attain liberation. Sathya Sai Baba explains: "The spiritual discipline for each age has been prescribed by the scriptures; for the *Kritha* (First Age), it is *dhyana* (meditation); for the *Treta*, the second, it is *dharma* (righteousness); for the *Dvapara*, the third, it is *archana* (ritual worship) and for the present age, the *Kali*, it is *Namasmarana*, the remembrance of the name of God" (Divine Discourse, Yugaadhi, March 27, 1971).

In some respects, these difficult times we live in are energetically also a time of great opportunity, as it is the time in which spiritual advancement can be made most quickly. The divine name can be any that suits your temperament and could include a name such as Jesus, Allah, or Amen, if the Hindu way does not appeal to you. If you cannot accept the power of mantra as a tool for God realization it is, at its most basic level, a simple way to help to tame the monkey mind.

How many of us can truly claim to have inner peace? When you close your eyes and watch your thoughts, you are confronted with a clatter of self-sustained activity. In meditation, or at night as you sleep, your mind may be whirling with thoughts, emotions, and fears that arise from a mind that is out of control and doing its own thing.

If you don't rule the mind, the mind will rule you.

As part of my training courses and workshops to help people with mediumistic potential to unlock and develop their gifts, I have often employed mantra as a means to help the sitters to tame their thoughts. Within Spiritualism, there is a great deal of misunderstanding about meditation and what it is. Most people sitting in a development circle will, at the meditation part, simply close their eyes and enter a state that is close to sleep or dreaming. They see interesting imagery and visual experiences which they assume all come from the spirit world, but which are mainly coming from their own unconscious thoughts and processes. On one level, it is good to get people to be aware of thoughts and to enter a state where they are watching thoughts rather than being swept along by them. But to remain exclusively in a state of mental flow of imagery is not, in my opinion, either conducive to mediumship or meditation.

What is needed to achieve both meditation and mediumship is a still mind and enhanced attention. In this way, the slightest thought that touches the still pool of the attention is see as a clear ripple upon the surface and, by influencing this surface, the spirit world is able to make its communications. It touches the surface of the mirror of the inner pool, and the communications are "seen" by the medium as thoughts other than his own crossing the field of his attention.

People with unsteady minds—and, let's face it, that's most of us—can start a period of meditation by first chanting a mantra aloud or inwardly. Using a mantra is like taming a mad monkey by making it run up and down a pole, or leading an elephant through the jungle by letting it wrap its trunk around a stick you carry. Once you have the mind fixed with a mantra, you can take control of it very easily.

I have stated that mantra in the age of *Kali Yuga* is considered to be the quickest way to enlightenment and to escape the endless cycle of birth and death. Mantra is also a powerful tool for worldly influence and to achieve specific goals. Magical mantras are chanted to the gods and also to the planets and stars. The most important mantras in astrology are the ones done to win favor with the nine planets known as *navagraha shanti*. Some of these ideas are incorporated in the remedies of the Naadi leaves, and one may be asked to recite mantras for each planet according to its position in one's birth chart. A weak or inauspicious position of a planet may require the person to recite the relevant mantra, either by wearing the gemstones, or by just worshiping the gem that represents the afflicted plane.

In the last canto of the 5,000-year-old holy text called the *Bhagavata Purana*, the sage Vedavyasa made fifteen predictions about our present age of the *Kali Yuga*. Just like the Naadi leaves, the text has some amazingly accurate insights into our modern age. Below are the fifteen predictions in English, from the text found between section 12.2.1 and section 12.3.51:

1. Religion, truthfulness, cleanliness, tolerance, mercy, duration of life, physical strength, and memory will all diminish day by day because of the powerful influence of the *Kali Yuga*.
2. In *Kali Yuga*, wealth alone will be considered the sign of a man's good birth, proper behavior, and fine qualities. And law and justice will be applied only on the basis of one's power.
3. Men and women will live together merely because of superficial attraction, and success in business will depend on deceit. Womanliness and manliness will be judged according to one's expertise in sex, and a man will be known as a *brahmana* just by his wearing a thread.
4. A person's spiritual position will be ascertained merely according to external symbols, and on that same basis people will change from one spiritual order to the next. A person's propriety will be seriously questioned if he does not earn a good living. And one who is very clever at juggling words will be considered a learned scholar.
5. A person will be judged unholy if he does not have money, and hypocrisy will be accepted as virtue. Marriage will be arranged simply by verbal agreement, and a person will think he is fit to appear in public if he has merely taken a bath.
6. A sacred place will be taken to consist of no more than a reservoir of water located at a distance, and beauty will be thought to depend on one's hairstyle. Filling the belly will become the goal of life, and one who is audacious will be accepted as truthful. He who can maintain a family will be regarded as an expert man, and the principles of religion will be observed only for the sake of reputation.
7. As the Earth thus becomes crowded with a corrupt population, whoever among any of their social classes shows

himself to be the strongest will gain political power.
8. Harassed by famine and excessive taxes, people will resort to eating leaves, roots, flesh, wild honey, fruits, flowers and seeds. Struck by drought, they will become completely ruined.
9. The citizens will suffer greatly from cold, wind, heat, rain and snow. They will be further tormented by quarrels, hunger, thirst, disease, and severe anxiety.
10. The maximum duration of life for human beings in *Kali Yuga* will become fifty years.
11. Men will no longer protect their elderly parents.
12. In *Kali Yuga*, men will develop hatred for each other even over a few coins. Giving up all friendly relations, they will be ready to lose their own lives and kill even their own relatives.
13. Uncultured men will accept charity on behalf of the Lord and will earn their livelihood by making a show of austerity and wearing a mendicant's dress. Those who know nothing about religion will mount a high seat and presume to speak on religious principles.
14. Servants will abandon a master who has lost his wealth, even if that master is a saintly person of exemplary character. Masters will abandon an incapacitated servant, even if that servant has been in the family for generations. Cows will be abandoned or killed when they stop giving milk.
15. Cities will be dominated by thieves, the Vedas will be contaminated by speculative interpretations of atheists, political leaders will virtually consume the citizens, and the so-called priests and intellectuals will be devotees of their bellies and genitals.

Not very cheery predictions, but most have already come to pass and even appear to predict the environmental problems we have today: "Struck by drought, they will become completely ruined," and, "The citizens will suffer greatly from cold, wind, heat, rain, and snow." It sees also the corruption in our churches: "Priests and intellectuals will be devotees of their bellies and genitals." Only one prediction appears to have not come to pass: "The maximum duration of life for human beings in *Kali Yuga* will become fifty years."

The *Bhagavata Purana* is focused on *bhakti* (religious devotion) to Vishnu, primarily focusing on Krishna, and it advises us that devotional chanting is the remedy that will help us. In *Srimad Bhagavatam* verse 12.3.51, it says: "Although *Kali Yuga* is an ocean of faults, there is still one good quality about this age: simply by chanting the names of Krishna, one can become free from material bondage and be promoted to the transcendental kingdom."

TESTING THE ORACLE

For me, the first consultation with the Naadi oracle was a spiritual earthquake. If it was right, it would have huge implications for my life, and—if I am right with my feelings—it is about to reveal many things for the world and future of everyone.

When people come to me for a mediumistic consultation to get proof of the afterlife, I advise them—no matter how convincing the reading with me was—to get further sittings with other mediums, visit their local Spiritualist church, read the literature, visit seminars, and so on.

For some, it is fine to have just the one sitting and get enough proof that their loved one is safe and well in the spirit world. For these people, the healing is done, and they can get on with their normal lives. That may be enough—job done. They may never need to see a medium again. In fact, the vast majority of people who visit a medium may not even be looking for evidence of survival; it is the "messages" they seek to help make their outer life easier and to help them let go of their worries. They want their troubles to be taken away. Unfortunately, noble as it is to lift this suffering, it can degrade the true philosophical purpose of mediumship, which is to make the person think about the reason they were put on Earth in the first place.

There are a few individuals who realize the momentous significance of what these messages from the spirit world imply. They tell us that life is not the end, and they inspire some people to begin a spiritual quest to know the meaning and purpose of their existence and why they are here. To these seekers, I suggest that they should not be content just hearing what the spirit has to say through me or Jane, but to start a quest to get more clarification, more guidance, and more evidence of the reality of the spirit, so that there are absolutely no doubts in their minds. They have to do some work, seek out rock-solid truth, get multiple confirmations that the afterlife exists, and assemble such a huge personal repository of direct experience and evidence that there is absolutely no doubt left. Then you can throw away beliefs and religion, because you know the truth for yourself.

I felt it was important to take my own advice and see if I could really submit the Naadi oracle to the same scrutiny by getting further clarification of its truth or otherwise. Perhaps there was something I had overlooked. Maybe I had inadvertently said something during the initial leaf search that allowed the reader to look me up on the Internet. Maybe I had let something slip in my replies, and they fed things back to me.

If you've ever sat with a poor-quality psychic reader, you may have experienced this yourself. Some readers will feed back things later in the reading that you told them at the start, or make a few open-ended guesses and let you fill in the rest with your own ideas. In other words, you hear what you want to hear, since you are projecting what you want to hear on to what they have to say.

I needed to get another Naadi reading. If a completely separate and unconnected reader were to say much the same thing as the first consultation, then I would initiate the things that the oracle was telling me to do with my life. I didn't want to make this into a self-fulfilling prophesy, but equally I didn't want to deny my destiny. The first oracle had identified my previous life in India and how—in this life, now—I was to open ashrams around the world, where I could teach the messages from the universe that would be given to me through the holy men that I would meet on my journeys and the spirit guidance that I would be given by the gods (which I interpreted as the spirit guides).

Maybe I was being conned big time, and my own monkey mind was an accomplice. This could be my ego on steroids, a spiritual megalomania. I've moaned about other mediums when I've seen average mediums suddenly get plucked randomly by ignorant researchers and put on television. It fires up their monkey mind with self-importance and transforms them into puffed up, self-righteous clowns. So was the same thing happening to me?

My great ego leveler—my wife, Jane—had her doubts about it all. You can find out too much about people on the Internet. How could I be absolutely, totally, one hundred percent, cross your fingers and hope to die, sure that there was not any skullduggery? Jane was not fully convinced. She was intrigued and fascinated, but not convinced enough to try the oracle for herself. The fact that it appears to predict when I will die is a bit of a put-off and may not be something everyone would like to know about their fate.

Meanwhile, I had started my research and managed to find a number of books and accounts from people who had consulted the Naadi *before* the invention of the Internet. They told stories just as incredible as my own. Similarly, people who had visited the Naadi centers in India had been given amazing messages from the leaves, there and then, and with no opportunity for the reader to do their research. Any form of detailed research would have been near-impossible, since just as today, people gave only their thumbprint and not their names.

I also need to help get rid of all doubts in you, the reader, if I am to write about this with any authority. And, just as importantly, from a personal viewpoint, I wanted confirmation of the direction of my destiny.

With some help from Vivek, my trustworthy friend of many years, I tracked down and set up a new reading. Again we used a proxy email address, and I set up a completely new Skype account and double-checked that there were no details about my name or any clues whatsoever as to who I was. A thumbprint was sent to the Tamil-speaking reader, who we knew could not speak English. A translator was also arranged, and again the interview would be set up over Skype. In my opinion, it would be pretty hard for anyone—particularly if they only spoke Tamil and had no information about me—to be able to research me on the Internet. Again, no payments were made, so that no clues could be gleaned from bank payments or money transfers.

For this second consultation with a new reader, I was a little better prepared and now familiar with the process of finding my leaf. I wasn't going to let anything slip or give away any information about myself. Again, I was to only answer with a "Yes" or "No" as they went through the leaves.

The bundle that contained the leaves relating to me was found from my thumbprint. Apparently I have a very rare thumb impression, with a whorl opening to the right and three dots that signify the third-eye center of Shiva. The Tamil-speaking reader and his translator became very excited by this, as it marks out a person with an unusual destiny and past life, who will do significant things in this life. To my surprise, they were pretty well jumping up and down with excitement at finding such an auspicious omen.

The second part of the reading had me answering "Yes" or "No" to the leaves' inscriptions, until we found mine. There were some pretty odd questions, and I wondered what strange messages they contained for the people who would later find their leaf in the ones we discarded.

"Do you trade in jewelry?"

"No."

"Do you own an industrial business related to metal foundries?"

"No."

"Have you renounced the world to follow a life of a *sadhu*?"

"No."

And so it continued for about half an hour, as I rejected many odd potential lives. Then a line of questions suddenly resulted in "Yes."

"Were you born in hospital, and were you a healthy child?"

"Yes."

"Does your mother's name begin with a vowel?"

"Yes."

"Is it the letter E?"

"Yes."

"Her name is Ethel, and she is living?"

"Yes!"

"Your father's name is Donald, and he is dead?"

"Yes!"

"Your first wife's name was Tina, and your present wife's name is Jane?"

"Yes!"

And so he continued reeling off the names of my family, and who was living or dead, or married or single, and eventually he said that my name was Craig, and he gave my birth time and date. This was exactly the same information, in much the same sequence, as my first reading. It was apparent that the leaves had identical information, even though I had approached this reader anonymously, and there was no possibility of collusion between this reader and the first one I saw.

With a beaming smile, he held up my leaf to the screen and was pleased to inform me that it was very detailed—three feet long, and with a great deal of information scrawled on it in tiny Tamil script. Once they had translated it, they would be able to give me a great deal of information about my past, present, and future.

SADGURU SRI SHARAVANA BABA

During the weeks while I waited for the Naadi to be translated and sent to me by audio file, I received a text message from Vivek (my spiritual fairy-godfather) telling me that a great guru was in the UK, and he felt that the guru wanted to talk with me. Somehow it was all connected with what was happening with the Naadi prophecies.

The series of texts came through on a gray and windy day, as I walked along a solitary stretch of beach that was strewn with ruins from the D-Day landings. Here, in a place where men had prepared to die in one of the great wars of the *Kali Yuga*, I was receiving spiritual messages from the great sages of India. The contrast in atmospheres was strangely surreal.

Vivek had just had an interview with Sri Sadguru Saravana in Croydon on one of his rare visits to London. He was to have one more appearance, which was at a private home just fifteen minutes' drive from my home in Eastleigh. Vivek felt that the coincidence was just too significant to miss, and he would put me in touch with the homeowner, then threatened to text me twice a day thereafter to remind me to go. There was no way he was going to let me off the hook! "You sit before him, and he will tell you everything. Take Jane with you. Please, please go. Trust me. He's just like Sathya Sai."

Vivek had mentioned Sri Sadguru Saravana before, during our many long chats on Facebook about Sathya Sai Baba and other miracle-makers from India. He had told me about this Indian man who could read minds as if he were reading a book. You didn't even have to ask him a question. He would just tell you what you needed to know. Some Sathya Sai devotees had been drawn to him, too, and some had seen him transfigure into Sathya Sai Baba.

The only problem now was to talk Jane out of Sunday lunch, shopping, and a movie, and get her to go with me on another wild goose chase. There was some resistance, because the last time I had taken Jane to visit a guru, we went to see one whom we both felt was far from spiritual. This was a man called Vishwananda, who claimed to be the reincarnation of Yogananda, and who dressed and modeled himself on Sathya Sai Baba, despite—we heard later—having been the only person ever to have been thrown out of the ashram.

When we stood together before this man, we both looked in his eyes and saw an ordinary man—someone whom we did not like at all. Talking to some his original devotees reaffirmed our doubts, and we could see why so many of his first devotees had deserted him. The one thing he did have going for him was that he not only had a beautiful singing voice, but he could turn traditional *bhajans* and mantras into wonderful, beautiful compositions.

Now, this is just my opinion, of course, and all gurus have their detractors, and some say that Vishwananada can deliberately hide his power from people. Skeptics and others have poured scorn on all the great spiritual leaders—including Sathya Sai Baba—so don't just take my word on this. Trust only your own, direct experience.

At the time, I was very concerned about the influence Vishwananada was having on my friends in the yoga group I attended. Everyone seemed to be getting sucked in, and I saw seemingly solid relationships being torn apart which, in my opinion, was caused by his divisive influence. It really worried me until I had a dream of Sathya Sai Baba, who put me straight. (If you ever have a dream about Sathya Sai Baba, you will come to understand that dreams about him are real encounters.)

Many of the dreams I've had about Sathya Sai Baba have been hilarious, and this was another one of those. He appeared to me dressed as Elvis Presley and was doing a rather bad Elvis impersonation. It was side-splittingly funny, even in the dream, to see Baba in the full Elvis garb—bling and sunglasses, too. After a few "Uhhhuh, Babys" and a bit of wobbly singing, he said to me: "Why have an impersonator when you can have the real thing? Don't worry about your friends. I will look after them."

Soon after that, Vishwananda announced to the consternation of everyone but Jane and me that he was closing his organization, called the Bhakti Marga. Most of the people I cared about then drifted away from him. (When I searched the Internet today, I see that the Bhakti Marga is back in business, but I'm not telling anyone.)

So it was this experience in mind, and with my own over-enthusiasm for all things spiritual, that I needed to prize Jane from her Sunday outings. Just because we were followers of Sathya Sai Baba when he was alive did not mean we should rule out seeing other gurus. I've always believed in taking personal responsibility for one's life, and that there are many gurus who can help us progress. It's simply the same divine light shining though many different windows.

Sadguru Sri Sharavana Baba was born in October 1979 in a village called Srikrishnapuram in Palakkada in Kerala (South India). He had a humble background and suffered a lot of cruelty in his early life. It is claimed that he has produced many miracles. He now has ashrams around the world, and the emphasis of his teachings is love, faith, devotion, surrender, and selfless service. His organization does a lot of work feeding the poor and clothing the destitute.

Jane and I had never really heard about Sharavana Baba, and most of the Westerners crammed into the front room of the house, which had been converted into a white-and-turquoise colored temple, with a thick, red silk carpet strewn with flowers, leading to a golden chair at the front of the room. Visitors sat on both sides, and mantras and *bhajans* were sung to the accompaniment of a harmonium and drums. It was a small but daunting temple with a lovely atmosphere. The Indians certainly know how to make a show when it comes to spiritual ceremonies and events—and all in an inconspicuous house, just down the road from us.

We'd arrived quite early, and we had a long wait since—as with all gurus—they tend to be fashionably late. I think it builds the tension a bit so that when they enter the room, there is a high sense of anticipation and devotional energy. But that's all part of the pageant and fun.

When Sharavana Baba stepped into the room, he took a few paces up and down, then walked directly over to Jane, who was sitting on a chair at the back, and placed a pink rose in her hand. Then he walked to the front of the room, where I was sitting with the others on the floor, and patted me on the head and touched my hand. I think everyone wondered what was going on—including us. We were the only people in the room he did this to. How did he know that Jane and I were a couple? I hadn't even seen him walk into the room, since I was looking toward the front. The first I knew was the friendly touch to the head and the thought running across my mind: "So nice to see you. Sorry for the wait." Jane had been thinking about the perennial problems with our children when Sharavana Baba gave her the rose.

Sharavana Baba

What struck me with Sharavana Baba was how jolly he was. When we conferred afterward, Jane and I both thought he looked like our daughter's first husband, who was a thick-set man with a swastika and prison tattoos all over his face and shaven head. This man was the exact opposite: kind, gentle, and radiating love. It felt a bit like a cosmic joke as Sharavana Baba sat in his seat and bounced around to the *bhajans*, whimsically twirling flowers. He was clearly a man who liked to have fun. Jane and I were both immediately enchanted by him. You could see he was a realized being who radiated joy. It was definitely worth missing the Sunday roast and the shopping trip.

Sharavana Baba spoke mainly Tamil, which was translated into short and simple statements in English. He held up a tangerine and gave a simple but inspired talk about the importance of the inner life and how, like the fruit, the outside may be beautiful, but the inside has the vitamin C—something you need but cannot see. He went on to talk about how if we focus on the inner life and get that right, then everything in our world outside will get better, too. It was much the same sort of message that other gurus teach, but expressed in a simple and beautiful way, with lots of happy smiles and jokes in between.

I never trust gurus who are too serious. For me, one of the marks of enlightenment is humor mixed with humility, for it is only the ego that takes itself so seriously.

At the end of the proceedings, everyone waited in line in front of Sharavana Baba in his golden chair to be given a personal interview. We were quite close to the front of the line and could see various people expressing their worries and distress, and getting comfort from the guru. Knowing how draining it can be working with people's spiritual problems and giving clairvoyant guidance, we could see that Sharavana Baba had a pretty daunting task on his hands, but he appeared never to tire. From the little one could overhear, it was clear that he was giving much more than general advice, but was giving detailed and personal insights into people's lives.

The lady in front of Jane and me was very distressed, but walked away comforted. When Jane and I kneeled together before him, a silly mood set in immediately. It was like talking to an old friend whom you've known for years, and whom you can rib a bit and pull their leg. To me, it felt like all three of us were sharing a very funny joke together. Yet during the conversation between the three of us, he was simultaneously talking directly to Jane and directly to me. It all took about fifteen minutes, but that short time was hugely mind-opening.

He said to both of us that we were very old souls and had more spiritual work to do. "You have visited many gurus now and in your time, and because of this you can meet people like me, and we all can be happy. The last time was two years ago"—which we took to mean the meeting with Vishwananda, which bothered Jane and nearly prevented her from coming along.

He said that we had all been together before in past lives. "Where's the rose I gave you?" he said to Jane. As she replied, "In my bag," Saravana Baba gave me a sideways, cheeky glance. The two of us, preempting what obviously should follow, simultaneously said,

"It's in her heart!" As he spoke, he lightly nudged his head against my forehead like two people sharing a cheerful moment. "It's in my heart, too," he said.

He looked back to me and said, "You have nothing to worry about with your family." Then he turned to Jane and said, "Stop worrying about your children," which had been a big concern of Jane, not only that day, but in the weeks and months before. For me, too, there had been a lot of health worries in the family of late. He spoke again to me, saying, "You have been held back for a long time." Turning to Jane, he said, "And you know your husband here has a great deal of spiritual work in store, starting at the age sixty-two, and there will be a lot of travel, too—for both of you."

These words were almost a paraphrase of the exact words written on the Naadi leaves and an important confirmation of the prophecies. "You do not have to chase it. It will find you," he advised.

I told him that this is what the Naadi leaves had predicted for me and asked him if he knew anything about my past life. He explained that I had been with Shirdi Sai Baba and also knew Sri Ramakrishna. (I thought he said Ramana Ramakrishna, as there was a lot of noise around, but Jane corrects me here.) He said I had been a devotee of Shiva in my former lives and lived at a Shiva temple in Tamil South India. (I missed the name, as it was too hard to pronounce and recall.) Again, this corresponded very closely with the Naadi message that I had been hoping to get confirmed from an independent spiritual channel.

He beamed a big smile and said, "I *am* the Naadi oracle!"

Our eyes met, and I chuckled: "So am I. I guess we all are!" (Words that came out of I don't know where.) We all joked together a little more, and he concluded our interview with an invitation to his ashram in Kerala.

A week later, we had a second opportunity to meet Sharavana Baba on Easter Sunday at a private house in London. By now, word had spread among the Indian population, and the small house was packed to the ceiling with people. My hope had been to ask the swami some specific questions about mediumship and the afterlife. Unlike most Spiritualists, I believe the next life is not the final destination, and I wanted to ask him—as I had asked other gurus—what his take was on what happens after death. It looked like I would not get the opportunity.

The evening was conducted mainly in Tamil, with a short discourse in English about the primary meaning of the teachings of Jesus and our spiritual place in this garden we call Earth. There were some prayers and *bhajans* (chanted, repetitive Indian songs), and then everyone was invited for a short interview. Again he beamed his lovely smile, hugged and patted us both, repeating again his earlier messages about the spiritual happiness we have and will share with the world.

There was no opportunity to ask detailed questions, as a large crowd was pressing for his attention. When we got home, I flicked open one of his books I'd bought, and the answer to the question I had intended to put to him about the transitory nature of Heaven was there in black and white: "As for the enjoyment of Heaven, it is also subject to impermanence, frustration, and failure. The sacrifices that propitiate the gods entitle the sacrificer to the same heavenly pleasures as the gods themselves enjoy, but only for as long as the fruits of his merits last. Thereafter he takes birth in the lower regions, according to his past actions and associations. So long as they are propelled by the *gunas*, the senses are active, they perceive diversity in the *atman* and impel action, the fruits of action, and bondage for the individual."

What was remarkable about both meetings with Sharavana Baba was that he seemed to know and anticipate our thoughts. What made it all so hilarious was that Jane and I also have pronounced telepathic skills, so it all became a wonderful cosmic joke of anticipating each other's thoughts. I'm not sure if it felt quite the same for Jane, but I sensed we'd all connected inwardly, and there was a childlike game happening, where we were all trying to be the first one to catch the thoughts floating in the air. Impossible to describe, really, but some of the mediums reading this may get what I mean.

Sharavana Baba not only knew and was able to preempt questions in our minds, but just as on the previous occasion, he held three intimate conversations simultaneously: with Jane, with me, and between the three of us together. Something was happening on a much deeper level than anyone observing the events could have recognized. Jane and I walked away from the interviews in a spiritual daze and feeling very inspired and cosmically charged.

We saw him for a third time when he visited the Crawley Amman temple near London. The discourse was in Tamil, but we were able to talk to him briefly afterwards in English, with occasional help from a translator. To me, he said: "You are at the turning point, and both of you are now on a divine path." Then he turned to Jane and, with a mischievous and funny look in his eyes, said: "How's your family? Now happy with family? Very, very happy?"

Since our last visit, our daughter Danielle had announced her engagement to an intelligent, loyal, and handsome Italian "god" and also become pregnant. In the past, she had undergone some horrendous ordeals, but now she was very, very happy, not just with the planned baby and marriage, but also since she had been told by the doctors after having her first baby, Willow, that it would be extremely unlikely she would ever have another child. Some time ago Jane, Danielle, and I had all simultaneously dreamed on the same night of Sathya Sai Baba talking to us at Danielle's house, and telling us that he would sort everything out. Now here was the same light shining through Sharavana Baba.

Sharavana Baba handed Jane a rose and, pointing to the stem, said, "Life has a few thorns, but as you can see, they are not much compared to the beauty of the flower."

MORE MESSAGES FROM THE NAADI

About a week after seeing Sharavana Baba, the audio file from the Naadi reader in India arrived by email—well, almost arrived, after several attempts over a number of days to get the big audio files through my email account. As I sat at my computer, struggling with technology, trying to get the emails on to my computer, I had an eerie feeling that the cosmic eyes of the Naadi's *maharishi* were looking at me. Had he "seen" this moment in time? One of the first predictions on the audio translation was that there would be a slight delay before "the native" (i.e., me) would be able to hear his predictions.

The narrative this time was much rawer and perhaps closer to the original text. Nonetheless, the leaves were being interpreted three times: once by the Tamil reader, then by the translator, and then by me! The previous consultation had been very clear, and although this new interpretation had a few differences in slant, the fundamentals were the same. I would be meeting many holy men and learning their secret knowledge. I would be building temples, the rich and famous would support my work, I would research the Naadis, I would show people how to open the third eye, and I would give messages from the universe to thousands of people. One heck of a tall order!

As well as confirmations, there were many new things in the prophecy that seem puzzling today (I'm writing in 2015), but could be portents for the future of the world. One that I will reveal now is that a whole country will be threatened by a toxic cloud blowing in from the northeast. The oracle did not say which country, but it said that my own seership would reveal the answer closer to the time, and I would be able to warn people of its direction, as well as do *puja* to help mitigate the problems. The oracle hints that this will occur when I reach the age of seventy-one, so it should happen in 2025. During this time, there will be many other natural calamities. This may be expected, given what we know about the consequences of global warming. But it is extraordinary to think that the Naadi leaves saw this thousands of years ago and can give us warnings and remedies to help us avert disasters. It is interesting also to note that Sharavana Baba has predicted that in the future, toxic clouds will trouble the world.

The oracle also predicts that the abilities of prophecy that I will learn from the saints, holy men, and yogis I will meet will enable me to give warnings of great tidal surges that will occur in the future.

Some of my research into others who have had Naadi readings reveals that other people's leaves have warned of great environmental troubles in our time. We can see the signs already in the strange weather patterns and the regular comments on the weather forecast that temperature, climate, and rainfall are the highest since records began. In many ways, this is self-evident, but people are feeling it, too. On my website forums, a great many visiting psychics and mediums express grave concern and have horrible premonitions of earthquakes, tsunamis, and chaotic weather ahead. At the same time, a great many more people are asking questions about why they have been placed on this Earth and whether they have lived before. Perhaps our unconscious concern is that we may mess things up for our own future lives.

According to some Naadi reports, there will be grave upheavals in our time that will stem from economic problems beginning in 2009. In fact, we now know that the economic problems started in 2007–8 and continue to blight the world. The financial troubles will be followed by political turmoil—something we are perhaps already seeing in the Arab world, though my personal feeling is that the real troubles will begin in China. At the time of writing, there are problems between China and Japan and South Korea, but I believe there will be an implosion in China. I feel that there will be a new revolution in China, which will ricochet around the world. Interestingly my wife, Jane, gave a fascinating reading to a relative of the Chinese leader Sun Yat-sen (November 12, 1866–March 12, 1925), who was the revolutionary first president and founding father of the Republic of China (1912–49). His spirit message seems to be that China will one day have a proper democracy. My feeling is that this will only come after terrible troubles and great upheaval within the country. Some of this will come from the Muslim population, but there will be forces pushing for change in Hong Kong and also unexpected places such as Mongolia as well.

Some of the Naadi predictions I have researched suggest that, after worldwide political upheavals, there will be warring factions fighting for supremacy in three regions of the world. The specific countries have not been revealed. In the excellent book *The Hidden Oracle of India* by Andrew and Angela Donovan, Angela's Naadis appear to reveal global shifts similar to those described by Edgar Cayce. I do not have access to the original script of her Naadi, but she writes: "The Middle East will experience two geological shifts when the Earth itself will move. Water will be involved on both occasions. Before and after these times, however, the people will be guided, aided, and directed to understand what is happening and learn from the experience."

With the advent of fracking, we are already seeing minor earthquakes in Texas and small tremors in the UK, too. My feeling at this stage is that the U.S. and Europe will experience the worst of the northern hemisphere earthquakes, though again I feel China will also suffer. According to the Naadi, the information about this type of thing will be revealed to me in the future through a vision of the god Shiva.

My oracle says: "To protect the people from these natural calamities the native would do some *pujas*, *yagnas*, and *homas*. The native would be able to foretell about the natural calamities related to storm or rain, or related to waves or seas and oceans. Some countries may face some problems related to toxic air or toxic storm, and the native would be able to foresee and foretell those problems to people. This would happen in the north or northeastern side of a country, which the native would be able to foretell to people. To protect the people from this calamity, the native would perform some *pujas*. Like this, the native would use two or three ways to protect the people from natural calamities."

My oracle later mentions the need to build villages for the poor. I have a feeling this is going to be a need on a global scale, as the current form of building we have becomes dangerous because of tremors. A new form of housing will be invented—similar to the old postwar prefabricated buildings—that will be used worldwide to house the many homeless of the future.

The Naadi leaves do not make any predictions beyond the year 2050, which suggests that either the world is no more by that time, or perhaps we will have advanced enough spiritually to foresee our own futures!

My intuitive feeling is that, despite the environmental issues and a growing problem with an overheating sun, the world will get through all this. More importantly, there will be a sustained and growing interest in spirituality. People will learn that thoughts are things, and that our thoughts, as well as our actions, have an effect on the world. Because of this, more people will turn to ritual, prayer, mantra, and meditation as means of helping to safeguard the future of the world.

THE SPIRITS SEE MY FUTURE

I was blown off my seat when the Naadi oracle leaf was identified as mine by giving the correct name of my first wife, then an accurate series of names, then my current wife Jane's name, and then my exact time and date of birth. How could someone writing this leaf thousands of years ago—in the *Dvapara Yuga*—have known all this? The names Tina and Jane did not even exist in those times, and although the Internet could reveal the name Jane to be that of my wife, I have never mentioned in my books, website, or anywhere else public that my former wife's name was Tina.

I should not be surprised, of course, as my own work as a medium often includes guidance and prediction, usually with the caveat that "all this is subject to free will." But the Naadi was so accurate that it is hard to see if any free will had ever applied in my life. My destiny appeared to be absolute.

A private consultation in the 1980s with the world-famous medium Doris Stokes was my first introduction to Spiritualism. Doris was an archetypal grandmother figure, and thousands thronged to see her public demonstrations of mediumship. She became the world's best-known medium and, in her simple, unassuming way, she popularized the knowledge that had previously been limited only to Spiritualists and other, similar organizations. She was famous all over the world, particularly in England and Australia, and she could fill the London Palladium or Sydney Opera House to capacity.

Briefly, what happened—for those who have not had the delight of reading my other books—is that I accompanied my bereaved sister, Viv, to a sitting with Doris to see if the spirit of her dead husband, Wayne, could give some proof that his spirit had survived death. Wayne was diagnosed with a vicious form of cancer three months after they were married, so our mission to get proof of life after death was emotionally pressing and sincere.

Not only did Doris give us startling proofs from the spirit of Wayne, but she gave rock-solid evidence about many of our family who had died. She also predicted my time in the United States, knew about my problems as a single parent, and saw how I would give up my graphics and advertising business to become a professional medium. With only the minimum feedback from me about my situation, she knew all about my life and future.

The medium Doris Stokes

She "knew" about my struggle as a single parent with a baby of sixteen months to look after, while working flat out through the day, and boiling Terry Towel diapers late into the evening. She described my grandmother in the spirit world and made some predictions about my business, how I would travel, and whom and when I would marry.

Two predictions came to pass almost instantly. At the time, I was running my own advertising agency, and she named a blue-chip company I'd be doing work for. A few weeks later, out of the blue, that company rang me up with a big order that was to put me on a firmer financial footing. Doris had even given me the name of the man who would place the order. She mentioned that I should look out for a company with a blue circle for a logo, which would be of great importance to me. Thinking in terms of graphics, I afterward approached Blue Circle Cement to see if they needed any advertising and graphics work, but my sales pitch failed. Many years later, when I'd left advertising behind me, I set up a business in conjunction with a company called Stream, which was originally named Psychic Circle and once had a blue circle as its logo.

Doris also said that I'd be going to the U.S. with my friend Stuart. Stuart Martin, a longtime friend, was offered a temporary teaching job in an American youth camp. As I boarded the plane to L.A., I recalled what Doris had said. She also told me about my work in the distant future with American movie celebrities, and a few other things that are yet to come to pass with a number of well-known people.

The most remarkable prediction that Doris made, although she always said that she couldn't see the future, was concerning my future wife. With startling accuracy, she named my future wife and told me when I would meet her.

Perhaps I shouldn't have been surprised that the ancient seers of India had also seen my destiny 5,000 years ago. When the events that Doris Stokes predicted had unfolded in my life, it was mind-boggling, but I still find it hard to take in the fact that one's destiny can be "seen" thousands of years in advance. The Naadi had mentioned that my "sister's husband is dead," and they knew all about my life with Jane, so it makes me wonder if I have any choices at all. Perhaps fate is fixed.

SEEING HISTORY

It was not long after my sitting with Doris Stokes that my aunt made the suggestion that I visit a medium in London that she'd heard good reports about. Peter Close, the elder brother of Brian Close, the English cricket captain, had just retired from his job as a sergeant with the London Metropolitan Police Force, and he was now working full-time as a medium. As a police officer, he'd had to keep his interest in Spiritualism secret, but now he was free to do private consultations. My aunt had an excellent reading, so I made the call, made a booking, and in a few days drove to London for a private consultation.

Peter gave me an excellent reading, which was packed with evidential proofs of the continuation of life. Many family members and friends came through, but one spirit communication was unexpected and quite shocking. Peter's face flushed as the spirit person made contact. "Oh, my goodness! This young man has been burned alive," he gasped. "He was involved with drugs, and it resulted in a terrible, slow, agonizing death."

When the spirit connection finished, Peter slumped into his seat as if something had gripped him by the lapels, shaken him, and thrown him into his chair. His face was bright red, and he was sweating profusely.

This was the communicating spirit of my friend who, like me and other friends at school, took LSD in our teenage years. For both of us, it was it an epiphany, but for my friend, who we now believe had preexisting mental problems, LSD changed into a fierce demon that catapulted him into a frightening, schizophrenic world. LSD took hold of his soul and tore it to pieces. Sometimes he believed himself to be Christ, at other times a dolphin, and sometimes he thought he was an acupuncturist and conducted some horrible experiments on himself.

Eventually my friend was sectioned by the police under the Mental Health Act, but during the assessment he caused a panic by setting fire to his "secret" notes, and in the commotion he escaped, hijacked a car from a nun, and disappeared off the radar for six months. Eventually he turned up at my apartment in London, carrying just a large leather bag and an ax. Not knowing about these events, I again tried to talk him into seeing a psychiatrist. We agreed that he could stay a few days, and when he was calm and prepared, I would accompany him to the psychiatric hospital.

Sadly, he slipped out one night, leaving a note explaining that he was okay and was going to go on the road for a while. Unfortunately, he ended up in a squat, where again he took LSD and was launched again into a weird world of mad ideas and dark, out-of-control feelings. He believed that fire could cleanse the soul, so he walked into a gas station, poured gasoline all over himself from the pump, and lit a match. He survived for seven days, alone and unidentified. He died in unrelenting agony.

"He wants you to know that he's okay now," said Peter. "You did all you could to help him, but now he has the proper help he needs in spirit and is recovering from his problems. I'm also being told that you are the person that my guides have been saying will join my development circle. You are going to become a great medium and will help many people—including people who have been damaged by drugs."

And so I joined Peter's circle, and my adventures in Spiritualism began. People are led into Spiritualism by many paths. Some learn about it through healing, many come to it because of a bereavement, a few read about its philosophy, and the curious see it first on TV, YouTube, or at the theater. Not many are led to it by the spirit of a burning man with a mutual interest in psychedelic drugs, talking through the conduit of an ex–police officer!

Other than my encounter with Doris Stokes, I knew very little about Spiritualism and had no idea that mediums were expected to demonstrate in churches. Although fascinated by the fact that spirits could communicate with the living, I was initially much more interested in proving to myself that some of the things I had experienced with LSD could now be proved to be real. My friend in spirit had perhaps spotted this, and the spirit world saw it as the way to start their mission through me.

I had stopped experimenting with LSD many years before, not only because now I was a responsible single parent, but also because I had seen what the drug can do to unstable people. For me, it had been an extraordinary, life-changing experience, but I understood that it was also a limited path because it is not possible to permanently sustain these awakened states. As I will explain later, it's not something I would encourage, but it did nonetheless have a profound effect on my thinking and inspired me to find out what life was all about. I felt at the time that developing mediumship could perhaps give me insight into these psychedelic states and give personal and empirical evidence to validate the reality of what I had experienced. I wanted to prove to myself and others that telepathy, for example, is not a hallucination, and that through extra-sensory abilities we can tap a huge hidden resource of spiritual knowledge. Mediumship was my way into this reservoir.

Peter's circle taught me how to connect with the spirit world, and in a comparatively short time, I was giving detailed messages from the spirit that included lots of factual information such as the first and last names of the communicating spirit, information about their former life on Earth, and lots of highly personal tidbits that only the recipient of the message could know—things such as nicknames, family stories, personal secrets, and so on.

At the time, I was running my own advertising agency. This spiritual interest was supposed to be a bit of a hobby and a way to verify the experiences I spoke about earlier. I couldn't possibly consider becoming a full-time medium or devoting more than one evening a week to my interest. My business was just beginning to boom, and I had some top-name clients. All things considered, for a twenty-four-year-old single parent, I was doing pretty well. But there was absolutely no spare time.

It was my destiny to leave all this success behind, to rage against this gray world, and give into my wild longing to run off with the immortals. Years later, in my sixties, the Naadi revealed the true purpose of my life and the secrets of providence in broken English: "So why do we get this birth? What is the purpose of this birth?

What is the reason, and what are you going to do? So you are going to give lots of messages to the people. And also, you are going to communicate with the universe. Sometimes you are in deep thinking, and in deep meditation you are connected to the universe. So you give messages from the universe. So in that message you going to share with the people. So with this type of messages you are going to get from the universe, you are going to write the books. Everything. All the people like your activities. All the people like your messages."

Destiny had it in for me. There was no escaping the fact that eventually I was—like it or not—going to become a medium.

Spiritualists do not believe in a predetermined future or predictions like these. One of the seven principles that are the foundation of the movement is personal responsibility. If we have personal responsibility, then we also have free will. And if we have free will, we can decide our own future. Although opportunities and obstacles will be brought to us by destiny, free will gives us the choice of how to react and the power to choose the path that will determine our fortune. Our free will and choices determine what will happen next. Or so it seems.

One evening, around the year 1983, while Peter was in a trance, I asked his spirit guide, Rama, about the destiny of the world and whether we'd blow ourselves to pieces with nuclear bombs. His answer was that the big powers would not go to war. There would be no full-on conflict between Russia and the U.S., but the troubles for the future lay with Iran, Iraq, and North Korea. The greatest difficulty facing the world in the future would be environmental damage.

Quite an accurate prediction for 1983, when Iran and Iraq were slogging it out between themselves and seemed no threat to the West. And apart from the Rangoon bombing, North Korea was not often in the mainstream news. Although 1983 saw some moves to protect the environment, with some people shouting about the troubles ahead, there was little news about the threat of global pollution.

I feel that this prediction still holds good and that we will *not* see a global nuclear war—even though it is clear that Ukraine could be a tinderbox for greater conflict on the borders of Eastern Europe. My feeling is that Russia will become very closely allied with China, and that together they will become a dominant world power. (There will be a revolution in China that will also cause problems.) China and

Russia will share arms and oil, and I believe may even make moves to use the same currency. Simultaneously, the European Union will gradually fall apart, with Greece, Portugal, and Italy dropping out of the euro and eventually going their own way. Germany, Austria, and France will continue to maintain a union, but on nothing like the scale of the former EU.

In 2010 I predicted on my website a huge revolution in the Arab World (the "Arab Spring"), and writing now in 2015, I predict that we will see further massive upheaval. The Arab world will tear itself apart, with Saudi Arabia unwillingly drawn into the conflict after a gunman attacks Mecca. At this time, there will be a huge earthquake throughout Iran that will cause great political instability. The Kurds will form their own country. Iraq will be partitioned, with some Shi'ite areas becoming part of Iran. The northeast of Syria will be occupied by Turkey. Egypt, Tunisia, and Saudi Arabia, with the diplomatic support of Turkey, will form an alliance that will bring greater stability in the Middle East by 2022. Oil will become less important than water, and huge new water reserves will be found beneath the deserts of Libya, Egypt, Sudan, and central Africa. Areas of the Sahara will see huge greenhouses built to feed a hungry world.

As well as teaching us mediumship, Peter's circle also opened me to other psychic skills that I wanted to deeply explore. As a stepping stone to psychically linking to a person and then to the spirit people surrounding them, a trainee medium is taught the skill of psychometry. Basically, you hold an object and talk about everything you can sense about the owner's past and present. I teach the same methods in my own circles, and I have explained some of these techniques in detail in my book *Psychic School*. But far from just being a stepping stone to mediumship, I believe the skill of psychometry can be used to link us to all sorts of extraordinary things.

Throughout my career, I have experimented with this ability to sense the vibrations from objects. For a show for the BBC, I read the history of objects in a museum, while the curator confirmed or denied my comments. One of the most interesting of all was when I was working with host Chris Packham, who blindfolded me, took me to a secret location, then handed me various objects and artifacts to work with. He handed me a violin and asked me to tell him all about it. When I said it was part of a set with a matching cello, and that it used to be owned by the writer Thomas Hardy, Chris said he had to sit down because he was in a "state of shock," and he said to camera: "That was remarkable. . . . In the *World's Most Skeptical Person's Award* in 2001, I was a runner up, but I just don't know what to make of what I've just seen. I think he did remarkably well!"

Psychometry can sometimes reveal extremely detailed information, not only about objects, but about places, too. When Jane and I visit historical places, we often sense and see things that others don't. We become aware of the vibrations from the past and pick up information that only historians know. At the Palace of Versailles—the royal chateau for Louis XIV in Versailles, in the Ile-de-France region of France—we seemed to just "know" the history of the place, and we were able to check our information with the guides. They assumed we were both very knowledgeable historians, but in reality we knew very little about its history other than a general outline.

Jane felt particularly moved when we saw the Queen's Hamlet, which was set in the gardens and was the place that the vivacious Marie-Antoinette—King Louis XVI's wife—would retreat to enjoy the pleasures of simple, rural pursuits, away from the pomp of Versailles. This tiny hamlet was created as a model village, where the extravagant queen would fantasize about being a simple peasant. It was built in the style of a real Norman village, with eleven cottages dotting the Big Lake, including the Queen's House, a billiard room, a boudoir, a mill, and a refreshments dairy. Each house had its own little garden, planted with Savoy cabbages, cauliflowers, and artichokes, and surrounded by a hornbeam hedge and fence of chestnut trees. In short, it was a mad fantasy world for a spoiled queen.

It was raining when we walked around the village, so it was free from the wall-to-wall Japanese tourists we had encountered in the main palace, and we could take in the atmosphere of the place. Jane was reminded of the exact same dream we both shared, from a time before we met, of being chased by armored soldiers with dogs into a pit, where we were attacked from behind and beheaded. It was interesting to us because we both have the same birthmark on the back of our necks, and when our daughter Danielle was born, she also had the same mark. Mine has now faded, and Danielle's is now covered in tattoos, but at the time we did think it rather strange.

Marie-Antoinette was beheaded, of course, and this may have

brought the idea to mind. There is nothing in my Naadi oracle so far about a past life in France, and Jane does not want her leaves read in case they say something horrible. Maybe Jane did have a past life in France or somewhere similar. She certainly shops like Marie-Antoinette!

I think if Jane did have an aristocratic birth, it would have been Russian. She's always had a fascination with the stories about Rasputin, and ever since she was a child, she has admired Queen Catherine the Great. When we were in Russia, visiting the Amber Rooms at Catherine Palace at Tsarskoye Selo, near Saint Petersburg, she felt she knew this place, too. Of course, this is probably all fanciful thinking, but I would love to know if the Naadi leaves could one day give us any clues as to who Jane really was.

When Jane and I go to places that are steeped in history, we are sometimes transported to other times and get glimpses of the history of the people who once lived there. Put me in a place that has powerful spiritual energies, such as Varanasi, Stonehenge, the megalithic temples of Malta, Jerusalem, or Assisi, and I become lightly entranced by the energies around me and can describe things that only expert archeologists know about. On a TV show for the Discovery Channel, after a long drive, the filmmakers and historians took me to an overgrown, flat plot of land in an obscure forest, and I was able to accurately describe and draw what stood there, as well as give insights into the people and their history.

DESTINED TO MARRY JANE

The most remarkable prediction that the medium Doris Stokes made, although she always said that she couldn't see the future, was concerning my future wife. "Jane Wallis," she had said. "You will meet your future wife, Jane Wallis, on March 6." It took a good few years, but it was on March 6 that Jane and I met at a demonstration of mediumship I was giving to an audience in Eastleigh. I relayed a spirit communication to Jane, who was sitting in the audience, with a message from her grandmother Barber, and I concluded by saying she was telling me that Jane was mediumistic, too, and that I should have a consultation with her. I am not in the habit of asking members of the audience for a consultation. Heads turned when I made the request. It was a bit embarrassing, but a meeting was arranged.

We met, fell immediately in love, and were soon married. Jane's surname was Willis, which was pretty close to Doris's prediction, but her grandmother, who had pulled the strings from the spirit side, had the maiden name of Wallis. Doris Stokes had not only got the date of our meeting correct but all the associated names right as well!

The Stokes family were also important to Jane. "I got to know John Stokes after Doris Stokes had passed to spirit," says Jane. "He originally came down to my home in Eastleigh to help a friend of mine who needed some spiritual healing. Not many people knew about John's healing gift. We got on with each other straightaway and often used to meet up, together with his adopted son, Terry, at his friend Terry Carter's house in Portsmouth. John was a lovely, kind man, and I thought of him as a second father." When we decided to get married, it was John Stokes whom Jane asked to give her away in church, as she'd been out of touch with her own father since childhood. We often wonder if Doris Stokes was there too, watching it all from the afterlife.

When the wedding invitations arrived, many of my friends and family assumed it was a joke. My parents must have recalled the time when they returned from vacation to see the family home boarded up and bedecked with a real estate agent's "Sold by Auction" signs. Can you imagine their joy when they discovered that their restaurant had been given a professionally written sign, renaming it "Ethel's Diner"? My mother calls herself Vick, but her real name is Ethel—a name she hated and had kept a closely guarded secret. Now just about the whole of Southampton had seen the silly sign, and restaurant customers would inevitably ask, "Who is Ethel?" It was a joy watching my mother squirm as she explained about her real name. (When the Naadi mentioned that my mother's name was Ethel, I chuckled—she hated the name so much, but it looks like she was destined to be stuck with it!)

So you could forgive my family for thinking that the "surprise" wedding invitation for April 1, 1988, at Bittern Spiritualist Church, Southampton, was another April Fool's prank. I had kept my mediumistic work a secret for a long, long time, and many of the family were unaware of my clandestine activities. As a single parent, I'd served mainly London churches as a medium so that my business clients would not think me crazy. When I started demonstrating mediumship in the early 80s, Spiritualism was still considered a bit of an odd calling, and it was still classed as necromancy and forbidden to be shown unchallenged on television.

A Spiritualist church? A wedding? An invitation with a Ghostbusters logo and the words, "Your presence is requested, and spirits will be served afterwards"? It had to be a hoax. Some of my relatives—who had never been inside a Spiritualist church—were visibly shaking at the prospect of going inside. I think they were expecting us to sign the register over an Ouija Board.

But of course it was not a joke. Jane and I had decided to marry soon after we met, but in reality our coming together had been planned centuries ago. Together we shared our lives, had a happy family, and eventually grandchildren, too. I call it "traditional," but some would say we have a fairly "old-fashioned" marriage, in which Jane does the ironing, gardening, housework, childcare, cooking, laundry, pet feeding, window cleaning, more ironing, washing up, floor washing, sweeping, mopping up cat-sick, bed making, dusting—and I supervise and make sure all her chores are done properly. Jane had been a registered psychiatric nurse at the time when nurses were expected to be cleaner, more hygienic, and tidier than Florence Nightingale on steroids, so she just cannot bear to see my half-hearted cleaning or feeble attempts at cooking. (When I met Jane, I quickly forgot my skills as a single parent.) Meanwhile, I try to make sure all the bills are paid. Jane helps me, and I help Jane, not only with worldly and emotional things, but spiritually, too.

John Stokes gives Jane away at Bittern Spiritualist Church

We also both work from home, with Jane doing face-to-face consultations, while I write books and magazine columns, build and run my websites, do seminars and workshops, and do mediumistic consultations by phone. Our work is tremendously tiring—not just because it is emotionally intense, but because it is energetically demanding. Even with yoga as my spiritual support, and quiet gardening for Jane, we both get exhausted by mediumship. Every day we are helping people in dire need, people who are sometimes at the point of suicide. They come for an hour's appointment, and you can be with them all day—how can you turn away someone whose life has reached melt-down?

Jane and I must love one another, since most couples living under pressure and under each other's feet 24/7 for years would probably have torn each other apart by now, but we rarely have big rows, and usually we have fun and enjoy one another's company. (I dare not say anything different—but it really is true! The Naadi confirms this, too.)

Marriage is a sacred bond for life, and it works if a couple is loyal to one another and prepared to suffer for one another. If Jane has a problem, I worry for her. If I have a problem, Jane worries for me. We help one another grow, but also keep each other's egos in check. As the number of anniversaries multiplies, we learn to adjust to one another and forget our egos. Life is full of challenges, and if you have a good marriage, you'll face problems and solve problems together, not scarper for the door when the path requires fortitude and perseverance. So long as you understand each other, you can learn to adjust your behavior. And if you apply spiritual principles to your bond, you'll know that everything is God, and maybe you'll come to understand that the love you are sharing together is part of the divine plan unfolding. I am Jane's god, and Jane is my goddess. In this way, a marriage can be happy and joyful—and the ironing gets done, too!

GIVING UP THE FRUITS

Making a conscious choice to give up my graphics and advertising business was a tough decision. I had built the business without any capital and against all the odds. For a long time I had struggled, first to become an artist, then a graphic designer, and eventually to run my own design agency. During the recessions of the Margaret Thatcher era, there was a time when there was so little working capital in the business account that I had to ask my staff to work for no wages, on the understanding that if we did not get a big order by the end of the month, we'd all be sunk. All we had was our expertise and a small, cramped studio and office with an expensive-sounding address.

Just when things looked like we'd had it, I had two calls in response to a somewhat brilliant ad and mail shot I'd designed. The mailshot was about how we could design a campaign to improve internal communications in large corporations through newsletters, competitions, and poster campaigns. It was written as mock-Stalinist propaganda, calling for the downfall of capitalism and the overthrow of the bosses. I sent it out to as many top executives and capitalist pigs as I could find. The coal miners' strikes and riots were still fresh in people's minds, and big companies were keen to find ways to prevent strikes and improve their relationship with the workers, so my mixture of humor and serious intent fell on fertile ground.

The first inquiry came from the chairman of one of the world's biggest airlines. When the call came through, I thought it was my friend getting his own back on a joke I'd recently pulled on him, when I sent him a fake compulsory purchase order to his home address. The airline would not be able to see me for a couple of months, and I knew that the business couldn't survive that long, since we were out of funds. Fortunately, a few days later a second call came in from one of the world's biggest petrochemical companies, but we still had the same problem—no big company would take us on with such crappy offices.

These were desperate times, so the solution we decided was to do as the Allies did before D-Day, when they built fake airfields, inflatable tanks, and manikin armies to distract the Nazi invaders. I called the chief executive of the petrochemical company and explained that our offices were based in Winchester, a cathedral city with few big office buildings available to buy or rent, so we were spread all over the town center in a number of small locations, all within walking distance of each other. I arranged to meet his team at a nearby fancy hotel "so they would have no problem parking." From there I would show them around our office network. On the day, I deliberately arrived a little late, as I couldn't afford to buy them a drink. Just before the meeting, I noticed that I not only had the familiar hole in my shoe, but now there was also a hole in my sock, and you could see my protruding toe. I frantically blackened the skin with a marker pen in the hope that no one would notice, and confidently walked in to begin the meeting.

First stop was a rented conference room we'd decked out with logos to give the impression that we owned it. Here we presented our design ideas and mock-ups of the proposed newsletters and company magazines. To my relief, they absolutely loved our suggestions. Little did they know that everyone sitting around the table had never met each other before. I'd pulled in stoned friends, bookkeepers, artists, unemployed sales people, and my daughter's nanny, who were all up for having a fun day pretending to be high-flying executives, art directors, and personal secretaries. We had a five-minute rehearsal. Some were told to be quiet but to look intelligent and appear to be taking extensive notes, and the others were to talk about their love of graphics and design (even though they'd never picked up a rotary pen or used Letraset in their life). It was really hard keeping a straight face when they talked with great authority and with a vast amount of jargon about things they knew absolutely nothing about.

We then marched the executives out of the office and followed the fresh, new signs to another building that was temporarily decked out with our corporate styling, signage, and logos. In reality, this was the typesetter's offices, who we agreed would get the exclusive typesetting order if they went along with our plans. David, my freelance bookkeeper (who was temporarily a "senior executive") had a convincing, posh-sounding voice, and it was his job to show our clients around our second office. We'd put logo-rich signage on the interior doors to give the impression we had all sorts of facilities at our disposal. David had a bit of a problem, as he'd never actually been in the building, and he walked up the stairs and opened a door marked "Dark Room" to reveal a broom cupboard. "Ha, ha! The guys love to have a joke," he quipped.

The typesetters did a brilliant job, too. They were told to only speak in technical jargon and, if asked a question, to always move the subject quickly to baffling topics such as pica measurements, the benefits of double-leading, kerning, x-heights, hot metal or photo setting, justified line breaks, and so on. There was a drink in it for anyone who could baffle the best. The prize, I believe, went to a seemingly normal conversation about Bézier splines.

Eventually the visiting directors, by now enchanted by our organization, visited our *actual* offices—"the engine room," as I called it—and the place they would come if we needed to meet in the future. My real team of two designers and a photographer spoke about their work in front of a flowchart-covered bulletin board, loaded with "anticipated" projects.

We got the order, but we had a clear conscience because, as we intended, nobody actually said anything false or told any lies. Our work proposal and costings were accepted on their own merit. We just made sure that there was a reassuring environment that inspired the imagination, in the hope that we'd be trusted with a job that we knew we could do well. The client gave us a two-month trial, loved the publications we produced, and suggested we sign for a five-year contract. With funds now in the bank, we were also able to also get the order with the airline, and soon after I secured deals to produce marketing packages for one of world's biggest banks and designed the annual reports and brochures for one of the world's biggest insurance companies. In the space of a few months, the business jumped in size, moved into "champagne and rubber plants" offices, had household names on the client list, a cloying bank manager, and a full order book. The staff got their wages, and I bought a new pair of shoes.

There are many times in life when things seem impossible. Not having money is a problem for most of us, but even if you have money from the start, there can be other hidden worries that spoil everything—ill health, failed relationships, a rotten childhood, tedious social responsibilities, a fun-free world, and so on. Worldly success seems to come most easily when there is nothing left to lose, throw yourself on the mercy of the universe, and see it all as a crazy cosmic dance. But this is not always easy to see when we are faced with the relentless grind of troubles. The key to material freedom is to understand that external things cannot bring permanent happiness. To be free, we need to accept that nothing can be held fast, and that everything is in a state of change. Don't be like my Jewish-Buddhist friend, who renounced material things but still keeps the receipts. We have to let go completely and not worry about results. If we give up the fruits of our efforts and do things just for love sake, then there is nothing to take away, and what appears to be taken from our life inevitably comes back in a fresh new form.

Business is a brutal way to learn lots of helpful lessons about what's important in life. It is a good training ground for a spiritual path, since it requires effort, courage, imagination, and determination—qualities that are also needed for spiritual advancement.

I dropped my corporate-marketing business when I met Jane so that I could follow a more fulfilling spiritual path and explore my mediumistic and writing abilities. Today I have an Internet business that sells books and psychic readings and, now sits in the background of my life and supports, but does not overshadow, my spiritual work. Business has taught me that in life there will always be material uncertainty, but we should never worry about change and loss as, with the right attitude, it all comes our way again. In particular, if we cultivate morality, we will not have any difficulties on our path through life. I remind myself of this by a notice I have printed on the top of my accounts receipt box that has a quotation from Sathya Sai Baba: "Money comes and goes, but virtue comes and grows."

NEXT WEEK'S NEWS TODAY

I have only once pulled a knife on someone. It happened when I was hitchhiking in light snow at night from Zagreb to Venice at the age of twenty and was picked up by a very suspect, sweaty, fat man. When the car headed in the wrong direction and the man started making sucking gestures with his finger and mouth, saying something in Italian about "jiggy, jiggy," I started to get worried. When he refused to stop and let me out of the car, and reached out to touch my leg, I had no choice except to pull out a knife on this Brylcreemed ruffian and shout, "Stop the car!" Actually it was hardly a knife. It was a banana knife that I'd brought back with me as a souvenir from my recent stay on a kibbutz in Israel, and it was totally blunt and so thin that it would snap if used aggressively. But it looked terrifying. The car screeched to a halt, and I threw out my rucksack and continued my journey to Venice on foot. As it happened, the incident was a blessing, for I entered Venice just as dawn broke and was greeted by my first view of the Piazza San Marco across crystal waters and an incredible sky. Canaletto had nothing on this.

This was not a particularly auspicious introduction to the gay community, so when Jane's friend, Danny La Rue, suggested that we do some readings for his charity at a gay club, I had a few nagging doubts.

Before becoming a single parent, I had traveled the world on underfinanced and sometimes perilous expeditions. Jane had also traveled everywhere, as her previous husband was a barman on the QE2, which meant that she had unlimited concessionary travel. While I was drinking out of streams and living on black bread, Jane was traveling the world in fabulous luxury, wearing glittery dresses, and sipping champagne under chandeliers. I have never counted cruises as travel, of course, since you see the world but don't experience it, but Jane loved it. (I'm a travel snob like that.) Nowadays I can take Jane to God-forsaken wildernesses and to the ends of the earth, just so long as there's a fancy hotel to stay in.

On the QE2 Jane got to know other regular travelers who frequented the first-class lounge—the Queen's Room on the Quarter Deck. Those were the days when only the rich could afford to travel by liner, and she got to know James Cagney, Lorna Luft, Pat O'Brien, and Frankie Howerd. She gave readings to Maureen Noland from the Noland Sisters and to the female impersonator, Danny La Rue, who had called us to take part in the charity event to raise money for AIDS.

Also involved in the planning was Tony, a gay man who had come to a reading with me in the past in which I had brought through his friend who had been brutally murdered. The communicating spirit had given so much information about the criminals involved, a Freemason connection, and of how the bloody body had been moved upstairs and put in the bath, as well as some information about the car models and plate numbers, that the police came to me undercover for a reading. When the spirit of the murdered man recognized the man who came for the consultation, he urged me to say, "You're the cop who put me in prison!" In reality, his language was a little more colorful than that, but the cop's cover was blown, and he nearly fell off his seat in disbelief. Afterwards he identified himself as a detective and said that he was satisfied that I was not a suspect, but that he was nonetheless astonished that I knew detailed information that was only known to the police. I was never told if the revelations the spirit gave led to an arrest, but I think it helped solve the case.

At the gay club, Tony looked after us, while Danny La Rue did his stage performance, and we gave personal readings in a separate area. I think there was a bit of ribbing going on, but knowing I was a bit nervous about the situation, even though the medium who had initially taught me mediumship in circle was gay and most male Spiritualist mediums are gay, they knew that I was uncomfortable and ensured that I even had my own personal restroom! It was a pretty extreme event. Jane didn't bat an eyelid, as she loves bantering with the gays. They all think she looks like Diana Dors and treat her like a star. I'm no Judy Garland myself, but it was an enjoyable and memorable event, though I admit it did feel a bit odd giving spirit readings to men dressed in gimp masks, ball gowns, leather thongs, and dog leashes.

During our time, we have had a lot of help and support from the gay community on both sides of the Atlantic and from the spirit world, too. Just recently Jane dreamed about our outrageous gay medium friend Mystic Ed (a.k.a. Francis Ward), whom we'd appeared with on a number of TV chat shows. Liberace dressed frumpily in comparison with Mystic Ed. In the dream, he exhibited his hilarious humor and walked her round a special Gay Celebrity Graveyard, with bling gravestones studded with diamante jewelry. Listen up, people of Beverly Hills—there could be a good living to be made from this idea!

Years after the AIDS charity event I've just described, our gay and lesbian friends also helped us tremendously by cheering for us when we were filmed doing mediumship at a theater by the BBC. Our presenter for the theater event was a female vicar from a breakaway Spiritualist group, who would wear the whole vicar regalia, including a dog collar, purple silk clergy shirt, and cassock. I will never forget the face of the BBC cameraman when she gave her female partner a deep kiss just before we went on stage. Nor will I forget the fact that she left her microphone on during the interval, and the whole theater heard her break wind! I thought I was the master of this, but these were truly remarkable acoustics.

The gay club event with Danny La Rue and Tony was one of Jane and my first public events together. Meanwhile, now there was no graphics and advertising business to feed us, we had somehow to make a living. Our way to achieve this was by doing readings at psychic fairs, readings, and home and "party plans." It all sounds easy, but it got complicated, since by now Jane had given birth to our daughter Danielle and had her hands full. Even though people booked readings, they often didn't turn up, and we were left with no money and a whole day ruined. Also, as a medium you can only really do a few readings per day, as the work can become completely draining.

For a while, "party plans" seemed to be the answer, and while Jane did readings at home, I put an ad in the press and started getting group bookings. I also started writing articles, had a column in two local papers, and once a week Jane and I went on local radio to give advice and demonstrations of our skills. All this created local interest in our work, and I started getting lots of booking for "party plans."

Party plans were booked in all types of homes, but sometimes I ended up late at night in areas where you would find your car with its tires missing and a pile of bricks for wheels. Sometimes I would give individual readings at these sessions, and sometimes it would be done with everyone in the room together. I remember that for one group I made a communication with the spirit of a young girl who had been murdered. I provided some highly evidential messages to give absolute proof it was her, and soon everyone was in tears. To lighten the mood, I asked the communicating spirt for some funny information, and soon found myself telling many of the people in the room about their shoplifting antics, what stolen clothes they were currently wearing, and when and where they'd stolen them.

Party plans were not the most upscale events. The worst one I went to saw me giving readings to a group of women individually in the bedroom, while everyone chatted in the lounge. Then there was an almighty banging on the front door and the barking of a Staffordshire bull terrier. The hostess burst into the bedroom and told me to get out of the house as quickly as I could, then helped me squeeze out through the back window. It was her ex-boyfriend, and he was so jealous that he'd never believe this was a psychic gathering, and that nothing untoward was going on in the bedroom. He was not long out of prison and would most likely tear me limb from limb, feed me to the dog, and ask questions later.

Clearly this was not quite what I had hoped for when I closed the door on my corporate advertising business to pursue a more spiritual path. And things were doubly difficult for Jane and me because we paid our taxes and did things properly, whereas all the other psychics in town were undercharging as their main income was from state benefits. Also, all these readings late into the night were beginning to make me really ill. You can read endless palms or tarot cards, as these require no psychic skills, but mediumship saps the very life from you.

Something had to be done, as clearly this livelihood was not working, and if I continued like this I'd probably be dead soon. A solution came when Jane and I managed to secure a regular spot on a mainstream television show called "The Big Breakfast," making news predictions for the coming week in a slot titled "Next Week's News Today!" Take a look on YouTube, and you can see two astonishing things from the shows: Jane and me making incredibly accurate predictions about upcoming events, and me as a fresh-faced man with some hair left!

I have told the story of our time on the show in my book *Psychic Encounters*, but the short version of it was that we now had a top TV slot that lasted over a year. On the basis of the prestige of this show, I was able also to secure a number of psychic columns in national newspapers, to get a few books accepted for publication, and—as Jane and I were so brilliant—had loads of TV offers. "The Big Breakfast" paid us peanuts, but it was a great opportunity. We had to get up at 3:00 a.m. to do the show and would not arrive home till late afternoon, when I'd drive off to do a party plan for a dozen people. In the morning, we would be giving impromptu readings or chatting with stars such as Patrick Swayze, Robbie Williams, Oliver Reed, Tom Jones, Frank Bruno, Jason Donovan, Billy Joe Spears, Kylie Minogue, Glenda Jackson, and Rupert Everett, and in the evening I'd be giving readings and chatting to the unemployed. But I don't forget that it was the ordinary people who enabled us to pay the bills—just.

It was still a struggle for many years after this, since money from books and media is intermittent, but eventually the Internet came along, and in time my website generated the regular income I needed. Although it was many years later that I consulted the Naadi leaves, it is fascinating to think that all this had been foreseen by the *maharishi* thousands of years ago, simply from the marking that the leaves "saw" on my thumbprint: "That thumb impression name is Irue Suri Neruleka. In that thumb impression there are six dots. So who are the people who have these six dots? They are people who are going to be involved in the spiritual or media field, so they are very popular to the people."

PARIS AND PRINCESS DIANA

Anyone who doesn't like Paris needs their head examined. We were a very lucky family, since we had made a very close friendship with a lady named Madame Francoise, who owned a beautiful house in Parc de Sceaux—a glorious area of Paris. As a boy of twelve or thirteen, I could stay there whenever I liked, and her forty-year-old son, Monsieur Guy, would run me around and show me the sights.

Just after the War, when my father was still a young man and had just been "demobbed" from the Fleet Air Arm, he helped set up a youth exchange with France to give young people the opportunity to learn about each other's countries. My grandmother was one of the key organizers, and my father helped by piloting the plane. They were able to find places for all of the boys except for Guy Francoise, who was a very difficult young man. Nobody would have him. My grandmother, who was a very altruistic lady, volunteered to take him. With three eccentric young men of her own, he would fit in fine.

They all became great friends, but Guy was very troubled and began thinking people were poisoning him and that the radio was talking about him. Guy was suffering from schizophrenia, and one day he completely freaked out, leaped up from the dinner table, and tried to get on to the roof. My Dad and his brothers tried to contain him and, in a mad dash down the stairs, the floor collapsed, with my Dad up to his waist in the rotten floorboards. Eventually they managed to trap Guy in the front room and called the doctor. "Whatever noise you hear, whatever happens, don't come in under any circumstances," said the doctor, as he went in with his syringe to give Guy a sedative.

There was an almighty racket, and eventually the doctor emerged in a disheveled state, holding a bent syringe. "Call the emergency services, now!"

My experiences of Paris were very unusual. Guy would drive the wrong way down one-way streets and park the car anywhere—right in the middle of the street, or diagonally into a quarter of a parking space with the trunk poking out into the street. As a teenager I found it amusing when he used to growl at huge dogs until they went crazy and the owners fought to control them. Sometimes he would make astonishing announcements: "Would you like to go to the House of the Naughty Ladies?" or lift up his shirt, point to his belly button, and reveal to the public that this is where his psychiatrist shot him. In the Musée d'Orsay, he tried to pick the paint off a Van Gogh. He had terrible table manners and would pace up and down throughout the meal. Invariably he would pick up the soup plate and swill it down without a spoon then, with a bright red face, declare that it was boiling hot. At a dinner party, I've watched him eat a huge brie cheese alone and seen the table collapse as he thudded his elbows on to it. Perhaps the most embarrassing incident was when he took one of the paintings from his mother's collection—an impressionist painting by Maurice Utrillo—and tried to unsuccessfully sell it at the flea market.

In March 2003, Jane and I were approached by a Los Angeles–based film company and asked to conduct a television séance to contact the spirit of Princess Diana. Somehow the producers had gotten to know about a reading I had given to one of her friends, in which I had unknowingly made contact with the princess. I'd given evidence about some of the letters Diana had written to her, a Romanov pillbox Diana had her given as a gift, and described their mutual friend, the writer Barbara Cartland. The proposed program would see Jane and me retracing the route, which Diana took in London and Paris before she died, and clairvoyantly picking up information about what really happened from the vibrations at the locations. We would then return to London to conduct a live séance with friends and confidants of Diana to see if we could get messages from beyond the grave or any other information that might help solve the mysteries surrounding her death. Simple.

The quest to connect to the spirit of Diana started in Paris, where Jane and I retraced the route she and Dodi Al Fayed took on the day of their death. I explained at the beginning of this book that when you set out on a quest that has spiritual significance, strange synchronizations happen, and our quest to seek the spirit of Diana was accompanied by many odd twists of fate. One of the most remarkable coincidences happened *en route* to Paris. By a sheer fluke, the driver of our limousine was the former personal chauffeur of Paris's other royal romantic exiles, King Edward VIII and Wallis Simpson.

Our first task with the TV crew was to use our psychic skills to see if we could get any clues about what had happened on that fateful journey in the early hours of Sunday morning, August 31, 1997, from the Ritz Hotel to the crash site at the Pont d'Alma tunnel. We were using a form of psychometry to link into the vibrations of place, and we made it clear to the viewers that this was a psychic skill and not, at that stage, a mediumistic link. We were taken along the journey from the back exit of the Ritz Hotel, across Paris, to the Pont d'Alma tunnel. *En route* we visited Dodi's flat on the Champs-Elysées, overlooking the Arc de Triomphe, and endeavored to tune in to its vibrations. Dodi's father, Mohammad Al Fayed, the owner of Harrods department store, also gave us permission to film in his flat in Mayfair, London, where again we described our impressions.

Both of us felt that the spirits of Diana and Dodi drew close to us as we visited the sites, but of course at this stage nothing we said could be verified. Even our impressions while being driven through the Pont d'Alma tunnel could not be confirmed or denied, as there was already a vast amount written about this in the papers. Nonetheless, Jane and I were convinced that there was no conspiracy and that what had happened was simply a tragic accident. If, indeed, we had sensed Diana and Dodi near us at these times, then we believe that Diana's thoughts went out to her boys at the time of her death, while Dodi's were for his father. Diana was not pregnant. I believe she forgives Prince Charles for his infidelity.

Psychometry of an object or a place is not proof of a spirit communication. The next stage of the TV project was for Jane and me to give private consultations to a number of personal friends of the princess. These people would be able to confirm or deny any communication and verify any unique evidence that Diana told us, thereby proving that it was not imagination. The venue was set as the Livery Hall of the Stationers Guild, near St. Paul's Cathedral in

London—the site of the wedding of Charles and Diana. This historic building had housed many royal events since its construction more than four hundred years ago.

To preserve the integrity of the program, only the head of research knew who would sit around the tables. Jane and I remained at our hotel until our cars were instructed to bring us to the Livery Hall. Jane worked with the first group of people, and I arrived later to work with the second group.

The producers understood that there were no guarantees that either of us would get anything through. You can't simply "summon" a spirit. I believe about a million dollars was invested in the program, and the readings were, of course, pivotal to the success or failure of the venture. Not being paid relieved some of the pressure on Jane and me to "perform," but it was an awesome responsibility nonetheless.

Not everything Jane and I gave was correct, and one of the journalists (who referred to himself as "a shocking cynic") and a musician said later in the media that they were not convinced, despite having made positive testimonials on camera immediately after the filming. However, most of what we had to say for the more open-minded sitters contained very specific information that was highly personal and impossible to come by through research, etc. There was no way we could have known these things except through clairvoyance. Later in this chapter I will explain how the spirit communicates using a mix of clairvoyance, clairsentience, and clairaudience—seeing, hearing, and sensing.

When Diana drew close, I became aware of her vivacious personality and of a somewhat mischievous mood as she took part in this highly contentious project. Turning to a young woman seated at the table, Diana passed me impressions of this woman continually writing. It turned out she was Louise Reid-Carr, Diana's personal assistant at the time of her death. Diana showed me the room where Louise used to work, and I described to Louise how she used to stand by the window taking notes beneath a painting that Diana disliked. The earlier sitting with Chrissie F. flashed through my mind, since Diana told me to say that Louise also had a close connection to the author Barbara Cartland. Louise confirmed that she was related to the author. But what clinched it for Louise was when I related that when Diana used to go in to see her, the princess would go up to her, reach her hand into Louise's pocket, and say, "Let's have one of those sweets."

Louise admitted, with a smile, that she always kept a packet of pear drops in her pocket. I could hear Diana say to me, "Tell her I want one of her sweets." The whole mood during Diana's communication was one of cheerfulness and fun, indicating that she wasn't in despair. I feel she hoped that by providing the proofs she had given to those present, her boys would also get the message, "Mummy's happy."

Interesting information also came through for a man who I later discovered was named James Thurlow. Diana said: "Ask him about the menus. Tell him how I always tore them up. Tell him how I used to laugh about it and make it into a bit of fun." He looked astonished when I relayed this to him, and he admitted that his job was to liaise with the chefs in the palace kitchens and discuss the menus for the day with the princess. I also said Diana had given him a special rolled parchment—a menu—when he retired, signed by her. He confirmed this, saying it was a hand-painted, Italian rolled parchment, which he had framed and is now proudly displayed on his wall at home.

I said that when he used to go up to Diana's quarters, it was up an awkward spiral stone staircase, and he'd often see her standing there frying eggs. He'd joke about how he'd cook all this food for her, only for Diana to go up to her room and fry eggs. James confirmed all this. I also told him that the princes weren't supposed to go up the spiral stone staircase, as this was the servants' entrance, but they did anyway and used to play marbles at the turn of the stair to the kitchen. I also related a story about how Diana had asked James to help in a frantic search on their hands and knees for a lost piece of jewelry—a funny event that James confirmed had happened.

It's the trivial things that most people wouldn't know that build up proof, and there is no doubt from watching the footage and his testimonial afterward that Mr. Thurlow was impressed. (The comment about the stairs and search for the jewelry was edited out of the first showing because I had a hacking cough that sent the sound meter off the scale, but was referred to in James's testimonial at the end of the show and included in the second screening.)

I found out afterward that Jane had given equally impressive proof to her group. "Diana began to speak to me about AIDS, and I asked one of the women at the table, whom I was drawn to at that point, why that might be," said Jane. "She told me she was HIV positive, and I later found out that she was Lynde Francis, founder of an HIV center in Zimbabwe. Diana also spoke of scar tissue on Lynde's leg that had nearly killed her. Lynde confirmed that she had had a skin graft after a snake bite in December, which had indeed nearly killed her. Diana also asked me to mention the earrings and say how glad she was to see Lynde wearing them again. Lynde explained that wearing the earrings was a big step, as she had been bed-ridden for many months and had regretted being unable to wear them. Diana then showed me some children's clothes and pointed to an image of a baby wiping flies from its eyes. I told Lynde this, and she confirmed the night the princess had bought clothes out of her own money and given them to children at the orphanage Lynde ran.

Next, I was drawn to a man who, I was later told, was Philip Godfrey-Night, who'd also met Diana and whose partner had died of AIDS. Diana wanted me to ask him about a plate of tea and cakes. He told me that when Diana met him at a hospice, she'd jokingly asked when she could come round for tea and cakes in his new kitchen. I also gave proof in that Diana was aware of a friend who was connected with the town of Brighton and who had died in his arms. She spoke of his good work with the terminally ill.

While I felt privileged that Diana had shown me what really happened, I also felt emotionally exhausted. But it was clear to me her death was an accident, not a conspiracy. After that connection, I felt confident that the séance would be a success—as it proved to be. I know people will criticize us for having taken part in this program, but we wouldn't have done it if we hadn't felt it was right. I felt Diana was happy with it, and we couldn't have done it without her blessing.

I have, of course, wondered if it would be possible to track down the Naadi leaves of Princess Diana, as they could hold the clue to why and how she died. Her leaves would reveal the truth or otherwise behind the conspiracy theories, but we may never know if her leaf is in the library. With a copy of her thumbprint and the public records about her life, it is in theory possible to find them. I know her birth time and that her Indian star is Jyeshtha, but the obstacle is that the Naadis always include a few very personal questions that only the person making the consultation can answer. Without this knowledge, it is near impossible to find her leaf unless

Prince Charles or their sons were to explore the oracle and the truth to be revealed through their own leaves.

We were in New York promoting the show on the news channels and chat shows when the shit hit the fan in the UK. "Good Morning America," the *New York Post*, and *People* magazine had covered the story objectively, but in the UK some of the press went hysterical. No footage had been released in the UK, and the program could never be shown in its entirety, as the critical séance scenes were cut because of British broadcasting regulations. Yet without any information to go on, and giving us no opportunity to respond, some of media attacked us viciously. Only the *Daily Mail* gave a proper interview and said anything positive about what we were trying to do.

Spirit of Diana hits the world headlines

When you know for certain that the spirit world is real, why should it be such a terrible thing to give proofs that the person who has died is happy in the next world? Apart from basic expenses, all of Jane's and my fees were given to one of Diana's charitable trusts. We were doing this simply because we are mediums, and it is important to reach out with the truth to as many people as possible. All that matters is to live with truth and love, and if the press doesn't like it, then that's their problem. As a medium, you have to do things that sometimes rub the establishment up the wrong way—just as Diana did in her life.

What really saddened me, though, was how a number of mediums also went on the attack so as to benefit their own careers. One medium—who had been discredited for fake physical mediumship and been caught holding the "floating" trumpet during a séance—toured the chat shows and spat out as much negativity as he could. He claimed that he'd seen the footage and that it was useless. If you'd like to form your own opinion, some of it is now available on YouTube.

When people go on a divine path, their journey will be challenged by the materialists and those with demonic intent. The history of spirituality is peppered with examples of holy people who have been betrayed or falsely accused of misdeeds. The most obvious examples are Jesus, who was betrayed by his favorite disciple Judas, or the Prophet Muhammad, who had to flee Mecca in A.D. 622 after he was warned about a plot to assassinate him.

There are many examples in Eastern mysticism where flawless spiritual masters have been attacked with the full force of the establishment or been betrayed by their devotees. For example, two mixed-up devotees tried to set up Sri Ramakrishna Paramahansa by sending two sex-workers into his room at night, but Ramakrishna would not fall into the trap, saying that he was unable to see them in any light other than as his own mother! Feeling deeply ashamed, the two prostitutes prostrated to the floor and left his chamber.

Sri Ramana Maharishi, the silent sage of Arunachala, was dragged through the courts by his ex-devotee Perumal Swami in an argument over money. Eventually the devotee became very ill and almost an invalid, and the cosmic boomerang took flight and others cheated him of all his money. He went to Sri Ramana Maharishi and begged for forgiveness and freedom from Hell. The master smiled and replied: "I have forgiven you, and I cannot forget you, even if you forget me. Even if you go to Hell, I am present there, too!"

The great teacher Swami Vivekananda, who was instrumental in first bringing Vedic teachings to the West, had all kinds of allegations thrown at him throughout his life, and some worked full-time to sabotage his mission. Sri Aurobindo was falsely imprisoned by the British for a year before being acquitted. Shirdi Sai Baba was criticized for taking money (*dakshina*) from devotees, even though this was spiritually a way of taking their karma and redistributing the wealth to the poor. And, of course, there was an attempted assassination of Sathya Sai Baba by ex-devotees and many horrible accusations made, but never any formal prosecution served.

The Diana séances saw us dealing with some difficult attacks from people you would expect to be supportive, but they also taught us how to bear with adversity and not to place too much importance on the media and its relentless thirst for shocking news. The mediums who went on the attack have all now faded into obscurity, while we continue carry what we believe to be the light of truth.

I'm sure we'll be attacked again in the future, and the Naadi leaves see this happening in my seventies, but they also show how to avoid it: "The native would be very famous for his services related to spirituality, but still there will be some obstacles in going ahead in spiritual knowledge. These problems occur because of conspiracy of some people. By worshiping God, by following the remedial methods given by Siva Vakiya Maharishi, all these obstacles can be eradicated from the native's life."

One of the upshots from working on the Diana and BBC programs was that my work as a teacher of mediumship became more widely known and in the years that followed I did a lot of work online and in real world workshops to help others develop their latent psychic skills.

OPENING THE THIRD EYE

Teaching people how to awaken to the spiritual path is not easy. Some people, when they read my books, come to my online courses, or attend my circles and workshops expect instant results. The ignorant assume that developing psychic and mediumistic powers is as simple as learning to swim. A few weekend workshops, and that's it—they can set up shop as a professional reader. They ignore my advice that to develop as a medium normally takes years of training in circles, then a few years as a fledgling medium within Spiritualism, and then another fifteen or so years demonstrating solo on the Spiritualist platform before you are almost ready to become a professional medium.

Most people get the occasional psychic flash, such as a dream coming true, knowing who is going to call you before the phone rings, a feeling of telepathy, and so on. Many also get the occasional mediumistic insight—communication from a spirit—and particularly during a crisis such as the sudden death of a loved one. Lots of people can learn to become a psychic, but mediumship is a very rare gift that we are born with and then cultivate over a lifetime of work and sacrifice. I tell my students that one in a hundred may have the potential to become a psychic, but only one in a million has the potential to become a medium. Judging by the numbers advertising their services in the directories and on the Internet, it seems that one in ten *claim* to have all these powers. Just as the Naadi oracles in India are blackened by fraudsters, so too my own divine calling is tarnished by thousands of wannabes and frauds.

Many people are attracted to become a medium because they love the glory, and for the unemployed, tarot reading is a shortcut to making a living in the black economy. Benefits topped up by the occasional reading make for an easy life. The problem is exacerbated by the fact that the public is gullible and does not recognize what is real proof from what is simply cold reading—that is, techniques to imply that the reader knows much more about the person than the reader actually does. (The skeptics say it is all cold reading, but that's another debate.) Television has not helped matters, as many of the "mediums" selected for TV shows are frauds or fools.

Today, my workshops and circles are less about becoming a medium and more about developing your spiritual potential. If psychic powers and mediumship also develop in the course of a student's progress, then I will help this to flower, knowing that the seed has been planted in an individual with true spiritual intent. In this way, I let loose on the world psychics with good character and a heart full of compassion, rather than greedy egotists who will use their gifts for misguided or wrong purposes.

I was startled when the Naadi leaves expressed my hidden concerns about how hard it is to teach people about opening the third eye and the ignorance that I have encountered: "So when this comes to your knowledge, then you can say to the people. But people may not listen, because it is difficult for you and the people, because you are already a spiritual person. But for a normal person, it is not easy for them to open the third eye. It is not many that understand spiritual things."

The oracle made a lot of sense, in that for me working with the third eye comes naturally, but it is often hard to get others to understand the inner processes and discipline required. The second set of palm leaves said the same thing: "And this guidance is even by the native. And such nature of the native is indicated by the third dot in his thumb impression. The third dot indicates the third eye of Lord Shiva. So the third dot in the native's thumb impression gives sudden changes in the native's life and sudden fortune in the native's life. The third eye of Lord Shiva is to perish the evils, devils, and demons. With the help of the third eye, Lord Shiva created Lord Muragan to perish the demons and to protect gods of the Heaven. So because of the third dot in the native's thumb impression, the native would do many favors to many people, and the native would lead a life of high status."

The third eye is the seat of our consciousness that is focused in the sixth primary chakra (spiritual center) called *ajna* chakra—or guru center. The external point of the *ajna* center is between the eyebrows, which is the trigger point for concentration when arousing this center, which is situated almost in the center of the brain in the region of the pineal gland and medulla oblongata. There are many *kriyas* (methods) to open the *ajna*, such as concentrating on the mid-eyebrow area; *trataka*—various gazing techniques; movement of the *prana* light in the spinal column by synchronizing it with the breath; and the inner chant of the *bija* mantras, combined with various *bandhas* (energy locks). Some of these techniques are secret, in that they are only passed on through the oral traditions from guru to pupil, whereas others are available through the yogic texts. All of the methods require a proper teacher and a great deal of perseverance, study, and practice. My Naadi says, "It is not easy for the normal person to open the third eye."

Just sidestepping for a moment: In the 1970s an eight-year-old guru named Guru Maharaj Ji (Prem Rawat) was proclaimed to be able to give instant enlightenment by opening the spiritual centers. All people had to do was visit his Divine Light Mission and "take the knowledge." If this was the case, my artist friend Gary and I wanted to find out and go through with it, so we decided to make our way to London and find out more. We were even prepared to shave off our long hippy hair, as this was one of the requirements of receiving knowledge.

This was another of those spontaneous, unfinanced expeditions. Hitching a ride, we got dropped part way up the motorway on a parallel A-road and had no choice other than to walk about twenty-five miles from Virginia Water into London. When we eventually made it to Hyde Park, where we planned to sleep the night in deckchairs, we had only enough money to buy two pints of milk and a loaf of sliced white bread. I do not recommend this. Our stomachs blew up like beach balls, and deckchairs are impossible to sleep on, often collapsing unexpectedly when you eventually fall to sleep. At about 4:00 a.m., the police moved us on, and we dragged our exhausted, dew-soaked bodies to the Divine Light Mission venue.

Guru Maharaj Ji did not show up, so his mother gave the discourse. She looked at Gary and me and said something to the effect of, "Why is painting so important to you—give it up." No guru—even if they were telepathic—was going to tell us what to do, and we both rejected the whole idea. We didn't like the tone—it was all a bit too much like mind-control, and we felt that "taking knowledge" could be a spiritual sidetrack. Looking at the allegedly "happy" devotees, some looked pretty mixed up, and we quickly decided that it was not for us. Later, the Divine Light Mission attracted a lot of media criticism and allegations of corruption. You can read about this on the Internet if it interests you.

The "knowledge" offered was based on four secret *kriya* techniques that in traditional yoga are normally only given to students after years of preparation. I will not explain the full techniques, as it is madness to do this without the proper instruction and preparation. The first is called "Divine Light" and involves pressing the eyeballs and third eye center, which causes the eye's retina to fire lights. (It is dangerous to press too hard on the eyes, so don't try it!) The second technique is called "Heavenly Music," in which each thumb is placed in the ear and the hands twisted upwards. The third is called "Holy Name," in which the *Soham* mantra is intoned. And the final technique, called "Nectar," is basically the yoga technique of *kechari mudra*, where you curl your tongue up to the roof of your mouth and into your nasal passage. Used correctly together, the full techniques—not explained here—will push *prana* to the third eye and open the awareness.

As far as I can tell, people were given these techniques, and they worked up to a point, but then they were further encouraged to devote their lives and money to Guru Maharaj Ji. In my opinion, the good in yoga *kriya* was being hijacked, and the techniques were incomplete, as they skip stages and hoodwink people by offering easy-to-achieve lights, sounds, and tastes. There is no shortcut to awakening. People think that kundalini yoga can offer a fast route to bliss, but in reality it is a lifetime's work. I recommend you read *Living with Kundalini* by Gopi Krishna, which is an extraordinary story about the mental states he experiences as his kundalini awakened—and some of the consequences when things go wrong.

The philosopher René Descartes believed the pineal gland to be the "principal seat of the soul" and viewed it as the third eye. Others have speculated that the two physical eyes see the past and the present, while the third eye reveals the insight of the future and clairvoyance. The yogi Swami Sivananda taught that by concentrating on this center, the karmas of past lives are destroyed, and the meditator will become a *jivanmukta* (liberated soul) and display all the eight *siddhis* (psychic powers—literally means "perfections"), as well as the thirty-two minor siddhis. The eight major *siddhis* are *anima* (reducing one's body even to the size of an atom); *mahima* (expanding one's body to an infinitely large size); *garima* (becoming infinitely heavy); *laghima* (becoming almost weightless); *prapti* (having unrestricted access to all places); *prakamya* (realizing whatever one desires); *istva* (possessing absolute lordship); and *vashtva* (the power to subjugate all). The powers of prophecy, clairaudience, remote viewing, and so on are on the list of thirty-two minor siddhis.

Ajna means "command" in Sanskrit, and from this center the bodily systems and states of awareness are controlled. From here we also get intuitive knowledge and, although not mentioned in the Indian texts, here also are centered the powers of mediumship. Again, great discipline is needed if this is to develop properly. In some people, the rush for psychic powers results in the pituitary gland becoming dominant over the pineal gland, and energetically this can cause great disruption in the body, mind, sexuality, and emotions. If the inner work is done with slapdash or forceful methods, the medium can become the victim of what have been called by some physical mediums as "intruding entities," which give false information and pollute the proceedings. In my opinion, it is becoming critical that Spiritualists learn from the East, as today many of the methods taught in circles and development groups would benefit from the centuries of knowledge and inner practices in the Indian holy texts. These are, in fact, echoes of the *sanatana dharma*, an ancient teaching that some say predates all religions. It is the natural, ancient and eternal way, which is God-centered rather than prophet-centered and belief-based, and it is beyond any historical date of founding. It is the first universal religion.

The Naadi oracle predicts that in 2017 or 2018, I will gain more knowledge about the secret knowledge of the third eye, and it explains how a saint will communicate to me in the form of a shadow. In my work as a medium, I have always avoided physical mediumship, as it has such a checkered history, and most of what I have seen has been either fraud or just plain silly. One demonstration Jane and I went to see saw us seated in a pitch-dark room, with one red spotlight pointing upward to the medium's face. The chiaroscuro lighting made her face look odd and distorted, and the slightest movement would be exaggerated and morph weirdly in the strange light. This was passed off as transfiguration and was claimed to be the faces of the spirits of loved ones communicating. I doubt if anyone would have seen anything if it had been in normal lighting. We left the event at the Spiritualist church a little angry, but also amused at the foolishness of what Jane and I dubbed "the gurning medium."

I am intrigued to know what the Naadi means by this "round figure" and "shadow" that will appear to me in 2017 or 2018: "In the native's sixty-four, sixty-five, the native will do meditation seeing a round figure. By that, the native will get more spiritual knowledge. By doing meditation and chanting, the native would see a form. He would see energy in a form of a shadow. After seeing that shadow, the native would get more spiritual knowledge. The native would get some message from a saint. The native would get the knowledge of Veda and *shastra*. In this period, the native will fulfill all responsibilities toward his grandchildren. The native will travel to different states, different cities, and different countries. The native will teach the art of spirituality to many people. The native will teach the art of living without medicine by doing some exercises or yoga or energy healing. The native will teach the arts related to meditation, vibration, and yoga."

I have described in my other books the incredible ball of light that appeared in front of us soon after Jane and I met, and I wonder if this is a reference to something similar. (See also the chapter in this book about Sivananda Saraswati.)

"The art of living without medicine" is also a mysterious message. The brain is capable of producing every drug the body needs, and the *ajna* center, I believe, could be the way of living without medicine and, combined with yoga and traditional spiritual healing, it could be the way to perfect mental and physical health. Legend has it that the ancients used to extend their lives by hundreds of years using these secret *kriyas*. For example, Hariakhan Babaji Maharaj, who lives in the Himalayas caves, is said to have been alive for thousands of years, and he sometimes appears among men to accomplish a goal for the welfare of mankind. He is usually seen as a young man, though details of his appearance vary, even when he is observed by several people simultaneously. He was the teacher of Lahiri Mahasaya, who became known in the West through Paramahansa Yogananda, and he was instructed to reintroduce the lost practice of *kriya yoga* to the world. In my opinion, it is best for most people living the householder's life to simply allow the *ajna* center to awaken naturally through concentration. In this way, the chakras and kundalini will spontaneously and gently play their part as mind and *prana* harmonize—the quiescent state that the yogis call *turiya*.

I am also intrigued by the fact that Naadi says here that the inner eye protects us from demonic forces. These could be symbols for the bad vibrations from other people and from the world around us that create dis-ease and illness. The *ajna* is not the final destination of the spiritual forces within us. We may awaken the kundalini, but its destination is the *sahasrara* chakra at the crown of the head. Only when the divine inner light is taken to the *sahasrara* chakra do we become the master of all forces.

From an astrological point of view, we are about to experience many new vibratory influences that will change us as we enter the new *yuga*. Soon scientists will announce what many of us interested in astrology have suspected, that the sun orbits a binary star and, together with our solar system, the two orbit a giant black hole that sits at the center of our galaxy. As we shift to a new galactic position, cosmic rays triggered in the sun and from the center of the Milky Way will influence and change our consciousness. It is not recognized by science, but if consciousness is quantum-based, then it is likely that the tides of particles in the universe would effect this subatomic world. We are being bombarded by invisible energy all the time from the remote on our TV control, our lighting, Wi-Fi, radio signals, and the solar wind (the continuous flow of charged particles from the sun, which permeate the solar system).

René Descartes proposed that the pineal gland and the third eye may be the seat of the soul, but if we go deeper still, we may find that our consciousness is located deeper still. The dendrites are a short, branched extension of a brain nerve cell, along which impulses received from other cells at synapses are transmitted to the cell body. The synaptic barriers of dendrite brain cells are too thick for nerve signals normally to cross. This means that nerve signals need to use quantum tunneling to cross the dendrite synaptic barrier. Could it be that our consciousness exists on the quantum level and perhaps is not generated by the brain at all? If this is the case, then we may also be energetically influenced by the particle clouds and gravity from outer space.

The *ajna* (third eye center) may play a part in connecting to these cosmic energies, which I believe are part of the *prana* or life force. The interior of the pineal gland has retinal tissue composed of rods and cones and is a remnant of a real eye—a parietal eye—that once sensed light levels and seasonal changes. Some animals today, such as the lizard-like reptile tuatara, have a well-developed parietal eye, with a small lens and retina. The eye is photoreceptive and associated with the pineal gland, regulating circadian rhythmicity and hormone production for thermoregulation.

In humans, we lost this third eye millennia ago, but perhaps it still responds not only to seasonal light changes but also other cosmic forces. It is known that the position of the moon can influence a woman's menstrual cycle, and studies have shown that lunatic asylums are more troublesome when the moon is full. Could it be that the pineal gland is being influenced by the moon and triggering the body's rhythms and neuroendocrine mechanisms through the release of melatonin and gonadotropins? Are the sun and the planets casting energetic influences that are also "seen" by the pineal gland and have an influence on this "seat of the soul"? If so, then the position of the planets and stars may be a powerful influence on the evolution of the collective human consciousness.

For me, one of the most potent forces for the awakening of my third eye came when I went with my wife Jane to visit the guru Sathya Sai Baba who I will now tell you about in the next two sections. Listen carefully, for it is said that simply hearing stories about Sathya Sai Baba brings good fortune and spiritual awakening.

SATHYA SAI BABA DARSHAN

As part of the remedies outlined in the Naadi leaves, it said: "After that, the native has to visit a temple of any saint, for example Sai Baba, and there the native has to worship the saint according to the custom in the particular temple." Although I have been a follower of Sathya Sai Baba for many years, I understood this to mean Sathya Sai Baba's first incarnation as Sai Baba of Shirdi—who was revered by both his Hindu and Muslim followers and is regarded by his devotees as a saint. I completed the *archana* to Sai Baba at—of all places—a temple room above a Primark store in Reading.

In 1999, Jane and I went to India to stay at the ashram of Sathya Sai Baba in Puttaparthi, near Bangalore. This had been a tough year for me financially, as eight years before I had given up my lucrative advertising business, and now Jane and I were scraping together a living by doing psychic and mediumistic readings. I was called to India in a dream and wanted to ask Swami about my life, my work as a medium, and in particular was hoping he could somehow help my father, who at that time was dying of bone cancer. We had absolutely no money and could hardly pay the bills, but somehow I miraculously managed to save enough money to take Jane and myself to India.

I have already written about how I came to know Sathya Sai Baba through dreams, how Jane and I were called to his ashram in Puttaparthi, and of the inner challenges and awakening that the visit gave us in my other book, *Psychic Encounters*. Now, writing sixteen years after our visit to the ashram, the moments I recall of sitting and watching Sai Baba walk among us—sometimes standing just inches from us—remain extraordinarily vivid in my mind. In India they call this sight of the guru *darshan*, a Sanskrit word meaning "auspicious viewing," and which expresses something that is more than is known with our five senses. *Darshan* envelops the mind, heart, and soul, and it enfolds you in an experience that is uniquely personal and very hard to describe. When Baba brushes past you, it's like everything that is "you" is laid bare. All my idiosyncrasies, stupidities, good qualities, talents, and memories, as well as my arrogance and failures, were exposed. You can feel the higher soul in yourself talking to God, while the monkey mind babbles on and on about how much it suffers and so on. One thing I learned more than anything is that being with Sathya Sai Baba is an inner experience. It's like walking with God, and it is something that does not begin or end at Puttaparthi, but remains with you forever.

My first glimpse of the bright-orange clad form of Baba, with the golden morning light of India highlighting the edges of his body and breaking through his bushy brown hair, is a sight that will remain with me forever. It felt almost impossible to be watching such a holy form move with such grace that he seemed to almost hover across the ground. Occasionally, the silhouette of Baba would stop and talk to someone in the crowd, and although I could not hear the actual words, there was a compassion and reassurance in his tone that reverberated in the hearts of everyone within earshot.

I was fortunate with my first *darshan* and many after to be seated in the front row, so that I could watch Baba from up close and marvel how with every gesture, the slightest facial movement, or tiniest glance he would trigger reactions in the transfixed devotees. At one time, watching all this, I became aware of how Baba was moving with the energy of the attention of the crowd. He would glide in one direction and then suddenly stop to create what I felt was like consciousness being effortlessly swished around and played with, like a child toying with water in a tin tray. Then Baba would give a cheeky smile and move again, with every eye mesmerized by his slightest movement, until another sudden stop and a glance at us. It was as if he was playing with energy, *prana*, consciousness, reality—it was all flowing with him.

I had a feeling of simultaneously experiencing multiple realities. On the one hand, I was seated on a hard floor, with every bone aching from the long wait, and at the same time I was part of an extraordinary situation in which reality was malleable. There was the "me" that wanted to get something to eat and use the restroom, and there was the "me" that was basking in eternity. Everyone around me was equally entranced, yet having a completely different experience. The extraordinary thing is that the experience is very, very personal. Sai Baba comes to you directly, without any intermediaries, priests, vicars, or mediums. Even in a crowded place, it is just you and him.

Sathya Sai Baba was famous for his materializations, and of course this caused lots of controversy and vitriolic attacks from the press and skeptics. Magicians say it is all sleight of hand and trickery, and I think sometimes it was, as Sathya Sai Baba didn't give a hoot about what people thought. I felt that what I was seeing was a multilevel reality, in which you could see either a miracle or a trick because both realities were happening at the same time. Sathya Sai Baba is like a mirror—you can see in it the divine or a delusion. It all depends on who is doing the looking.

I know that this may sound like self-brainwashing—someone desperately trying to convince himself of something that may not be true—but if a person has a hard-wired materialist mindset, then it would be impossible for them to experience a miracle, so an alternative reality is presented to them. This is a space that science cannot fathom, because in the realm of miracles, something is both true and untrue at the same time.

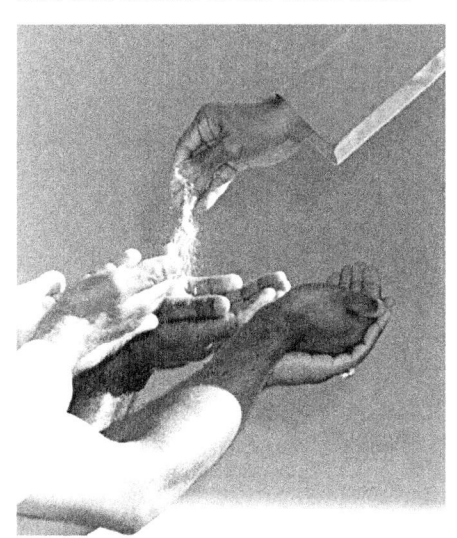

I watched Sai Baba materialize *vibhuti* ash from his fingers right in front of my eyes at about an arm's length from me. There were no hidden pellets, distraction techniques, or sleight of hand. I could clearly see *vibhuti* appearing from just in front of his fingers. When the impossibility and magnitude of what I was seeing struck me, I heard a loud "crack!" as something within me had—in a positive way—just snapped. I understood in that moment—with my whole being and not just my mind—that the materialists' construct of reality is completely false. God was not just in Sai Baba but in me, too. God is everything, and there is absolutely nothing to fear.

When doing mediumship, extraordinary proof may be given to one person in the audience, but those same details may appear as cold reading to a materialist. Sometimes something very, very simple may be the absolute clincher to prove the reality of a spirit communicator, but that same information can sound hollow to a skeptic. For example, when a medium said to my cousin, "I have a big lady here who loved fairies," it would sound to a skeptic like something that could apply to most Spiritualists. But when you know that my lovely, big fat aunt owned an original painting by Cicely Mary Barker from the famous "Flower Fairy" illustrations, and that before she died told my cousin that this would be the evidence she would give as proof of survival, then the simple message takes on a new dimension.

The fact is that you will never know the truth unless you *directly* experience it for yourself. You can go on the Internet and read lots of incredible tales about Sathya Sai Baba's miracles, love, and wisdom, and you can also read lots of terrible things, too. My suggestion to anyone who is new to Sathya Sai Baba is that you read the books about him, but also simply ask in your heart for a dream. If your quest is sincere, a dream—not dropping-off-to-sleep thoughts and fantasies, but a real Sai Baba dream encounter—will eventually come. Write it down immediately, before any details fade, and use this alone as your answer as to whether Sathya Sai Baba is who he says he is. Forget the rest. Just trust your dream.

My field of mediumship also has huge controversy surrounding it. You can watch YouTube videos of Jane and me giving evidential messages of love to people in an audience or at a private sitting, but of course it could all be a set-up—an elaborate trick, with people planted in the audience, and stooges faking tears and alleviated grief. It's not until you get a personal spirit message from a medium that gives irrefutable proof from your own dead loved one that you can chuck your beliefs, doubts, and preconceptions out of the window. When you get a highly evidential message about things that no one could possible look up or guess, then you know for certain that life continues after death, and all this nonsense the skeptics throw at the mystics—cold readings, trickery, cognitive dissonance, the Barnum Effect, communal reinforcement, unconscious retrospective falsification, and so on—all this can be seen for what it is: intelligent men and women trapped on an intellectual merry-go-round. Mystical things are outside of the scope of empiricism. They have to be experienced directly.

At the ashram, I felt that everyone was having not only a completely different experience but also seeing a completely different reality. For some, Sai Baba was God incarnate; for others, he was just a man; and for a few, he was a pervert. Just as some saw miracles, so others saw conjuring tricks. In the case of Sai Baba, you cannot say, "Did this or that happen?" It *all* happened, but what happened was only dependent upon your viewpoint. If you went as a skeptic and refused to change your mind, you would leave as a skeptic, as this is the reality you arrived with and will leave with. Similarly, if you came looking for God, then that's what you found. The presence of Sai Baba simply defied logic. It turned everything we know about reality upside down.

SATHYA SAI BABA'S NAADI

On April 24, 2011, at 7:40 Indian Standard Time, Baba died at the age of eighty-five, leaving nearly forty million followers worldwide in a state of shock and disbelief. An estimated half-million people attended the burial, among them Indian Prime Minister Manmohan Singh, Congress President Sonia Gandhi, then–Gujarat Chief Minister Narendra Modi, cricketer Sachin Tendulkar, and Union Ministers S. M. Krishna and Ambika Soni, as well as other politicians, celebrities, and public figures. Many prominent spiritual leaders also expressed their condolences, including the Dalai Lama, who said: "I am saddened by the passing away of Sri Sathya Sai Baba, the respected spiritual leader. I would like to convey my condolences and prayers to all the followers, devotees, and admirers of the late spiritual leader."

Mata Amritanandamayi ("the hugging saint," Amma) said: "Sai Baba inspired, blessed, and guided millions of people around the world, even though he stayed often in one place only, as he didn't travel anymore. Like to one light, many, many moths fly. This is the guru's light. We offer our salutation to that Divine Light that merged into the Brahman Light. Those who saw him were blessed ones; those who heard about him were lucky ones; and those who only tried to find negative qualities in him are lost in darkness. I wish for all *bhaktas* of Sri Sai Baba to carry the light of their guru within their hearts and continue the spiritual work in his sense. The guru will be with you all the time, even when he has left his physical appearance. Be sure, the Divine Light will come again. My humble adoration to that Divine Light, and blessings to all spiritual seekers around the world."

Sai Baba had predicted that he would be healthy throughout his life and die at the age of ninety-six. Many devotees were asking that if he was an *avatar*, God incarnate, as so many claimed, then how could his word fail? He is to have a third incarnation as Prema Sai Baba, but if the date of his death is incorrect, then the rebirth as the third incarnation must also be wrong.

Swami, dead too soon? It seemed impossible. One explanation for the Sai Baba's unexpected departure was that his predictions about the time of his death were in the timescale of the Hindu Nakshatra Kala Ganana, a timescale based on stars, and something he had referenced his discourses. Sathya Sai Baba was around eight-five solar years according to the Roman Gregorian calendar, but he was ninety-six lunar years according to the old Vedic Hindu calculation based on sidereal months.

Sathya Sai Baba may have given a few cryptic clues to this when he joked on his eightieth birthday celebration and said, "Today is my ninetieth birthday," and everyone present began to laugh. Nobody took it literally. It's not a particularly funny joke, considering that at times Sai Baba can be hilarious. His so-called jokes are usually—in retrospect—a form of *leela*, which translates from the Sanskrit as a "the divine play of God," and which I would explain as Zen-like humor that packs a cosmic punch.

Sreejith Narayan, in his brilliant book *Sai, Thy Kingdom Come*, argues that all of the above is way off the mark, and he points out discrepancies in the lunar-timescale theories. He has meticulously checked all of Sai Baba's discourses and found a great many quotes and references made by Baba that indicate that the divine joke is even more mind-boggling. Sreejith Narayan believes—and he makes a very convincing argument—that Sathya Sai Baba plans to return in the exact same physical form. Many devotees are now expecting either a resurrection of his physical body, or for him to return in multiple bodies simultaneously. Sathya Sai Baba will return and live till the age of ninety-six solar years.

Everyone is trying to interpret the where, when, and how of the Sathya Sai Baba return, but perhaps what he is talking about is something that is incomprehensible to us. Sreejith Narayan has quoted a number of things Sathya Sai Baba has said about his return and also of the nature of the anticipated Golden Age. Baba says: "It is not what anyone alive can imagine. It is beyond all comprehension. I can say that its beauty is magnificent beyond all dreams" (*Sri Sathya Sai Bal Vikas*, volume XV, number 9, September 1996). And in another discourse, Baba says: "You do not know, so many great things are going to take place. Everything seen, heard, or felt will turn sacred. All this is going to happen soon. Do not miss this sacred opportunity and waste it. Once lost, you will never again get it. Once obtained, you will never lose it" (*Divine Discourse*, Prashanti Nilayam, October 14, 1999).

Imagine that everything you can see around now is alive with divine consciousness, all you can hear is sacred, and the very feelings that are arising in you right now—the perceiver—are also immaculate divinity. Surely this is what divine realization is all about: realizing with the whole of your being that the knower and the known are one Divinity. Most people can only get a glimpse of what this is like with the power of their imagination, concentration, and meditation, but it is hard to experience it with the totality of our being. Perhaps the Golden Age will be a change in the energy of the planet as the sun moves through the *yugas* on its 250-million-year orbit around the center of the Milky Way. The shift in cosmic influences may allow our individual consciousness to wake up and be charged with the power of direct realization of divine truth. If this happens, it would change you forever.

Okay, now hold on to your hats! Things start to get even stranger. As you may have guessed from my enthusiasm about my Naadi leaves, I am pretty well convinced that what they say is true. They painted a picture of my life in remarkable detail, though at this point I do not, of course, know if their future predictions will come to pass, and of course I have "free will" and so have the option to resist, change, or mess up a future path. Nonetheless, from what I have read, most people who consult the leaves are as baffled as I am by their accuracy about their life history, and the predictions do appear to come true.

There are ten Naadi leaves translated by different *rishis*, who all tell the miraculous life story of Sathya Sai Baba and of his return after his death. Each *rishi* has written from a different viewpoint, depending upon their understanding of the events they "saw," events that baffled the writers of the already baffling Naadi oracles. Sathya Sai Baba's Naadis have been published in the book *Sacred Nadi Readings:*

Sri Sathya Sai Baba by Sri Vasantha Sai, together with her own Naadi prophecies. (You can get her book and *Sai, Thy Kingdom Come* by Sreejith Narayan as free PDF files on the Internet, or better still, go and buy a hard copy from Amazon.)

One of the predictions about Sathya Sai Baba in the Kagabhujangar Naadi says: "He descends in *Kali Yuga* as Truth, to save the world from destruction. He came in a physical form and preached many subtle truths. After he left his physical body, he went to the heavens. Yet this is not death; it was not the time for him to die. He came here to remove destructions, so left the physical body and went to *Swarga* (Heaven). There he showered his grace on the nine planets, the *devas*, and the celestial army."

The Naadi continues by saying that a big light will emerge and enter the body of Sri Vasantha Sai. Her own Naadis tell her that she is the reincarnation of "Radha, born during the time of the Pandavas." (Radha, also called Radhika, Radharani, and Radhikarani, is a Hindu goddess who is almost always depicted alongside Krishna, and who features prominently within the theology of today's Vallabha and Gaudiya Vaishnava sects, which regard Radha as the original goddess or *shakti*.)

Sri Vasantha Sai's Naadis are fascinating to read in that they predict that she will merge with the form of the returned Sathya Sai Baba and become one with him. Sai Baba is pictured here as Krishna returned and merging with her. In the coming years, the Naadi predicts that she will become progressively younger and eat very little food. In her next incarnation, she will be born without a stomach and will live without needing to eat.

On the same Kagabhujangar leaf, it says of the return: "On this day, where you look the wind and rain will come. Then Swami will come in his form in Andhra Pradesh in Prasanthi Nilayam, in the same month of his birth, on the day of the Thiruvathirai star." I'm interested in why the Naadi talks about wind and rain in all directions. In my own Naadi leaves, it talks about how "the native will be able to foresee the natural calamities related to storm or rain, or related to waves or seas and oceans," and also how "some countries may face some problems related to toxic air or toxic storm, and the native would be able to foresee and foretell those problems to people." This happens when I am seventy and seventy-one, which is in 2024–25. If the world is suffering from terrible storms at this time, then perhaps this is the time when Sai Baba will appear, when "where you look, the wind and rain will come." In the Agasthya Naadi for Sai Baba, it also stated that "the Lord's arrival will be preceded by a great, thunderous storm."

It would be interesting in my next book to compare the Naadis of other people to see if their readings also talk about storms and toxic air. By comparing the dates, it would be possible to ascertain times when these things would happen in the future. If you have had a Naadi reading that hints at world events or future conditions in the world, or has mentioned Sathya Sai Baba, then please get in touch with me through my website at **psychics.co.uk**, and we can compare notes.

Some months before consulting the first Naadi reader, I had a dream that I was at Puttaparthi doing yoga *asanas* on the floor of the *mandir* where Sai Baba used to give *darshan*. I notice that with every *asana* I do, the orange-clad swami moves a little closer to me, until he is standing over me, lifts me to my feet, and tells me to address a huge crowd that has now gathered in the once empty *mandir*. A cameraman with an old-fashioned movie camera stands in front of us as I speak. Sai Baba and I are both wearing ridiculous goggles and both joke around as we address the crowd together. The footage is transmitted, and the cameraman is amazed to see that there is a vast amount more footage than we actually took, and in many of the scenes Sai Baba has completely disappeared or is just an orange blur.

This dream could be interpreted in a number of ways, and at the time I felt it had something to do with my work with television, with the goggles as symbol for the "goggle box." But I wonder since the Naadi reading if the goggle or gas mask could be a symbol for the toxic air predicted in my oracle. A number of devotees of Sai Baba have spoken to me of their dreams about the return of Sai Baba, and some say that they have been given warnings about massive environmental changes.

In the Gorraka Naadi, it goes into details about Sathya Sai Baba's future mission after resurrection and his future rebirth as Prema Sai: "Swami left the body, but the people on Earth are still thinking about him. At the age of eighty-eight, people on Earth will accept him without doubt, blemish, or shortcoming. He will live for seven years. He will perform a big *yagna* with the blessings of the five elements. Then, he will travel to all places. Not only India, but he will cross seas to the foreign lands. He will do all this for seven years. In the seventh year, his consort in Mukthi Nilayam will merge into him. His *atma* will then separate, and he will also leave. He will take all his devotees with him, like going on a journey together. After two years, he will again take human birth [as Prema Sai]. In that birth, he will have child."

The many controversies and accusations about Sathya Sai Baba are also spotted in the Narada Naadi leaves: "Then, on another side, there are some who have spread false rumors about you, and tell of you in an incorrect way. There are many who have done this to you. Yet you never find fault in any."

In the Agasthya Naadi, it reveals how many today are arguing and making false claims: "There will be some dispute and quarrel as to who is in charge. Some may even claim that they themselves are the *avatar*." Sadly, there are a few dangerous clowns dressing up as Sathya Sai Baba, looking for funds, and mediums who claim to channel Sathya Sai Baba from the spirit world. I have spoken about this before, but again I say that Sathya Sai Baba does not need to speak through mediums. He can come to everyone directly. I saw this message written up on the canteen wall when I was at his ashram, and he says much the same in his discourses about mediums who may in the future channel his spirit: "Take it from me, I am not given to such absurdities! I do not use others as my media" (*Sathya Sai Speaks*, new edition, volume 2, page 167).

I had an interesting dream about Sathya Sai Baba that was part of a longer dream that saw me talking with Swami about various personal issues. In the dream, I find myself walking with Sathya Sai Baba through a giant cloister of a college or cathedral, and we talk as we walk around a rectangular open area of grass, surrounded by open galleries. I notice that there are Sai Baba devotees squabbling and trying to divide up the lush lawn with fences. I am a little shocked, as the grass area is meant for everyone. Sai Baba looks over at it with no concern and nonchalantly says: "Oh, don't bother about all of that. I'll sort it out when I return."

So maybe there is a hint in my dream that he will return—maybe soon, and hopefully in my lifetime. Of course, devotees of any guru have to be cautious of their own wishful thinking. There are many cases where devotees of other gurus do things such as mummify the body, bury them in salt, or await the resurrection for thousands of years. It's hard to let go, but I am sure that Sai Baba would not want us to fall into the same traps. It would be far better to spend our time putting a guru's teachings into practice through service, meditation, and inner transformation than awaiting an external guru to do the work for us.

In Muddenahalli, some interesting things are happening. A young boy called Madhusudan, who claims to see Sai Baba, relays messages from Sai Baba directly or from dreams, and for many devotees—including Isaac Tigrett, the founder of the Hard Rock Café—this is the way some feel that Sathya Sai Baba will make his future communications from the subtle body. The devotee and writer Phyllis Krystal took an interest for a while but recently withdrew, saying: "My difficult life situation and weakened physical condition unfortunately let me drift from my inner contact with Baba. I started to rely on this outer source. I wish to return wholeheartedly to what Swami taught us over and over again, to seek him in our heart instead of somewhere outside."

From May 12–21, 2014, Sathya Sai Baba is said to have materialized in his light body in front of over a hundred students at Kodaikanal, a famous hill-station in the state of Tamil Nadu, India. Every day, he spoke on various topics.

Sathya Sai Baba has told everyone, on many occasions, not to become attached to his physical form, yet he has also promised that he will return. Many feel Sathya Sai Baba will be physically resurrected in the same physical form. Some say that he will appear as a form of consciousness within us, and others that he will not return until he takes a new birth as Prema Sai. At Muddenahalli, they are also making claims that Prema Sai has been born in 2013, and that Sathya Sai Baba has been seen in his light body. The full revelation will not happen until Sathya Sai Baba has been in his light body until the earthly age of ninety-six. That's in about 2022.

I completely trust the dreams Sai Baba sends us, and I suspect that if a return were to happen, it will be announced though everyone's dreams simultaneously. Perhaps there's a cosmic joke (*leela*) intertwined here somewhere that none of us can comprehend. I was first called to see Sathya Sai Baba though a dream, and I hope that when Prema Sai is born, it will be the same. The truth can be revealed to us all *directly* and requires no intermediaries. It's easy, really: Love the love; forget the form.

BHAVISHYA PURANA AND BHRIGU SAMHITA

The Naadi oracle is not the only ancient Indian text that apparently foresees the future of the world or foresees the coming of Sathya Sai Baba. Among the 5,000-year-old Vedic Purana texts, which are narratives of the history of the Universe from creation to destruction, is the eleventh, called the *Bhavishya Purana*, and this one tells us of the future. Some believe that the Puranas deal with ancient histories, not only on Earth but on other planets, too.

The *Bhavishya Purana* was written by Sri Veda Vyasa Muni, the compiler of the Vedic texts, and some claim that his work foresaw the coming of Jesus Christ (as Isha Putra), Muhammad, Iranian prophet Zoroaster, Adam and Eve, Moses, Noah's Ark, and Hitler. For India, it predicted the fall of the Sanskrit language and the advent of new languages. It saw the life of the Buddha, the Hindu philosopher Madhavacharya, the founder of the Maurya empire Chandragupta, the Indian emperor Ashoka, the Sanskrit poet Jayadev, and Hindu monk and social reformer Krishna Chaitanya. The predictions also include the British (called Gurundas) occupation and the rule of Queen Victoria over India, and they name Calcutta and the Parliament.

For some, the text could prove upsetting, for it also says that Jesus spent time in the Himalayas and contains the highly controversial claim that that the prophet Muhammad (III.3.3.5-27) was a demon called Tripurasur, who was earlier burned to ashes by Shiva and had taken birth again in form of Mahamada (interpreted by some as the Muhammad).

Akin to the Naadi oracle are a series of other writings called the *Bhrigu Samhita* in Hoshiarpur, in the foothills of the Himalayan Mountains. This library is alleged to be the oldest astrological treatise in India, and it is said to contain the life-story of those who are destined to arrive there. I have not consulted this one personally, but I believe it is similar to the Naadi leaves, except the person's birthdate rather than thumbprint is used to foretell the future.

The writer Dr. Paul Brunton, who wrote *A Search in Secret India* and was one of the first Westerns to meet Ramana Maharishi, knew of its existence in the early 1930s. (Ramana Mahrishi was the guru mentioned earlier in this book that Sri Sadguru Sharavana said I followed in a former life.)

Brunton spoke to the famous astrologer Sudhei Babu about the lost oracle of Bhrigu: "Do you know if there is any English translation of the book?" asked Brunton. The astrologer replied: "I have never heard of one. Few even are the Hindus who know of the existence of the book. Hitherto it has been kept secret."

"When was it written?" asked Brunton.

"It was composed thousands of years ago by the sage Bhrigu, who lived so long ago that I cannot give you a date."

In the *Encyclopedia of Occultism and Parapsychology* (fifth edition, edited by Gordon J. Melton) it says of the oracle: "The original Bhrigu (he is reverently referred to as 'Bhriguji') was a Vedic sage and is mentioned in the *Mahabharata*. As the Bhrigus were a sacred race, it is difficult to identify the compiler of the *Bhrigu Samhita*, but according to legend he lived 10,000 years ago and had a divine vision of everyone who was to be born in every country of the world. He compiled this information in his great treatise on astrology, originally written on palm leaves. No complete manuscript is known, but large sections are rumored to exist somewhere in India."

I spoke with Nischala Cryer, a writer and director of the Ananda College of Living Wisdom in California, who told me: "I do believe in its validity. Many years ago my teacher (who died two years ago but had lived with Yogananda for many years) had a reading, and it was surprisingly accurate. There were things written in the book of Brighu that could not have been known, and it was exceedingly precise. For instance, he noted that my teacher was one of three children, and that his mother also had a baby girl who had died during miscarriage. From what I've heard, you have to be ready for it, and that is something to meditate on. Others haven't found it necessarily useful, so there you are. A friend who is a Vedic astrologer had a reading in India many years ago, when she was a young woman. It was very distressing to her, so people react differently. I think you have to ask the question, 'Why would I want to know?' It takes the fun and mystery out of the Earth plane. I've thought about doing it when I'm older—maybe."

A printed version is said to comprise some 200 volumes, but most Indian astrologers who use the system work with loose manuscript pages. These are supposed to give the name of the client compiled from Sanskrit syllables approximating names in any language, with details of past, present, and future life, as well as previous incarnations. In addition to his fee, the astrologer usually proposes the sponsorship of a special religious ritual to propitiate the gods for past sins. Indian astrologers reported to be using the *Bhrigu Samhita* include Pandit Devakinandan Shastri of Swarsati Phatak, in the old city of Benares, and Pandit Biswanath Bannerjee of Sadananda Road (near the Ujjala movie house) in Calcutta.

As with the Naadi leaves of South India, many fake readers have jumped on the spiritual bandwagon. Sometimes authentic leaves in the hands of an unscrupulous reader will warn him of the consequences of their misuse, and there are tales of readers losing their lives or families, or being punished in terrible ways by events. I was told of one reader who charged for a *puja* that was never completed and who burst into flames. Palm-leaf expert Kim Paisol from Denmark tells of how a true reader will always follow the instructions given from the palm leaves. "Some readers may be suddenly asked to hand over their collections to a stranger, who will come at a given time. Others may be told to throw their collections in the river, as its time is now over. A good Indian friend of mine told me that his great-grandfather, who had been directed to read from such a *Bhrigu Samhita* collection for more than thirty years, was suddenly told one day that its time was now over, and he was ordered to throw it into the nearest river. As he was a man of integrity and faith in God, the collection was therefore taken to a river, thrown in, and disappeared with the current."

Also of interest are the divine revelations found in the writings of Mahamati Prananath (1618–94). He attained the highest state of realization, and a series of verses flowed from him that are said to reveal the divine plan of God. These were compiled between 1657 and 1694 into fourteen books, called collectively the *Taratam Vani*, which contained a total of 18,758 divine verses in several Indian languages. Mahamati Prananath was constantly surrounded by his devotees, since no one knew when the next verse would be spoken.

I was able to correspond with K. C. Vyas, who has made an in-depth study of the texts and wrote *Seventeenth Century Revelations* about the *Taratam Sagar Ke Moti* (Pearls from the Ocean of Taratam). He notes that many of the world predictions made in the *Taratam Vani* have been supported in the astrology verses of the *Bhrigu Samhita*. "Bhriguji confirmed the claim in the *Taratam Vani* that 12,000 highly evolved human beings would, one by one, reincarnate, to claim the spiritual rewards that God has kept in reserve for them. As per my understanding of the *Taratam Vani*, furnished in my two research theses, all this would happen up to the twenty-ninth century."

So clearly there are many clues about future times in these other oracles of India, and I hope to continue my research and unlock their secrets, too. Perhaps more is yet to be revealed when I make my tour of the Himalayas and meet the "masters and yogis" that my Naadi leaves predict: "The native will get knowledge of even those things that are kept as secrets by saints for centuries. Naturally, the native will get more knowledge about Lord Shiva."

I hope that I have not strained my credibility with all of these strange stories from India. For many Westerners these tales about oracles, miracles and saints are greeted with a credulity that is less common in India. So to balance things up a little I would like to tell you next about how Jane and I have had our beliefs challenged and how sometimes our well-intended work is twisted by the media and skeptics. In the next section I'll be taking on the skeptical scientist Richard Dawkins.

RICHARD DAWKINS

It is very hard for a skeptic to get their heads around the idea that the fundamental principle of the universe is love. Love is the fabric on which the whole tapestry of life is woven and is my closest word to describe that misunderstood word, "God."

When Channel 4 asked me to take part in the TV program "Enemies of Reason" (not the working title they gave, of course) with Richard Dawkins, I knew from the start that this was going to be no easy task. Richard Dawkins is a materialist scientist, the author of *The Selfish Gene*, and he believes that the theory of evolution proves that there is no divine meaning to life, no spirit world, and no creator God. When the body dies, consciousness is snuffed out, and that's it. We are no more. Anyone who thinks otherwise has simply ignored the evidence and is blinkered by their beliefs.

To take on Dawkins on TV, with no editorial influence on my part, was a daunting prospect, but throughout my career as a medium, I have often felt called to stick my neck on the block and fight the Spiritualists' corner. I have had many television debates with leading skeptics and generally held my ground pretty well. It always annoyed me that so many famous mediums have been more interested in safeguarding their own comfortable position than taking on legitimate challenges. Most have been complete cowards, apart from a few exceptions such as the British mediums Steven O'Brian, who bravely demonstrated on the chat show "Wogan," and Keith Charles, who took up a TV challenge with the American conjurer James Randi. The "mediums" on some of the absolutely silly TV ghost and haunted house shows are rarely interviewed on chat shows other than by the commissioning channel, which clearly wants to protect its assets.

Jane and I have had some challenging encounters with the skeptics. I have hosted an evening-long TV debate in Scotland called "We, the Jury," in which I stated the case for mediumship in a courtroom setting. We've been on a great many chat shows and faced the usual skeptical challenges and the scorn of some hosts, particularly over our American program about the live TV séance to contact the spirit of Princess Diana. American shows we appeared on—such as "Good Morning America"—I feel are much more tolerant than the sometimes vitriolic UK magazine shows. In Iceland, Greece, and South Korea, we found people were genuinely intrigued to know what we do rather than tear things apart from the very start of the show. In Britain, mainstream TV assumes that mediums are all frauds and fair game to be attacked at will by skeptics, commentators, magicians, hypnotists, conjurers, comedians, and anyone else who would like to pour scorn on this holy work.

One of the most despicable television set-ups was for a show that was eventually called "High Spirits with Shirley Ghostman." I had my suspicions when the researcher explained that all they wanted to do was showcase our mediumship and show the world what wonderful work we do. They went to great lengths to reassure Jane and me that this was a legitimate program, and that they simply wanted to explore the work we do as mediums.

Of course, it was a trap that I fortunately spotted as soon as they started filming. It featured character-comedian Marc Wootton in heavy disguise, playing a slightly vicious medium, and in the final show it included—according to Wikipedia—"a parody of the act of controversial psychic Derek Acorah, and contain[ed] actual satirical references to the television show '6ixth Sense with Colin Fry' in Shirley's opening speech to the audience."

The show was designed to ridicule the mediums who took part, mock Living TV's mediums, and also dupe the skeptics into thinking that Shirley Ghostman was a real psychic. The psychologist Richard Wiseman was completely caught out.

I found out later that the audience was filmed as they watched a horrifying video showing operations, slaughterhouses, and the like, and images of their shocked and appalled faces were then cut into the sequences, as though they were reacting with horror at the people involved in our show. If you believe, as I do, that mediumship is a holy office and can help the world be a better place, then you may share my disgust at the way the television industry behaves.

Many scientists and academics are highly skeptical of the existence of psychic powers and often dismiss the whole topic as complete bunkum. These include conjurers such as James Randi and Derren Brown, who are active members of CSICOP (Committee for the Scientific Investigation of Claims of the Paranormal), whose mission is to "promote scientific inquiry, critical investigation, and the use of reason in examining controversial and extraordinary claims."

Skeptics argue that "extraordinary claims require extraordinary evidence," but most ordinary people believe that they have had a telepathic experience, so does this then mean that they are all deceiving themselves? Telepathy is not extraordinary; it is commonplace, as are clairvoyance, predictive dreams, and so on. Skeptics like to present themselves as sound and reasonable people, but from my own experience, most are very far from fair-minded, and are trapped in their precious science and misconceptions about reality.

Richard Dawkins, DSc, FRS, FRSL, is an ethologist, evolutionary biologist, and writer. He is an emeritus fellow of New College, Oxford, and was the University of Oxford's Professor for Public Understanding of Science from 1995 until 2008. With these credentials, and his lifelong experience of debating at universities, he's a pretty formidable opponent for anyone to challenge. I could never win against a man like this—I felt his mind was made up—but I could at best achieve "stalemate."

My part in the program was to give a demonstration of mediumship at Camberley Spiritualist church. Next day, we filmed a debate between us in a graveyard in London. A lot of footage was filmed, but of course only a fraction could be used for the show, and of course I had no say in the editing. I felt the part showing the demonstration of mediumship missed out critical parts that showed evidence of survival, and the screened debate misrepresented what I had to say.

Fortunately, some years later, someone posted the unedited parts of the debate program—what in the media they call the "rushes"—on YouTube, and you can see how much the edited show and the raw interview differ. (The two clips are posted on my website at

psychics.co.uk.) It is a great shame that I am unable to get hold of the uncut footage of the demonstrations. These showed some very strong evidence for the continuation of life. The backstory to this show, I feel, gives the reader some idea of what mediums are up against when they go on mainstream media and the ignorant bigoted skepticism we have to deal with. As we are talking about things that to them are impossible, they consider us to be either fools or frauds. When real evidence of survival is presented—such as accurate mediumship or scientific proofs—their reaction is hostility.

Battling it out on TV with Richard Dawkins

The solicitor Victor Zammit comments: "Richard Dawkins may be a good theoretical biologist, but he knows absolutely nothing about what is admissible evidence when it comes to afterlife or paranormal matters. To my knowledge, he never stated where, when, how, and why the objective afterlife and paranormal evidence presented cannot be admitted as objective evidence—or why he thinks the evidence is not valid. He tends to be descriptive . . . ignoring my research, and ignoring the best paranormal research of paranormal professional writers and truly brilliant researchers, such as Dr. Dean Radin."

The press was surprisingly sympathetic to the New Agers who were prepared to take up the Dawkins challenge. The *Daily Mirror* said: "As you'd expect, Dawkins puts his case calmly, rationally, and politely. So it must have been a bit sick-making when he discovers a perfectly logical, scientific reason why some of this hocus-pocus actually works."

In an interview in the *Times*, Dawkins admits: "So how many of these practitioners are crooks? The psychics, I think, mostly are," he says. "But with one Spiritualist, I couldn't make out if he was a charlatan or not. It's possible that they sort of know that they're cold reading, but they still think it's the spirits channeling through them."

Neil Davenport's news column said: "In reality, it was Dawkins who came across as shockingly naive. The program also showed that he possesses the sense of humor of a wooden chair leg."

The intellect is a good friend but a naive master. I feel that Richard Dawkins is intoxicated with his belief in science to the point that he lives under a sort of delusion by denying intuitive thinking and any possibility of transcendent experience. He's spiritually lopsided. I have to ask the same question that was printed in the *Guardian* TV section: "Why is Dawkins always so cross?"

A number of Spiritualists were angry at the fact that at the Camberley Spiritualist church event, Richard Dawkins conveniently ignored important proofs of life after death. A few wrote to Channel 4 to complain.

Suzie D. from Camberley wrote to me about my demonstration of mediumship: "You came to me first, and this was the first time I had seen you. When we have readings, we only ever answer 'Yes' and 'No' during the reading, and this time was no different.

"You started off by saying that you had a female, and that she was having trouble speaking. She had a lispy voice, and you could barely hear her, and you felt it was my mother. My mother had her throat cut twice in operations and did have a lispy voice, and she did have trouble projecting her voice.

"You then became confused because you said she was doing a stirring movement, and you said you did not understand, as she was saying over and over, 'The treacle's mine,' 'The treacle's mine.' This was an outstanding amazing statement, as the area I lived all through childhood was fondly known as 'the treacle mines.'

"You gave many other factually correct details, but the most amazing of all was that you said my mother came out of her door and saw two Morris Minors. She said they were black; I said no—(they had black roofs, and the man restored them, but they were gray). You then mentioned the neighbor's name, which was correct. Later my husband reminded me that although the Morrises were originally gray, he had the doors and wings replaced, and they were indeed black.

"The whole reading was accurate and could not be interpreted to be made to fit or desperately misunderstood, as Richard Dawkins implies to those who seek Spiritualists, and we were interviewed by him after, where we told him your reading was 100% accurate, even about the Morris Minors changing color.

"How can Mr. Dawkins, who should be, as a man of science, open to things that may not be able to be understood because we cannot physically prove these things, blatantly deny that he found any proof or evidence that evening? There have been many examples in the past and present of things that may not have a concrete basis to provide evidence of proof, such as string theories and black holes. Did eminent theologians and scientists just ignore these things because of the inability to give concrete proof? Or were they just better men than he?

"To summarize, what I found the saddest of all was that on the program he said that he found no evidence of proof of mediumship, or séance as he referred to it, and yet in my interview with him he clearly was given acknowledgement of evidence that was true. Yet he chose not to show any of this on the program and was selective, perhaps because it did not fit with the whole ethos of his program. Surely such a professional should have had the integrity and honesty when making such a program to show all sides and not just make the evidence fit for the glory of a television program!

"I want to thank you once again for your outstanding reading and the evidence that you provided."

I've given up on the skeptics, and it is not my intention to continue arguing with these closed-minded people any more. There is very little you can say to convince them even to examine the evidence of the "paranormal"—though that, too, is a suspect word, as we are talking here about the true reality and not something that's an appendage to the materialist understanding of reality. People like Richard Dawkins cannot entertain the idea that the spiritual world is preexistent to material reality. In the process of the universe becoming conscious of itself, it has used evolution to become manifest on the material plane.

Richard Dawkins has got everything topsy-turvy, for

consciousness was here first and has descended to become the material world and the process of evolution. In one of my Naadi readings, Shiva is described as the "atom," pointing to the idea that Shiva is both the material and the unmanifest. In mantras, Shiva's form is described as *sat-cit-ananda*—"being-consciousness-bliss." It is the inner experience of Brahman, the absolute that is beyond all form and beyond even the boundless bliss of ultimate reality. He is transcendent calm (*nishprapanchaya shantaya*) and free from all support and luminous (*niralambaya tejase*).

The work of spiritual people starts in this non-material place, where science leaves off, and where science cannot reach. The nature of consciousness, what it is and how it is created and sustained, remains an unexplored part of science. Modern psychology seems to be at odds with itself and nobody has a solid theory as to what consciousness is all about. But it is something that fascinates us mystics and I'm pleased to say that some of my books about the psychology of dreams became best sellers! In the next section we will explore the strange world of dreams and how they can help us to understand the meaning and purpose of our lives.

DREAMS AND TROLLS

We can get messages from the universe through mediumship, psychic abilities, spiritually advanced teachers, meditation, astrology, and the Naadi oracle, but one of the easiest ways everyone can access this vast repository of spiritual knowledge is through dreams. Not only do dreams sort and sift the information, emotions, and experiences accumulated through the day, but they are also a doorway to clairvoyance and mediumship. I have been deeply interested in dreams throughout my life and have been particularly drawn to Jungian psychology. My book *The Hidden Meanings of Dreams* became a bestseller was translated into many languages, including Icelandic, and I was invited by the publisher to talk about the book and demonstrate some of my psychic skills on Icelandic television. Although Iceland has a small population of just over 300,000 people, it has more books read, per capita, than anywhere else in the world. I arrived there in November, when there's only about six hours of daylight.

When a person begins their inner journey to discover who they are, they are faced with the dark, strange landscape of the unconscious mind, which looms before them like the dark and barren world of Iceland in winter. No wonder so many of the great myths that were written here went on to influence Norse and Germanic mythology, as well as modern writers such as J.R.R. Tolkien, who based many of his characters in *Lord of the Rings* on tales from the Volsunga Saga. The psychologist Carl Jung recognized that these myths and legends contained the residue of historic events, but were also a symbolic expression of processes happening deep within the human psyche. Walking in the landscape of Iceland is like walking through the unconscious mind.

Wild frozen rivers in Iceland

Most of the dreams we have are simply the resonance of unfulfilled desires. In real life, we cannot have everything, as that would be impossible, and if we could, it would cause catastrophic social problems. But the energy that we have invested in that desire continues to have momentum when we sleep, and it finds energetic expression though our dreams. Dream fantasies are a way of allowing the emotions to settle by expressing unresolved desires through the language of symbolism, allegory, and metaphor. Most dreams are simply a free movie show that expresses our deepest wishes and problems, and offers solutions to help the emotions to cool down, memories to set, and the mind to find rest. Dreams are also messages from the subconscious mind that is working out practical problems, creating ideas, and identifying health issues while we sleep. This is why "sleeping on it" helps us to make big decisions, since dreams reveal simple solutions to complex problems in an instant.

Sigmund Freud theorized that the primary function of dreams is to reduce anxiety and so maintain sleep. Repressed desires and memories of terrible experiences also have a powerful psychological energy that we take with us into sleep, and these complexes and crippling problems will try to resolve themselves in dreams and nightmares. Freud and others saw dreams as a way to access hidden psychological problems and, by analyzing their hidden meaning, he could use them as a form of therapy to help a person access, and face up to, their psychological difficulties. Freud certainly opened the door to the psyche, but whether his psychological theories have any validity is still a matter of debate. Some writers have argued that Freud became a self-proclaimed messiah and that psychoanalysis is a pseudo-science and a disguised continuation of the Judeo-Christian tradition. Others say that Freud was wrong about just about everything he proposed, and his work is more about his own hang-ups than a proper critique of human psychology. Although now out of favor with academics, Sigmund Freud's provocative theories have nonetheless had a huge influence on psychology, neuroscience, and culture, and he's often credited with kindling a revolution.

It was the French psychiatrist Pierre Janet who first proposed that we have an unconscious mind, and it was Freud who took the concept to the next level by breaking it down even further and encouraging his patients to talk about their problems, feelings, and experiences, regardless of how irrelevant, absurd, or upsetting they sounded. Freud's huge contribution was that he showed that human experience, thought, and some behaviors are determined not by our conscious rationality, but by irrational forces that are outside our control, and originate from the part of us we call the unconscious mind.

Freud's student Carl Jung developed this idea and proposed that by exploring the unconscious mind we can discover aspects of our personality that can be integrated into the whole self. Jung proposed that we have a personal unconscious, similar in nature to Freud's ideas, which contains temporarily forgotten information and repressed memories, but we also have a *collective* (or transpersonal) unconscious, which is a level of the unconscious shared with other members of the human species. The collective unconscious comprises latent memories from our ancestral and evolutionary past. Jung argued that the persistent recurrence of symbols from mythology in dreams supports the idea of an innate, collective cultural residue that lives within us.

It was Jung's mystical approach to the unconscious that inspired me to keep a dream diary and explore my own unconscious mind through dream recall and self-analysis. For about four years, from the age of seventeen until about twenty, I wrote down in the tiniest writing I could manage every dream I could remember and any recurring dreams and dreams from childhood into a heavy, bound book, with a mystically designed cover. Deciding that the whole process was a little too self-indulgent, I eventually threw the heavy book away when trying to walk alone, with no food, for five days on a closed road from Thessalonica in Greece to the former Yugoslavia. I surmised that it was both physically and psychologically too heavy.

In my rucksack was not only the diary but three hardbound copies from Carl Jung's *Collected Works*, so it was all terribly heavy, and ahead the road stretched for miles and miles, winding across a Greek landscape that seemed to go on forever. When I reached the border with Serbia, the guards had been watching me for hours, as my tiny figure wound its way along the closed road and huge, empty landscape. As I arrived at the checkpoint, they all broke into slow applause and then took me aside and frisked me for drugs. This may have had something to do with the fact I sported a beard and long hair, and wore a headband, a Che Guevara T-shirt, and a pair of stars-and-stripes bleached jeans. Or perhaps it was because I was the only customer of the day. With the all-clear, the mustachioed guards smirked as they opened the gates to Serbia to reveal a road that seemed to go even further than before, winding across lonely hills into the horizon.

But I struck it lucky. *En route* I encountered a group of Australians standing by a clapped-out van, arguing with a group of Afghans who were trying to buy it. Hoping to hitch a ride, I got talking with one of the Australians and suggested that I—as an independent and respectable person—broker the sale, but if a deal was struck, then I should get a ride as my payment. So I got a ride all the way to Zagreb, with the Afghans arguing the whole way as to why I was there and whether they should throw me something to eat or throw me out. I was not at ease as I dozed off in the back and could not be sure what all the metal stuff was that they had loaded into the van. As I dropped into troubled sleep, I had an irrational suspicion they were arms smugglers.

At Zagreb I bought the best cup of coffee of all time, was able to afford some black bread, and slept the night with the vagrants on the benches at Zagreb station. One generous tramp opened his tobacco tin and gave me his finest cigarette, made from stubs rolled with newspaper and held together with saliva. Now everything was complete!

But I have digressed. The fact is, I regretted the decision to chuck the dream diary, since the book, it turned out, contained many dreams that predicted the future. I can only recall the fragments of the prophecies, and it would have been useful to have had the book now as confirmation of these precognitions.

Carl Jung touched upon the power of dreams to predict the future in his autobiography. As a scientist, he could not speak about mystical topics for fear of ridicule, and he waited until he was ill and close to dying before dictating his final thoughts and stories about his life. Today he would, I hope, find people who are tolerant to his ideas that dreams may show us the path to knowledge of the Self and a direct realization of God.

I believe that dreams open us to Jung's collective unconscious but also to other aspects of reality that I describe in my other books, like a spiritual mycelium that connects us to everything that ever has or will happen. Through dreams, we can meet people from the spirit world and gurus from other levels of existence, and we can get glimpses of the potential future and access previous lives.

When the Naadi talked about my past life in India, it certainly seemed to resonate with events in my life so far, and it explained why some of the things that happened. But I have also dreamed about times and places that I am convinced are other incarnations, and I hope that some of these things may be revealed as I am given more access to other pages in the oracle. There are people and places that have emerged in my dreams and been touched upon in hypnotic regression that seem to me to be vivid memories of former lives. A life in Rome is very dominant in these memories, and I can recall tiny details about life at the time that are sometimes startlingly reaffirmed when visiting sites with a knowledgeable guide. When Jane and I toured Italy, I immediately knew the streets of the Roman forum and could navigate Pompeii. I can remember from dreams what I believe are the suburban baths at Herculaneum, where I joked with friends long dead about what a fool the emperor was.

How many reading this have had dreams that whisper of the secrets of our former lives? I remember my father describing a dream of being a Native American, and of how he could recall the vapor of the breath from the horses in the early morning light, or the dreams of a friend who tells of riding with Genghis Khan and of the scenes of brutal killing that vomited into his dreams.

We all have these moments of recall that are enveloped with strong feelings and emotions for people and places that now exist only in our fading dreams. Perhaps we are born with the same souls time and again. In this new life, we take on new roles, and sometimes a simple glance, a turn of the body, or a gesture from someone we love may remind us of times gone by and of the lingering memories of cherishment that still echo within us.

In the subconscious world, time becomes fluid, enabling us to gain access to the future. I have quoted many examples already in my other books, but it also raises the question that if dreams can come true, then is everything predetermined? A traditional image to explain this is to see the potential for the future like an apple seed. I can plant it in the ground, and destiny dictates that it will become an apple tree. This is the karmic process in action, since it will not become a coconut tree. The apple tree is determined by the seed, but whether it will produce sweet apples or wither away is determined by many factors. So, too, in our lives we can influence the fruits of the future and improve our lot by tending the seeds that bring results. Only by digging much, much deeper can we make the apple change into a coconut tree. For most people, living a normal life, it is enough that they secure a happy destiny by watering the seeds of their lives with happy, pleasant thoughts and optimistic energy.

Looking at the ominous landscape of Iceland, I was reminded of how the journey to explore the unconscious begins for many people when life feels meaningless. Here in this magnificent, cold, lonely place, I was reminded of legends, myths, and fairy tales, elves, tricksters, mythical beings, and heroes that Jung tells can be explained as personifications of unconscious processes within the psyche. But many Icelanders believe otherwise, and as we drove through the various valleys, my hosts spoke to me about the sagas that told of weird creatures that still haunt these ancient Viking lands. Locals were convinced that an ordinary intersection in Reykjavik was a place haunted by a troll. Every time we passed the point on the way to the

TV studios, we would greet the invisible troll, as this would bring us luck and a favor. All good fun, of course!

Late at night, on my way home to the airport, I idly watched the completely empty streets pass by the window of the taxi. As we slowly navigated the icy roads and passed the haunted intersection, I was flabbergasted to see a bald-headed, naked figure looking directly at me through piercing white eyes. His skin was ocher and covered in fine hair. I sat up abruptly as it slowly lifted its right arm and pointed back to the hotel route. In shock, I looked again, but there was nobody there. The wide, open streets were completely empty. No vagrant or naked flasher could survive in these cold temperatures, and the streets were completely clear, with nowhere to hide.

I was shaking from this hallucination, or whatever it was I'd just seen, and puzzled why it gave such a strange look and pointed back to the hotel. In a whirl of sudden wakefulness, I realized that I'd packed my bags but had left my expensive TV suit in the wardrobe. There was just time to return to the hotel and catch my plane. Clearly, the Icelandic troll had granted me a favor.

So far we have looked at mediumship, considered the premonitions of the Naadis, talked about reincarnation and delved into dreams. In the next few sections I will be exploring the ideas and philosophy taught by the saints I have encountered on journeys to India and other sacred places. We will find out what they have to say about higher consciousness, LSD, the Naadis, the persistence of the personality after death and discover what they have to say about mediumship and the life beyond death..

A HUG FROM AMMA

They call Amma (Mata Amritanandamayi Devi) "the hugging saint" because she quite literally hugs everyone who comes to see her, whether it be a small group or a crowd of thousands. She is from Kerala in India and is revered in her own country as a healer and guru, and is credited with many miracles. Her organization is doing a huge amount of humanitarian work. Amma says that this work also helps the doer: "As you help those in need, selfishness will fall away. And, without even noticing you will find your own fulfillment."

I have read a few postings on my Internet forum from people who have been hugged by Amma, but some say they felt absolutely nothing. I was prepared to accept that the lady had power, but it was also possible, of course, that her devotees were deluding themselves. And on top of all that, I am, in normal life, not a particularly "hugs" person. In fact, the last time I suggested a group hug was when some angry farmers were about to chuck my rambling friends and me off their land.

Someone advised us that if we wanted to experience Amma's energy, we needed to open ourselves to her. So while we sat in line waiting, I closed my eyes and energized my chakras using one of the *kriya* techniques we learned in yoga. Jane was finding it a little awkward to sit on the floor, since she tore the ligaments in her leg some time ago, and they were taking a long time to heal.

Eventually, we came to the front of the line and kneeled in front of Amma. I noticed that the right-hand side of Amma's face was bruised black and blue where she had brought her cheeks into contact with so many thousands of people. As Jane and I are a married couple, we were invited to hug her together: me first, then Jane, then both of us simultaneously. Amma squeezed us tight and whispered some Vedic words into our ears. She then let go and threw some rose petals over us. Her eyes twinkled as she made what sounded to me like a very mischievous giggle.

Jane stood up and, to her surprise, her leg was absolutely fine. I stood up and nearly fell on my face. I had to sit down pronto. My leg was completely numb! "Good God," I joked. "If she's transferred our karmas, I may get the urge to go shopping or whip the vacuum cleaner round when we get home!"

I certainly had the feeling of being the butt of a cosmic joke, but I expect it was really caused by me sitting in an awkward position. There was, nonetheless, a wonderful energy projected by Amma. I felt for a while afterward the same way you feel when a really top-notch spiritual healer has been working on you for a half-hour or more. I felt light, energized, and very relaxed, and yet all this had occurred in just a few moments of hugging. Clearly, Amma is a very special lady, and if you are prepared to open yourself to her vibration, she projects an incredible healing energy.

In India, the name Amma means Mother, and it is often used as a familiar form of address. The hug given by the guru Amma was certainly saturated in motherly love, and it came at a time when I would be away from Jane for a while, touring India with some yogi friends. It was an "everything will be all right" sort of hug. She started giving hugs as a way of comforting distressed people she met and now extends this to everyone she encounters. "I don't see if it is a man or a woman," she says. "I don't see anyone different from my own self. A continuous stream of love flows from me to all of creation. This is my inborn nature. The duty of a doctor is to treat patients. In the same way, my duty is to console those who are suffering."

As far as I am aware, there are no published Naadi leaves for Amma, but in the book *Famous Women, Astro-Portraits by Women Astrologers* by Dr. (Mrs.) Titiksha Mithai, edited by K.N.Rao, there is a chapter on Amma's horoscope. Her astrology recognizes her spiritual status: "The Navasma chart also reflects divinity. Virinchi yoga gives Self-realization and a face gleaming with divinity." Amma was asked by a devotee what was the purpose of astrology, and she replied: "When one is completely surrendered to the guru, the planets stop acting, and the guru takes over completely. When that happens, there is no need for astrology or *pujas*." However, she also told the devotee that few attained this level of surrender, so a knowledge of astrology can be beneficial for most people. I note that at some of her events Jyotish astrology readings are available, and to these she has given her blessing.

Mata Amritanandamayi Picture by Audebaud Jean louis

On a spiritual level, a hug from Amma is more than a nice hug from a chubby lady, since she is working with you on a very deep soul-level that frees the female *shakti* energy of the spirit body. In our body, there's a number of spiritual channels called *naadis*. (The Naadi oracle is named after these divine energy channels.) In the spiritual anatomy described in yoga teachings such as the *Hatha Yoga Pradipika*, there are claimed to be as many as 72,000 spiritual channels running through the spirit body, with six main channels called *ida*, *pingala*, *sushumna*, *brahmani*, *chitrani*, and *vijnani*. When we fall ill, the life force in these channels (*prana*) may get blocked or be out of balance. The physical problems of the body are a reflection of the health of these spiritual channels, which can be disrupted by shock, despair, and all the disasters of daily life. We carry this hurt with us through this life and into future lives. Yoga can help free up this trapped energy as well as the residual trauma from past lives. Visiting a guru can do the same, and a hug from a holy woman like Amma brings all sorts of mysterious energetic transformations to the soul.

According to my Naadi oracle, I have a lot of negative energy following me from my past lives. One says I was a male *rishi* with a bad temper, and in the other it says I was a woman *rishi* who deserted her family for a spiritual life. The oracle says: "She got married, and she lived a pleasant family life with her husband and her children. She was very much interested in spirituality. She was worshiping Devi Durga. After that, there were some changes in her life, and she almost became a saint. And at a very young age, she left her family life, and she did not fulfill the responsibility toward her husband. Later she did not fulfill the responsibilities toward her family members, and she also almost became a saint.

"So her husband was badly affected, and he cursed the lady. That is the native. And apart from this, a few ladies cursed her. The lady left her husband and children, and led a spiritual life.

"The native has got the curses of the husband and also the children. After that, the lady realized that what she did in her young age were sins. She admitted that what she'd done in her young age—that is, the sins she committed in a young age—and wanted to get eradicated from the bad effects of the sins. And she realized that what she'd done was unfavorable to her husband and her children, [and] were sins. In the past, the lady was interested in family life. She got married. She was blessed with children. But after entering into spirituality, the lady got the curses of the husband and also her children.

"She also prayed that in the coming births, she would lead a family life and fulfill all the responsibility toward the spouse and children, and then involved in spirituality with the spouse. Like this, the lady prayed to Lord Shiva and Goddess Parvathi, and got such a birth as a male child."

Considering the fact that my sister thinks I'm the world's worst misogynist—though this may have something to do with her brother "complimenting" her on how sophisticated her mustache looks—it is hard to get my head round the idea that I was a woman in a former life. However, my circumstances did lead me to learn to be a mother during my time as a single parent. "Just desserts," some would say, for all the comments I have made in my time about chaining women to the kitchen sink, the dangers of women drivers, and so on, but the Naadi would suggest that it was all part of my karma.

My daughter Celeste and I had a lot of fun as hopeless Dad and sensible daughter. At first, being a single parent and trying to run a graphic design business from home, with me sitting at my drawing board while rocking the cradle with my foot, was tough going. One moment, I am doing typography paste-up, and the next I'm changing a diaper. With only limited, male multi-tasking skills, it was important never to get the tubes of cow gum and the Sudocrem confused. In time, I was able to organize everything with military precision. I could do a week's shopping in twenty minutes, could change a diaper in thirty seconds (hint: duct tape is quicker than pins), and once baby was asleep, I could design brochures, ads, and trade exhibits. Eventually, the night shift paid off, and I could employ a nanny, and soon we were all in a happy routine.

There was absolutely no way on earth I would take the easy option and go on benefits. Somehow Celeste and I got through, and it was nine happy years of single parenting. Seeing what the Naadi says about my sins, I think there may have been a bit of karmic clearing going on in the early days of being a parent. I have never been so exhausted in all my life, and all this responsibility on young shoulders was sometimes hard to deal with. But of course this is what lots of women have to deal with—not only as single parents, but as regular parents, too. Jane was also a single parent with her first child, and with the help of her Mum she was able to support herself as a psychiatric nurse by night and be a mother by day, though she doesn't make as big a deal of it as I do!

For me, "motherhood" was thrust upon me, and I discovered that childcare is a huge spiritual exercise. Although I was better off with a nanny, I do think that people who see childcare as secondary in importance to a job have got it all wrong. In the first five years of a child's life, we mold a child's character, and through that we have more influence on the future generations than anything else. It is the most important job there is.

In this age of selfish, "me first" values, there is a lot we can learn from spiritual teachers like Amma. "Most people are concerned only with what they can get from the world, but it is what we are able to give to others that determines the quality of our life," says Amma.

NEEM KAROLI BABA OF RISHIKESH

Totally exhausted after the plane journey and the terrifying, long bus journey, we stopped at a temple outside Rishikesh. This place had been a magnet for hippies in the 1960s and 70s, for it was the abode of the guru Neem Karoli Baba, or as he is better known in the West, Maharaj-ji. This guru was visited by Richard Alpert, a Harvard professor who, together with his colleague Dr. Timothy Leary, conducted the first experiments on the effects of the hallucinogenic drug psilocybin on human subjects. Alpert and Leary were dismissed from the Harvard University in 1963—Leary for his conduct in general, and Alpert for illicitly giving psilocybin to undergraduates. Together they became the gurus of the psychedelic era and continued their experiments with LSD from a private mansion in Millbrook, New York. Millbrook became the locum of the hippy movement, attracting intellectuals from across America and the world, including people such as Allen Ginsberg, the Grateful Dead, and Ken Kesey.

But there was a problem with these experiments with consciousness-expanding drugs: the states of awareness could not be maintained. Dr. Richard Alpert began to get depressed. "I realized that no matter how ingenious my experimental designs were, and how high I got, I came down," said Alpert. "At one point, I took five people, and we locked ourselves in a building for three weeks, and we took 400 micrograms of LSD every four hours. . . . What happened in those three weeks in that house, no one would ever believe, including us. And at the end of the three weeks, we walked out of the house and, within a few days, we came down!"

Richard Alpert toured India in the hope that he could find an

Indian holy person who could explain LSD. He eventually met Maharaj-ji, who gulped down a load of LSD—915 micrograms, enough to send a small army into orbit. And nothing happened. Maharaj-ji just continued as normal, as if nothing were different. He explained to Alpert that LSD gave you *siddhis* (power), but that if a person attained the states of consciousness that meditation and yoga brought, then even a powerful drug like LSD had no effect on the yogi's awareness. Alpert became a devotee of Maharaj-ji and took the spiritual name Ram Dass, which means "servant of Ram" (God).

Neem Karoli Baba of Rishikesh

I took LSD a number of times when I was a teenager and during my early twenties, and it had a profound and lasting influence on my thinking. This was in the 70s, when the Beatles were still going strong, and magazines like *Oz* and *Ink* were circulating at school. Aldous Huxley's *Brave New World* was one of our set books, and it wasn't long before I also read his book about mescaline titled *Doors of Perception*. I soon also discovered the books by Timothy Leary, Dr. Ralph Metzner, and Dr. John C. Lilly. My friends and I in the upper-sixth form didn't take LSD for "kicks" or as "knockout drops," as the headmaster claimed during our interrogation when it all came out later. We were genuinely interested in exploring consciousness. We were also keen artists (I was later offered a place at St. Martin's Art College) and wanted also explore this new way of seeing the world.

LSD was not something I took lightly. I had researched it and thought very carefully about what I was going to do.

For me, LSD turned out to be a very positive influence, and my life is richer for the psychedelic experience. But I would be reluctant to wave a flag for its legalization or want it to be freely available to everyone. Some of those friends who got busted at school had their lives destroyed by acid. Some years later, one went crazy, thinking he was being pursued by a clockwork train and, as I mentioned in a previous chapter, one killed himself by covering himself in gasoline and lighting a match. On a bad trip, one of my friends saw dead babies in polythene bags pinned to the wall, and another thought he was the crucified Jesus who had resurrected as a dolphin. I believe that in all these cases, there was a preexistent but undiagnosed mental illness, but it was made far worse by the illicit use of LSD. For most people, and for some in particular, it is clearly a very dangerous path.

I'd taken LSD four times before, but on this occasion I took a very large, four-tablet dose of strong acid in the hope that I could once and for all make some sort of breakthrough and get to the bottom of what it was all about. I went through what Tim Leary had described as the somatic, cellular, and atomic states of awareness. At lightning speed, I entered abstract states that are simply impossible to describe and became aware not only of the fact I was thinking, but I could "see" how the cellular structure of my brain changed every time I had a thought. Reality was unfolding in sometimes terrifying glory.

When you take acid, you don't just sit back and watch lots of lovely colors and patterns float by. Your whole being is engaged in the experience, to the extent that you question the very existence of the person who is having the experience. Sometimes you can even forget your own name. This large dose of LSD transformed the objective world in unimaginable ways, while simultaneously my inner world leaped into spaces that were impossible to comprehend or describe. To me, it became evident that the whole of physical reality was a mathematical structure, as I experienced a tsunami of psychedelic perceptions and fell into alternative realities that were both magnificent and terrifying. I had no choice but to go with it and let go into whatever incomprehensible state of being presented itself. I found within me a fearless attitude, for I knew that if I resisted or tried to hold on to what I thought was "me," then I'd be done for. It was a case of go with it or go mad. Out of this an important realization emerged: it's all me, so why fear anything?

In those days, the prevalent scientific theory told us that LSD was a type of catalyst that speeds up naturally occurring chemical processes already happening in the brain rather than starting a new process. The depth of the experience you have is therefore not necessarily dependent on the quantity of the drug you take. Nobody is certain how LSD works, but recent theories claim that LSD binds to, and activates, serotonin receptors. It may inhibit neurotransmission, stimulate it, or both. It used to be thought that minuscule amounts of it are stored in the brain or spinal fluid, and this could cause "flashbacks," but there's no evidence to support this claim.

Even with this large dose of the drug, I could not get to the bottom of what this experience was all about or what the source of my consciousness was. I wanted to know what I was, and who it is that is aware. But I remained still in the realm of body, perceptions, and mind. I had the intuition that there was another step that would take a superhuman effort to scale. I could sense that there was another order of reality beyond all the incredible things that acid was revealing, but I couldn't quite push the door open. Most people who took acid were simply fooling around with their senses in a dangerous way and going nowhere, but I wanted answers to existence and felt that acid could help me to directly know the truth. Even a huge dose didn't provide the power to open that door.

I was going around in circles—almost there, but not quite. Then something really odd happened. The whole trip just stopped, and I was returned to ordinary, gray reality in an instant. It felt like a fuse had blown in my head, and I was back to a version of reality that was as close as my brain could construct to allow me to get my feet back on the ground. This enforced normality was even stranger than the impossible-to-describe states that I had just experienced.

A few weeks later, my parents went away on vacation. With the permission of my grandmother, who babysat while they were away, I held a party in the "Peach House" at the bottom of my parents' garden. We scattered around some empty beer cans, so that it would look like a standard party, bought my grandmother a box of chocolates, invited a few "smoke screen" friends who we knew would really get drunk while remaining friendly—and the rest of us dropped a small amount of acid.

We'd been tripping into the night and had already experienced the incredible kaleidoscope of fractal patterns, Fibonacci spirals, and incandescent colors that are the hallmark of most acid trips. In the early hours of the morning, most people had gone home, the drunks had behaved themselves, and some were now lying face down on the lawn. The four of us that remained on the trip started talking about life, the universe, multiple realities, philosophy, and everything. It was so inspiring that I commented that I wished we'd taken the acid later in the day so that we could directly explore all these ideas and notions. Fortunately my friend Andy had one more acid tab left, and we divided it between the four of us.

About a half-hour later, just as the second hit of acid started to have its effect, Andy said he wanted to show us something, and that we were to place our full attention on him. He then tensed every muscle in his body and face, then fell into a ball on the floor. To our heightened perceptions, it seemed that he was made of Plasticine modeling clay, since his body squeezed into a ball and his face imploded into a singularity. A wave of horror and fear swept between the rest of us, and I looked at my friend Mike, and together we said the words, "Ohhhhhh, shit!"

But Andy was fine. He stood up, and his whole being shone with divine radiance. His face was serene, like the face of the Buddha. Andy had broken through. He had opened that door. He was fully awake!

"Do the same," he said. "Tense every muscle in your body until you are ready to burst, and then just let go!"

When I closed my eyes, tensed everything until my heart pounded, and let go all the *prana* energy in my body, including in my spine, it released all at once. Together we were catapulted into what seemed like the black void of endless space, and we could see one another in our peripheral vision. "Let go, let go, let go," I inwardly heard Andy say.

Letting go did not just include the muscles and energy, but to get this release to happen, we had to let go of everything, forever. It was a form of dying. I let go of my body, my mind, my memories, my relationships with people, my childhood, my hopes, my perceptions of who I thought I was, and then encountered a huge emotional resistance until I finally let go completely of Craig Hamilton-Parker.

Finally "I" was gone. The whole lot was gone! I was no more.

What happened next is not in the realm of time, space, or human experience, and so it is impossible to describe, even to people who have taken acid or experienced deep meditation. All I can give are poor descriptions of the periphery, but not the "experience" itself. You could say it was like falling into an infinite ocean of divine light that extended infinitely in all directions, but even that would be inadequate. You could say it was becoming one with everything, so that my being included the huge vastness of the universe. But again, that misses so much because even the scale of the universe, with its infinite tracts of time, is small in comparison. It was more than the light of ten thousand suns or the coolness of ten thousand moons. Brahma, Shiva, and God—all these words fall short in describing this light that was beyond time and space. It is infinite bliss, ineffable, infinite, light upon light, stretching forever, beyond the beyond.

"When all is dissolved, all that is left is love," I said, as I emerged again into material reality.

I looked at my friends. Their faces shone in bliss. My attention turned to Andy, and I realized we had complete telepathic communication. My mind was one-pointed. If I looked at any single point, everything around it would disappear to the exclusion of that one point. If I looked at Andy's right eye, the same thing would happen. If I switched my attention to his left eye or to his third eye—which I could see clearly in his forehead—the same would happen. When we both connected with one-pointed attention, Andy's face would squish into an odd shape, and a great stream of visible thoughts would pour between us. We could exchange the most complex information about any topic at all. We could project images, words, and feelings, or unravel long sequences of memory, or reveal the residual energy of a problem that needed sorting out. The closest I have come to this in "normal" awareness is when two people do the spiritual exercise of *trataka* on one another's faces.

The things I am trying to describe here are simply beyond my verbal powers. Occasionally we would stop the *trataka*—for lack of a better word—and speak to one another, just to make sure we were both on topic. I remember being almost apologetic. "I'm sorry, Andy, but I've not understood you, and we'll have to communicate with words for a while. Do you mind?" So we'd talk a while, get back on track, and then slip back into full telepathic conversation—

sometimes while bursting into laughter.

I recall Andy saying: "Have you ever seen the kundalini? Watch this!" and immediately an energy visibly rushed through his body and unfolded above his head in a magnificent mandala of light and extraordinary psychedelic patterns. "Try it yourself!"

As we had these bizarre discussions, interspersed with laughter and sporadic sentences, one of our friendly, drunk friends dragged himself off the lawn and into the "Peach House." He couldn't make sense of what was going on in the room, yet somehow we could tell him everything he was thinking. He sat in the corner flabbergasted by our strange communications as he held the two empty Watney's Party Seven cans next to his stomach and blearily puzzled as to how he had managed to fit it all in.

When dawn broke, only the four of us from the trip remained awake. The dawn was magnificent, and as its primordial light filled the sky and the sound of birds pierced the stillness to herald a new day, I felt that I, too, had been born anew. The world would never be the same for me again.

Toward the end of a spiritually directed acid trip, the wild patterns, telepathic thoughts, and perceptual shifts settle, and the world returns to what is closer to a "normal" reality, with just a hint of the paisley-patterning and richness of color seen before. This in-between state is vitally important, for it helps to bring the psychedelic experience into the counterfeit reality of normal life. Everything about the world around me remained breathtakingly beautiful and was awash with a feeling of peace. I remained vitally aware that it was all simply divine love unfolding in an unhurried and eternal cycle. Everything that would ever emerge from this great peace would always bring good news and happiness of the highest kind. It was simply thus.

And yet I knew that I would forget all this wonder and become the same old twit I'd been before. Acid had allowed me to storm heaven, but I knew that the immensity of this moment would eventually leave me. My soul "knew" that I had known this "suchness" before at times, in childhood, in meditation, or whenever I sensed a glimmer of the Divine in normal daily life. It was all so simple. I recognized it like a person I had loved but completely forgotten about and couldn't recognize until they drew close. "How could I have forgotten you?"

Eventually, the clarity of that moment would be obscured as I once again became clouded. Just as it is hard to recall a dream on awakening, so too the acid experience can be hard to recall because it can only be experienced but never remembered. For a time we awaken, but we gradually fall back into sleep again. The mechanical mind—my own ignorance and behavior—was calling me back to my daily somnambulism.

"I must remember this! I must remember!" I repeated to myself, and yet this very act of remembering pushed me farther from union with the direct flow of Truth. Although I had experienced freedom in this moment, now, very gradually, my own attachments were surely and quietly pulling me back.

We all exist in a strange paradox. We cling to what we love, and yet these attachments keep us from experiencing the real world. We know this as we die. There is initially a wrenching from the world, and we may inwardly cry as we are forced to relinquish all we have achieved in life—our family, our home, our success, our fame and titles, wealth, health, or whatever it is that has driven us through life. After a fleeting moment of life, all is torn from us, and we may feel we face a lonely void.

But there is still something left. What remains is love. When everything is "as it is," we realize that it is all simply love unfolding, and so it is that the most important acts we do and the most important achievements we make are the acts of love.

Love is our connection with the infinite. Love is God becoming God through us. And it was with this understanding that I realized the futility of taking acid. LSD gave me the "power" to enter and move though spiritual states, but once I separated from union with those states, I would fall back again into my own ignorance. My task—and your task, too—is not just to realize God, or merge with God, but to *be* God. This is what I believe Patanjali means by *nirbija samadhi*—realization "without seed," that is, without any desire, without knower and known, and without me and God. Nothing remains except God.

As the trip progressed, I moved in and out of various states of consciousness and occasionally back into the union with what the Buddhists call Tathātā and translates as 'thusness' or 'suchness'. But I was coming down. I could still taste the nectar of paradise and would carry the memory forever, but I was nonetheless coming down.

At the age of seventeen, acid had taken me into a world that few people understand, even after a lifetime of study and spiritual work. The next morning, still tripping slightly, I took my mock English A-Level examination, and the questions were about the poetry of W. B. Yeats and William Blake. I don't remember the exact questions, but they were all about their view of the nature of the self, reality, and so on. I caught Andy's eye across the room, and we both snickered when we saw the questions. To the bafflement of my teacher, I scored top marks!

My acid experiences were the beginning of a mystical inner journey, and somehow I had to get back on the path and learn how to stay there. Fortunately, I was not alone in this spiritual dilemma, which charged me with an overwhelming desire to return to a state of "higher" consciousness at any cost. I was quite prepared to do whatever it took—sit in a cave meditating, become a *sadhu*, get crucified—but where to start?

Some yogis claim that *siddhi* powers can be gained by chemical means. For example a hallucinogenic ritual drink called *soma* was used by the early Indian and Iranian societies and is frequently mentioned in the *Rigveda*, which contains many hymns praising its energizing and spiritual qualities. It is described as the "plant of immortality," which contained the "elixir of life," and it was prepared by pressing juice from the stalks of a certain mountain plant that is now extinct.

In the *Rigveda*, *soma* is said to have given the yogis the ability to create objects from the mind, levitate, astral travel, and expand the awareness to the whole universe, extending their consciousness beyond the physical body. *Soma* is also said to have had the power to regenerate the body and extend life indefinitely, as long as one continues to drink it. It is clear that India knew all about tripping way before Albert Hofmann synthesized lysergic acid diethylamide on November 16, 1938.

My path was similar to that of Ram Dass in some ways. Although I had not dedicated myself to a guru like Neem Karoli Baba, I did find that yoga, meditation, and *kriya* could help me to integrate the psychedelic experiences of my teens. LSD is definitely not a hallucinogenic drug: it reveals *reality*. In the years ahead, Spiritualism and my psychic work were to become the vehicle to help prove not only that there is life after death, but also that my teenage psychedelic experiences were not some crackpot illusion, but very real.

Spiritualism and yoga were initially my anchors, though maybe I'd have been best to take Neem Karoli Baba's advice when he said, "It's better to see God in everything than to try to figure it all out."

The teachings of Maharaj-ji from the book by Ram Dass *Be Here Now* was a lifebelt for many of us who were trying to understand our overwhelming experiences with acid. Ram Dass helped to show us that the spiritual states we discover on an acid trip were the same as those of Maharaj-ji. The difference was, he was in them all the time. He advises us to not get high, but to *be* high.

As I looked around the small temple to Maharaj-ji, I thought how I'd have loved to have met this guru. I then "heard" a voice say, "You just have!" I looked around, but I was alone. My group were far from me and out of earshot. I had heard an absolutely clear objective voice—not an inner impression of a voice that comes through clairaudience, but an audible voice "out there." An auditory hallucination, perhaps, though I believe I heard the guru speaking to me from the beyond.

Googling "Neem Karoli Baba" reveals that many other people have experienced him connect with them on an "inner dimension." Maharaj-ji appears to be continually visiting people and helping them since he "left his body" in Vrindaban in 1973, so it is perhaps not surprising that when an ex-hippy like me stumbled upon his ashram, he would, with his legendary humor, give me a cosmic startle. I believe his message for me was that working with my intuition and doing *sadhana* is far better than the perilous path of the acid trip.

Staying for a while with the colorful adventures of my teenage years, in the next section I will be talking about how creativity can help to integrate the psychedelic experience and can serve as a trigger for the first stages of natural clairvoyance

HIPPIES IN MARRAKESH

In my teenage years, nothing mattered to me more than being an artist. At school I was obsessed with oil painting and sculpture, and despite the fact that I passed all my science and other exams with flying colors and could have picked the university of my choice, I wanted nothing more than to be an artist. I approached art with the single-mindedness of a *sadhu*, and I was prepared to sacrifice anything, and to give up everything, to be an artist.

During the process of identifying my Naadi, the first leaf stated that I had once been an artist—a simple line of words describing something that had once consumed my life. This was inflamed further when I took LSD and realized the vastness of the human perceptions and how blind we were to the world around us. Through my opened perceptions, the world I saw was filled with a billion colors that resonated with sound and form, and cascaded into intricate webs of multilayered patterns. The mind, too, was now opened to vast landscapes of imagination and possibilities that I somehow had to express on canvas.

Painting also connected me with my intuition and the spirit world. When immersed in a creative activity, ideas would appear out of nowhere and fill my awareness. They were fully formed and extraordinarily beautiful visions that I simply had to hold long enough in my mind's eye to copy. It was the ultimate in plagiarism—all I had to do was reproduce what I was seeing. Today, when I work as a medium, these same "oven-ready" images and words come to my mind when I make a spirit contact. I just seem to know everything about the person in spirit and about the person sitting in front of me.

I cannot explain where they come from. Proofs of survival and messages of hope simply emerge out of the universe. Similarly, when I was painting, I felt my hand was being guided by a muse that communicated ideas and information in a similar way to the way we mediums receive messages from our spirit guides and helpers.

The psychologist Hans Eysenck and others have suggested that there is a link between alleged psychic powers and creativity. Imaginative, creative people and patricianly artists score better in ESP tests. Some argue that psychic people are on the edge of madness but use their intelligence and working memory to cope, and to stop them from being overwhelmed—like a person who, to borrow the philosopher Soren Kierkegaard's phrase, "drowns in possibility." High-risk takers, optimists, and extrovert personality types also tend to score higher in ESP tests (such as Zener card tests for telepathy) than people with a neurotic disposition or systematic thinkers.

When it comes to testing miracles and psychic phenomena, I believe there are other factors that need to be taken into account that transcend the materialistic viewpoint. As I explained in the chapter about Sathya Sai Baba, it may be the case when presented with the impossible, the observer enters a reality that most suits his spiritual position. A materialistic reductionist will see a result that corresponds to his scientific standpoint, whereas a devotee may witness the impossible made manifest. This is why, when Jane and I have worked on television and had the rare opportunity to have a say in the selection of the crew, I've always asked that they select people who are genuine believers in the paranormal, or at least people who are not antagonistic to it. If possible, the crew should have personalities that are extroverted, creative, and optimistic. The skeptic will, of course, say we need gullible mugs to hoodwink, but our objective is to create the right conditions so that the energy around us is supportive and conducive to good mediumship. For every show we've made, there's always been the obligatory skeptic present, such as a magic circle conjurer, comedian, or unconvinced psychologist, but having the supportive energy of the production team does help. This is also why—aside from people who cheat—genuine mediumship shines when working in front of an enthusiastic theater audience but can struggle under the cerebral mindset of a research team. In terms of consciousness, they are completely different worlds.

From my anecdotal evidence, it would appear that many mediums have an extraordinary ability to visualize. In my own case, I sometimes see eidetic images—that is, images in my mind's eye that do not appear to be the creation of my imagination, as they are fully formed and unalterable. I "see" inner images in 3D, with great clarity, and from multiple viewpoints. At the early stages of meditation, I may see streams of imagery, or lights floating across the screen of my awareness, and sometimes when I go to bed, just before I drop into sleep, I witness an effulgence of imagery called hypnagogic dreaming.

Seeing a constellation of images as you fall asleep is not a pathological problem, and while a few people might experience them frequently, most people experience them occasionally. Although called hypnagogic dreams, they are very different to normal dreams in that dreams come in episodes with a narrative, coherence, and a theme, and they reflect our wishes, fears, and experiences. But here we feel like a spectator, with little or no control over what emerges into our awareness. Although I have found ways to manipulate the flow and direct it to an extent, the imagery remains nonetheless a torrent of impossible-to-describe landscapes, faces, patterns, strange scenes, and weird cartoons. Usually the panorama has brilliant and saturated colors, as if everything is bathed in an incredible luminosity that emphasizes every detail of what unfolds before my eyes. Sometimes images will zoom toward me and burst into detail, only to fade to make way for another super-real image with a life of its own. There are no apparent connections in the random and incredibly detailed flow, and we can only marvel at the stupendous ability of the mind to generate these wonders.

Many creative people have been inspired by these visions from the threshold of sleep. Edgar Allan Poe spoke about them as being unlike anything he had ever seen before, and he said that they had "the absoluteness of novelty." He would often snap himself into wakefulness and take notes that he could use as creative material in his stories and poems. Others who have been inspired by hypnagogic dreams include Coleridge, Wordsworth, Beethoven, Richard Wagner, Walter Scott, Salvador Dali, Thomas Edison, Nikola Tesla, and Isaac Newton. All have credited hypnagogia and related states with enhancing their creativity.

I am sure that an ability to visualize may play a role in clairvoyance—a word which comes from French meaning clear-seeing (*clair* clear, from Latin *clarus* + *voyance*, from *voir* to see, from Latin *videre*). Jane and I also have the gifts of *clairsentience* and *clairaudience* in which we inwardly "sense" or "hear" information about a communicating spirit. During meditation it is also possible, once the mind is in a one-pointed concentration state, to encourage the mind to think entirely in imagery, or if you prefer sound, so that thoughts become like music resonating through the brain's primary auditory cortex. I have explained in detail how these spiritual perceptions work in my books about mediumistic and spiritual development. My point here is that artistic ability may be a useful skill that is somehow linked to extra-sensory perception, and that becoming an artist may have been the important trigger I needed to catapult me into my unexpected career as a medium and spiritual teacher.

After an interlude attempting to set up an alternative hippy commune, followed by a year spent on a kibbutz, I decided to make a serious attempt at becoming a professional artist. Initially I set up a studio in my hometown, which I funded by working sixty hours a week cooking hamburgers. Stinking of stale lard, I would finish at 3:00 a.m. and continue painting through the night. I'd sleep into the day and awake to start another impossible shift. I had a few other dedicated artists working with me, and together we hoped to become a movement. The studio doors were open to anyone who wanted to be creative. They could spend the day with us and use our materials, so long as they actually produced some art. The problem was that it became a Mecca for the disinterested hippy unemployed, and there were times when you couldn't access an easel or sit at a bench, since the place was filled with stoned corpses. A year of flipping burgers while everyone got stoned and crashed was getting too hard to handle. I tried also to branch into graphic design for bands to supplement the income, but most of the time the clients, such as the Hell's Angels, either couldn't pay or wouldn't pay. Eventually, some of my artist friends left, and the studio closed.

Plan B was to take a vacation in Morocco with some friends who were sculptors and then take the Magic Bus through Spain to Amsterdam, where I'd find a place to crash and make a new start by setting up a European studio. In 1976, it all seemed so simple to a young man of twenty-one with crazy ideals.

In Marrakesh, we made friends with some guys in the Moroccan army and joined them for a trip down to the southern border of Morocco, near the Spanish Sahara. It was a perilous idea, but we figured we'd be all right, as some of us had been learning karate in Winchester, England, with a Japanese madman, who had been thrown out of the Karate Federation for crippling his students.

Before one training session, I had washed my karate clothes with a pair of red socks, which was shamefully out of place to his Samurai mind: "Hey you! Man in Pink Gi!" he shouted. "You now flee spar with me!" and he proceeded to put me through a bruising ordeal and relentlessly knock me to the floor. In winter, he used to have us doing knuckle press ups and barefoot marathons in the snow. Soon after my "free spar lesson," he broke my friend's jaw, and he was eventually stopped from doing lessons at all. If we could survive this small but daunting karate P.O.W. camp, we could certainly take on any problems we'd encounter in Morocco. And my friend Julian was built like a concrete coal bunker and spent hours side-kicking a wooden pole in his garden, so we could come to absolutely no harm.

It is a good idea to plan trips though the desert, and to take a map and plenty of water. Enthusiasm is no substitute for expertise. Of course, we ran out of water as soon as our feet touched the sand, and we were forced to buy some rancid water from a traditional water salesman, dressed in bright red and wearing a funny cross between a Mexican hat and lampshade. Once we were far from civilization, the sun went down as quickly as you'd switch off a light, and we hurried to a convenient hollow in the ground where we could sleep beneath the radiant stars of the moonless night. We threw off our rucksacks and shoes into the carbon-black night and prepared for an exhausted sleep.

I think it was Julian's wife who spotted the first snake and alerted us with a hysterical scream. The Moroccan soldiers were not much help. They panicked: "Snake pit! Snake pit!" they exclaimed as they ran off into the desert, taking the last of the water with them. All we could do was find a safe-looking spot, stand barefoot, and wait till dawn so that we could retrieve our scattered possessions in the comparative safety of the morning light.

We had no map, but next day we followed a trail that eventually brought us to a small village of a few houses. We were all now completely dehydrated and had sunstroke. It hit our karate fanatic Julian the worst, and as he was such a huge guy, it was doubly difficult to keep him upright. We all had violent diarrhea and were intermittently stopping to go wherever we could find a wall, bush, or tree. Of course, I was the one the villagers spotted, and instead of the warm reception and "Ice Cold in Alex" drinks we hoped for, we were greeted by a row of angry, white-clad Berbers with their hands on their traditional, curved knives.

It's a shame that I had not known of the Naadi revelations of my weaknesses at this time, for instead of inviting the hospitality which I knew from my experiences in Israel that Muslims extend to people in need, I lost my temper. Even the fact that we were wearing traditional *djellabas* and a fez didn't seem to hold any weight. Here were a bunch of despicable, diseased hippies that were not to come to town. "*Allez! Misérables!*"

I'm not sure how we survived the next three days under the trees by a river on the outskirts of the village. By day we were all hallucinating from the sunstroke and relentless diarrhea, and at night we could see the whites of the eyes of the village children watching us from the bushes. Eventually the weekly bus arrived, and we were just able to drag Julian up the dirt bank to the road and board the bus. It was not an easy trip. When one of our group begged the bus to stop so he could find a bush, the ugly driver with a mouth full of terrible gold fillings simply said, "Mister, you shit your pants!"

We survived, and now I could start my new life as an artist. I took the ferry to Spain and boarded the Blue Goose Magic Bus to Amsterdam.

The planets were not auspicious. My dream of establishing an artist studio in Amsterdam quickly fell to pieces, as I rapidly ran out of money. My time was spent scrambling to find temporary jobs and get enough money together to feed myself and keep out of the relentless rain. I worked at Dam Chips, a factory that made frozen potatoes and chips, and I lived for four days exclusively on water and paprika-flavored chips. When the money ran out completely, we would, every day, do the free tour of the Heineken Beer factory, at the end of which tourists were given a free beer and some cheese and crackers. At one point, things looked so bad that I actually considered getting a regular job and, together with a new friend, we both applied to be writers with Time Life Books (Amsterdam). They needed people fluent in English, but I couldn't understand why they didn't give us a chance at the preliminary interview. On the way out I noticed that my long-haired, bearded friend wasn't even wearing shoes, and I probably looked just as bad.

I did eventually make it as an artist. I managed to make it back to the UK and went back to flipping burgers and painting. I then teamed up with a friend, Gary "Skip" Conway, who was a spastic and, although he had little control over his hands, was nonetheless a pretty good artist. He was mad about jazz, and I was interested in exploring painting with an airbrush.

We got talking over a burger and decided we'd do an exhibition together. Soon we convinced Rowney Paints to sponsor us and got further funding from the Arts Council. We roped in an avant-garde jazz composer, Monty Warlock, who wrote excruciatingly hard-to-listen-to jazz compositions, and the three of us produced an exhibition titled "Paintings and Preludes." This featured our jointly painted abstract works that represented the mood, form, and rhythm of the music, in a synesthesia of perceptions.

We planned the paintings together. Gary did the masking, and I did the airbrush painting. We launched the exhibition at Southampton Municipal Art Gallery, and it toured other galleries in the UK, eventually ending up being exhibited in Harrods department store in London.

I believe that the creative drive is somehow linked to our natural clairvoyant intuition and for me this was one of the most important forces that pushed me towards self-discovery, mediumship and my quest for realization. I no longer paint as writing is now my master but yoga stayed with me and has served to balance the powerful energies that the psychedelic phase of my life unlocked. My story will now jump forward 30-odd years to my trips to India and my television work with Jane.

SWAMI SIVANANDA SARASWATI

Just up the hill from the place I stayed at in Rishikesh is the ashram of Swami Sivananda Saraswati (1887–1963). Sivananda was a medical doctor before renouncing worldly life for the spiritual path, and his teachings drew upon all the formal doctrines of yoga. During his lifetime he authored over three hundred books on yoga, based not on theory but on his own personal experience. I would highly recommend them. They are thorough, accurate, and extremely well written. Sivananda's main philosophical message was: "Serve, love, give, purify, meditate, realize. Be good, do good. Be kind, be compassionate. Inquire, 'Who am I?' Know the Self, and be free." On the walls of the temple, this message was summarized to "Be good. Do good."

Sivananda Saraswati does not ask you to give up your home, wealth, and job, and to escape into a cave or jungle. Instead, he assures us that it is possible to attain divinity while living in our present surroundings and discharging all our worldly duties. He assures us that the yogi who keeps up meditation while performing actions is a powerful yogi indeed. He also took an interest in Spiritualism.

Speaking about the researches of famous Spiritualist Sir Oliver Lodge, he wrote: "To the student of Eastern philosophy, bred and brought up in the sacred scriptures of India, the existence of a soul and its transmigrations are only the beginning of his philosophy. To the West, it has come to be almost the end of their researches till now. . . . Modern Spiritualism has given wonderful demonstrations regarding the existence of disembodied spirits, who continue to live even after the dissolution of their gross physical bodies. This has opened the eyes of the rank-materialists of the West and the atheists."

He also, however, warns of the apparent dangers of mediumship, because our focus on the spirit world may weaken our self-regulation and distract us from the goal of finding divine awareness. "No one should allow himself to become a medium," writes Sivananda Saraswati. "The mediums have lost the power of self-control. Their vital energy, life-force, and intellectual powers are used by the spirits which control them. The mediums do not gain any higher divine knowledge."

He has a point, and I also feel that many mediums forget that the goal in life is not the spirit world but awareness of our oneness with God. Mediumship without the aspiration to divine knowledge is poor spiritual practice. Sivananda Saraswati was writing at a time when Spiritualist mediums were producing physical mediumship—a form of objective mediumship where the medium exudes a substance called ectoplasm, which manifests as a voice box, spirit hands, or a full human form.

This is a highly controversial form of mediumship that has seen a great deal of deliberate fraud, but also, I believe, some real results. I have spoken to many Spiritualists who have seen it and, since they are intelligent people with good values, I believe them. Unfortunately, everything I've personally witnessed to date is chicanery.

In my next book, I will be exploring the world of physical mediumship in detail, and I have places booked with a number of physical mediums who are working today. I am, of course, hoping that I will able to see tangible evidence. In my own circles, we have seen "spirit lights" that are seen by everyone taking part, and so they are unlikely to be retinal flashes caused by sitting in the dark. Sitters have also claimed that when I have done trance mediumship, a thin, luminous mask has appeared over my face, showing spirit people. As not everyone in the room saw this, I am inclined to say that this could be an optical illusion. There was, however, one incident of tangible, objective phenomenon that happened to Jane and me, which I first wrote about in my book *Psychic School* and I reprint here:

"Perhaps it was something to do with the conjoining of our spiritual powers or the energies of the places we chose to visit during our courting, which included Spiritualist churches, séance rooms, and a memorable, mind-boggling encounter with the Dalai Lama. Our auras were most certainly primed with spiritual energy, and we both knew that this period of our lives was especially important—a turning point when synchronicity happens and events take unexpected and strange turns.

"The president of our local Spiritualist church, where Jane and I had met during one of my public demonstrations of mediumship, had arranged for us to exorcise poltergeist activity causing trouble on a converted fishing boat. It was moored on the River Hamble in Hampshire, England, close to the ancient site where King Henry VIII once built his navy vessels from the oaks of the New Forest. Anticipating the following night's plan to cross the dark river and board this strange ghost ship, we tried to relax and get some sleep at about 11:00 p.m. As we rested, we were startled by an explosion of blinding light in the center of the room. 'My God, what's happening?' Jane called out, as the light proceeded to fold in on itself and hover in a luminous ball, then expand to form a circle of light in the center of the room. The circle was about four feet across and at eye level.

"We stared like startled animals caught in a car's headlights. My immediate thought was that it was lightning—perhaps even ball lightning—but we were indoors, and it was a clear evening with no threat of thunderstorms. Yet the room certainly had an electric atmosphere. I could feel the hairs on my arms standing on end.

"Jane and I sat speechless as the light hovered for what seemed like an eternity but could only have been about thirty seconds. Then the circle reformed into a tight ball and shot across the bedroom and out of the door, toward the living room. I leaped out of bed, chasing after it into the adjoining room. Seconds later it disappeared, leaving no trace. The light was no clairvoyant vision, or 'inner knowing,' but as real as this book you are holding. It was tangible, but with no explanation. Jane and I were astonished. Our limbs felt strangely heavy, and we were both slightly nauseous.

"I believe that what we experienced was linked to the fact that we were both, at that time, living in a highly charged spiritual state. Maybe a protective angelic force was revealing itself in preparation for our encounter with the poltergeist the next day. I don't know. The fact that we felt slightly sick afterward could imply that the energy had something to do with our bodies, perhaps a spontaneous projection of some form of ectoplasm—the invisible substance sometimes produced by mediums and made luminous by spirit communicators."

I'm not sure how Sivananda Saraswati would have explained that. In his hard-to-get book *What Becomes of the Soul after Death*, Sivananda Saraswati recounts a number of interesting Spiritualist casebooks and makes observations and comments about these super-physical experiences. Spiritualists interested in Eastern mysticism will find it intriguing.

In India we visited the shrine in Sivananda Saraswati's ashram where mantras are still being chanted twenty-four hours a day, and have been for the last fifty years. The monks take it in shifts. When the India yogis say they're going to do something, boy, do they deliver!

In the temple itself, I became immersed in watching the auras of the monks and people worshiping. I have been able to see auras all my life, and I still find it hard to understand why everyone cannot see them, for to me they are self-evident. Most people in the temple had normal auras, but my eyes were drawn to one monk who was immersed in meditation. Around his crown chakra, at the top of his head, I could see a red circle of light slowly turning. I had the feeling he was visualizing the dance of Shiva and was practicing an energy *kriya* of some kind. Unfortunately circumstances did not allow me to talk to the monk to find out what he was doing.

The visit to Sivananda Saraswati's ashram was an inspiring day, which was made even more memorable by the events of that evening, as we sat by the banks of the moonlit Ganges, listening to a private concert by the sitar player Hari Krishna Sha. He played for us into the night, and he explained the spiritual theory behind Indian music and how, when we listen to the *ragas*, the musical scale corresponds to the inner sounds of the chakras (Sa, Re, Ga, Ma, Pa, Dha, and Ni). The *ragas* are designed to stimulate specific chakras and allow the kundalini force to rise, energizing and nourishing the chakra system. Indian music also resonates with the chakra to maintain its optimum spin and balance, which brings healing energy to an organ associated with a specific chakra.

As we listened to his exquisite sitar music, we allowed it to literally dance up and down our spines.

The movements of the prana forces in the spine expounded in the yoga teaching and that Swami Sivananda Saraswati explained and clarified in his own teaching, follow natural cycles and move between the rhythms of the solar and lunar activities of the energy channels called ida and pingala. At specified times in the day and night there is a change in the levels and dominance of each energy that corresponds with the energies influencing us from the Sun, Moon planets and stars. Close to midnight, when we listened to the music of the chakras, there is a changeover in the external and internal energies and all becomes tranquil within.

In an ashram, the most important time for practicing yoga is the early morning which means an hour and a half before sunrise. It is called brahmamuhurta, 'the period of Brahma.' The deeper aspects of yoga are not normally practiced at midnight without the presence of a guru because at this time the unconscious mind is very active and negative and frightening thoughts may rise into your awareness. As in the west the Indians call this the 'witching hour' because the 'ghosts' in the mind become active.

And all this brings me conveniently to my next little story set back in the UK at the birthplace of William Shakespeare at the witching hour.

STRATFORD-UPON-AVON GHOST HUNT

Glendower: "I can call spirits from the vasty deep." Hotspur: "Why, so can I; or so can any man: But will they come when you do call for them?"
—William Shakespeare, *Henry IV Part One*, Act 3, Scene 1.

In Shakespeare's *Henry IV*, Owen Glendower fancies himself an adept in magic and prophecy, and he tells of the miraculous events that attended his birth, but is mocked by Hotspur, who finds this pretentious man annoying. Unfortunately, I also have a similar impatience to Hotspur when it comes to our modern-day equivalents—that is, TV ghostbusters—and often say a bit more than I should about the fakes and frauds that strut and fret their hour on our TV screens. Today anyone can call themselves a medium, even if they have never demonstrated within Spiritualism and gone through their rigorous selection procedures. At a Spiritualist church, if a medium is a nutcase or simply no good at what they do, then they never get booked again. In this way the fakes get weeded out and the mediocre get left behind. But on TV they are rarely looking for the truth—they want *entertainment*, and the dafter the better when it comes to ghost hunters.

Normally I turn down shows about ghost hunting, unless there is a serious intent to the investigations. I have on a great many occasions rejected top ghost-hunting shows and prefer to leave this sort of thing to the twits we know and love. If it wasn't for a warning message from an Inupiat Alaskan psychic, I'd have probably turned down the filmmaker Louis Frost before he'd finished asking. I'd been giving the Alaskan lady a mediumistic reading by telephone, and she was a real fan, and some great evidence was flowing. When the reading was finished, we chatted for a while. She said that she was a shaman and also got insights into people's destiny, and she told me a number of very evidential, unpublished facts about my life. Then she said: "In about seven to eight months' time, you will get a call to work on a ghost-hunting show. Despite the way you feel, do *not* turn it down, as it will lead to better things."

The call came in seven months later, and instead of telling Louis where to go, I just said that I'd love to take part. I'm not against ghost hunts, but I am against mockumentaries—TV programs in which events are presented in documentary style to create a parody. These shows are aimed at people who have no knowledge about the reality of psychic phenomena and are taken in by the Hollywood horror genre. It's very entertaining but a complete fantasy, and no more real than Harry Potter or Scooby Doo.

I'm no spoilsport. The horror genre is great fun. I have been paid by agencies to promote and give advice for a number of well-known movies, including *The Sixth Sense*, *White Noise*, *House on Haunted Hill*, *The Gift*, *The Others*, *Dragonfly*, and *Jeepers Creepers*, but these films do not claim to be true, whereas the shows on TV claim to be real. It all started in 1999 with the movie *Blaire Witch Project*, directed by Daniel Myrick and Eduardo Sanchez, which gave the impression that it was recording of "recovered footage" about real events of a group of three student filmmakers who disappeared while hiking in the Black Hills near Burkittsville, Maryland, in 1994. Supposedly they were there to film a documentary about a local legend known as the Blair Witch. This gripping, low-budget film style is now mimicked by TV producers and has spawned the rubbish we now see on reality TV, which consists of pseudo-psychics jumping at shadows, mediums channeling monkeys and crazy entities, lots of ghostly camera effects, and orbs passed off as real spirits. You mugs dribble over it, while these con-artists become millionaires!

When we went to do the ghost hunt at the Falstaff Experience, we were greeted by a ghost-hunting team who had clearly been selected not for their mediumistic ability but because they were larger-than-life characters. Some of them were hugely arrogant and claimed to see ghosts wherever they looked, or felt cold spots in every corner and every stairway. Some were completely deluded, while others were very nice twits. It was a bit sad, really, as this was clearly a mockumentary.

Some mediums really believe in what they do but are completely away with the fairies. One of Jane's and my favorites is a lady named Betty, who is an adorable person but, in my opinion, has completely lost the plot. Her specialism is deep trance—a deeply bonkers sort of trance. She will speak with the voice of a Chinaman, which is totally odd when you look at her white, powdered face with a bright-red slash of lipstick. She has badly fitting false teeth that stay put as she moves her red mouth, saying: "Gleetings flom the spilit world."

Betty often brings a huge lighthouse with her with a dodgy bulb, wired with highly flammable old-fashioned flex and a brown plug. Dangerously poor wiring causes it to flash occasionally during her performance, giving everyone empirical "proof" that spirit is present. The badly painted hardboard lighthouse, she explains, was built after a vision she had of a "spirit lighthouse" that she saw guiding the souls of the dead into the next life.

Occasionally she would interrupt her hilarious trance discourse, and we'd get an ad slipped into the philosophy. "This sister is available for aura readings if you would like to book her. She also needs a driver to take her to her next Spiritualist church. You'll have to pick her up by 5:00 p.m." And then the spirit discourse would continue its mad way, as if nothing had ever happened.

Jane and I almost had to leave the church audience once, as we were nearly bursting with suppressed laughter. Betty came out of trance to give a spirit message. Pointing with authority, she said: "I'm coming to the man at the back." Everyone looked round to see who she meant. "You! You!" she squealed. "You! The man with the murky aura." She said a number of other wacky things, but the best was, "Do you know that in your past life you were a murderer?"

All we can hope is that this was not the man's first visit to a Spiritualist church, for I'm sure he'd never come back.

All of the above is fun, but Betty should never have been on the platform in front of people who were seriously looking for proof of life after death. So, too, these modern ghost hunters do just as bad a job of convincing us that the spirit world is real.

At the Stratford-upon-Avon ghost hunt, it was the usual nonsense, with people jumping at shadows and making fools of themselves. This was "gold" to the program makers, for people at home would find this entertaining and fun. Louis had the great idea of mixing comedy with real life ghost hunting and contrasting the two themes in the same show so for one moment the viewer would be shocked by the absurdity of some of the ghost hunters and then the scene would switch to Jane and me making serious points about the myths and misconceptions that surround this genre.

Jane and I were interviewed about what we hoped to achieve, and we pointed out that just about everything there was to know about this haunted house was available on the Internet.

The medium/entertainer Derek Acorah had been in there, too, with the "Most Haunted" team, and had channeled the spirit of a medieval serial killer named John Davies. Acorah gave a great performance and presented a frightening example of possession. The only problem was that there is little or no proof that John Davies ever existed. He was a fictitious character that had been added to the website by a previous owner of Falstaff House to make the ghost stories more interesting. Sadly, we heard a similar story from the owner of Athelhampton House in Dorset, who told us that the monkey Derek Acorah "channeled" on TV was simply a story made up by her grandfather to scare them when they were kids.

Sadly, ghost hunting tends to attract people who are self-deluded, fraudsters, entertainers or mentally unstable. It is the stuff of fantasy and delusion. Ghosts do not haunt places; they haunt people. The real phenomena I have seen appear to be projected from people who are deeply disturbed, highly anxious, or have mental illness. The human energy field has a power that can project energy, and I believe that this is what may be the cause of poltergeists and other phenomena. Ouija boards and the like also tap our own spiritual energy, and the messages spelled out on the board are, in the vast majority of cases, simply fears and delusions transmitted from the unconscious mind.

There are some very rare cases of ghostly phenomena, but again most of these appear to surround people rather than places. Jane's and my encounters and casebooks have been covered in my other books, but as a rule I would advise people to be very suspicious of the claims made by foolish ghost hunters, with their pseudoscientific methodology and crazy equipment.

For our part in the program, Jane and I went around the building and endeavored to pick up on obscure facts about the history of the building and reveal information that only the owners knew and could verify. In this way, we tapped into the residual energy of the building. We encountered no ghosts. I know that this is not quite as exciting as someone spitting slime, cursing, and threatening to drag us all to Hell, but the fact is, we needed to make people aware of the many misconceptions surrounding ghost hunting.

The simple fact of the matter is that when we die, we become spirits and move to the next level of existence—the dimension we call the spirit world. No spirit gets trapped or is unable to cross over. Once in the light realms of the spirit, we stay for a time and enjoy a well-earned break from the trials of life, but we will eventually be reborn to continue our life on earth and grow toward divinity.

People have some funny ideas and misconceptions about spirits and ghosts and there's just as many bonkers ideas doing the rounds in India too. Here they talk about supernatural creatures called the *bhoot* which is the ghost of a dead person that is perturbed and restless due to some factor – such as a violent death - that prevents them from moving on. Bhoots are able to transform into animals but are usually seen in human form. If you meet one, you can tell it's a bhoot as their feet are backwards facing.

When I heard that the Indian teacher Mataji Vanamali was to visit the UK, I was keen to find out more about Indian beliefs about spirits, ghosts and life after death and jumped at the chance to interview her with my camera crew.

MEETING MATAJI VANAMALI

Mataji Vanamali says that she is not a yogi or a sadhu, but a gopi or vassal of Lord Krishna. She was blessed and given mantra upadesam by her guru, Sri Jayendra Saraswati, who is one of the leading religious figures in Hinduism today. While in Rishikesh, we visited her at her home, which doubles as an ashram called Vanamali Gita Yogashram, described on its website as "poised on a cliff, overlooking the fascinating Ganga as she gushes down the rocks." It forgets to mention that it is located next door to the leper colony she helps to maintain. Apart from its spiritual activities, the ashram also does service to the poor people of the village. About 150 of the village children have been adopted by the ashram and given clothes, food, and help with education. The ashram has also started a project to provide small cottages for very poor and deserving families of the village. Don't be put off by my jibe about the leper colony if you plan to visit. The ashram is homely and clean, and it is located in a lovely setting.

A number of miracles have happened around Mataji Vanamali, including sacred *vibhuti* ash appearing on her locket of Shirdi Baba, and her Ganesh statue drinking milk. And there's the story of the report of a statue of Shiva that materialized when her brother, Vanamali Gita Yogashram, put his hands into the waters of the Ganges.

I would probably not describe Mataji Vanamali as a "living saint," but she was certainly a lovely lady with a tremendous insight into Indian philosophy. I believe she has memorized all of the *Bhagavad Gita*, and she certainly had a tremendous grasp of the English language. Mataji Vanamali gave us an interesting talk about the *Bhagavad Gita* and spoke of how we need not need be a mendicant and seek seclusion in the caves and forests, but that we can attain the Divine as a householder. Her books about the lives of Krishna and Shiva are extremely detailed, yet easy to read.

When the time came for questions, I was keen to ask her about the Indian beliefs about the afterlife. She appeared intrigued when I explained I was a Spiritualist medium, and I explained: "In our work, we endeavor to prove that the personality survives death. I know that Hindus believe in reincarnation, but I have also read about, for example, Brahmaloka." Thinking about my earlier experience in the temple of Maharaj-ji (Neem Karoli Baba), I asked: "Can some of the holy men and women continue to help us after their death?" (Brahmaloka is defined in the *Encyclopedia Britannica* as "that part of the many-layered universe that is the realm of pious celestial spirits.)

Mataji Vanamali replied that Brahmaloka is just one aspect of the after-death state. There are seven planes above the Earthly plane and seven more below. But none is as important as the Earthly plane itself, for it is only in this world—in a human body—that we can attain liberation. Life on Earth is a divine opportunity. And yes, many of the gurus and masters opt to remain in the astral worlds and are able to communicate with and help their devotees on Earth. A good answer, I felt, that corresponded very closely to my own conclusions, which I have written about in my books about the afterlife.

A few years later, Mataji Vanamali visited Prem's yoga sanctuary near my home in the UK, and I was able to interview her in depth. I brought along a cameraman and posted the full video on my website. We talked about how the inner world creates the outer world, and how factual knowledge about any subject can come through the intuition of a spiritually advanced soul, even if they have had no education. I then asked her about life after death and whether the human personality can survive death.

Vanamali: "The opposite of life is birth, but life goes on forever. Individuality as we know it does not persist—for example, the body disintegrates with death—but what continues are a bundle of what we call *vasanas* and *samskaras*, which are a bundle of the total experiences and desires which the individual has gone through in this life. And this is what propels an individual to a new life, because Nature dictates that as you desire, so you shall receive, but what you receive may not be the exact same thing that you desire. You may demand, but what you get is not exactly what you wanted."

Craig: "You are saying the tendencies, but not necessarily the sense of personality, persist after death?"

Vanamali: "The personality cannot survive. If it does, imagine a next birth where the husband is reborn as the wife and the wife reborn as the husband. So Nature does not give us that sort of memory. But the *vasanas* (which means "perfumes") are the subtle aura of what you desire, and these propel you. That's why the last thought as you depart this world is considered very important."

Craig: "I assume that you cannot change that last thought because it expresses your very essence?"

Vanamali: "Exactly—that's what the *Gita* says. It's not like a deathbed confession, in which a renegade can suddenly decide to confess. That is not how Nature works. The last thought will always be the very essence of our being. And that is why Krishna tells Arjuna, 'Any one of these arrows may be your last, therefore think of me at all times, and even if you have to fight, let your thoughts be on me—that divine essence. Therefore if at any time you fall, your thought will be of me, and you will come to me.' If a mother is thinking of a child she is leaving behind, she will definitely return to the child in her new life to be closer to that child."

We spoke for a while about the evolution of consciousness over many lives, from animal to human, and how the spirit leaves the body at death through different orifices. I explained how my wife, Jane, watched a wispy green light leave the mouth of her step-father as he died. I wanted to persist with my questions about the possibility of the human personality surviving physical death, so I pressed a similar question as before.

Craig: "Don't you think that the personality, as we know now, could survive in the *lokas*—the multiple spirit planes—and what about the *Brahma Loka*, where the gods prevail? As a medium, I believe that in the *lokas*, our personality survives temporarily with a sense of self, but then when we come back to be reborn in Earthly life, we bring with us just the basic tendencies. If we brought the whole of our previous personality into this birth, then we would be living the same life over again and fall into the same traps."

Vanamali: "Exactly."

Craig: "But the personality, I believe, survives and, as a medium, I believe I connect with beings in the *loka* planes—which I believe are a temporary abode of the spirit. In this assertion, I differ from some other mediums who believe in an eternal life in the next world. I certainly wouldn't like to be having tea and cookies in Heaven for eternity! I don't think I'd even want to be me forever!"

Vanamali (chuckles): "The personality doesn't survive the body, but as you say, the tendencies will survive."

Craig: "Yes but from my experience as a medium I believe that the personality survives—at least in the *lokas*."

Vanamali: "But only for a certain time, and even then it's only due to a certain need or necessity on the part of that person to come back. If there is an especially strong desire or an especially strong bond with somebody on Earth, in that way they remain for a while."

Craig: "Of course it's hard to know what the personality is at all. We think of ourselves as being a particular personality, but behind that we are the light of consciousness."

Vanamali: "The apparent personality can survive, and that's why people see ghosts and so on, but they exist for some reason of their own, or because of terrible deaths and a desire to avenge. And, of course, the great saints who want to come back to help humanity—there again, you find people seeing the actual form of the saint. That again is desire."

Craig: "So from the Hindu perspective, if there is a *need* for the personality to survive, then it will continue."

Vanamali: "Yes."

This interview highlights many of the difficult things I've had to square as both a Spiritualist medium and as one with a keen interest in Hinduism and Eastern religions. On the one hand, I have the irrefutable evidence that I have gathered from my mediumship, which proves to me without a doubt that the personality survives death. As Spiritualists, we sometimes stand completely alone against all the world faiths that have similar but differing views about what happens to the soul after death.

When I talk about the continuation of the personality after death, I am describing something akin to a soul, which has a sense of its own individual identity as something separate and self-sustaining. However, when we meditate upon the nature of this personality or soul, we realize that it could be illusory. The maxim I use to determine what is my true identity is to recognize that anything I can witness is not "me." So the body, for example, is not the real me, since I can witness having a body. Same, too, with the memories. These are not me; they are something "I" am aware of having. The thoughts offer the same conundrum when I observe them in meditation. There are thoughts moving in front of the screen of my attention, but I do not know from where they arise, and sometimes the thoughts are not even my own—they are dropped into my head by the spirit people, or I sense them from other people by telepathy. When Jane and I say the same thing at the same time—which happens many times a day—we have to wonder who is implanting the thought in whom. If it's about shopping, then it is definitely Jane's thoughts taking dominance. If it's about getting something to eat, it's me!

Craig with Vanamali Mataji

So who is it that survives death? There are a number of "selves" inside us. There is the physical self—the body; the mental self—the thoughts, feelings, memories and so on; and there is the energetic self—the subtle body *prana*. And there is the self above all this that does the observing—the witness. This "witness self" is probably the real me and the part that will survive death and drag with it all the other stuff—what Vanamali called the *vasanas* and *samskaras*—which includes the karmic tendencies in the body, the memories and mental tendencies, and my material and spiritual desires for the future. All this interacts to create this field of awareness that I call my personality. It's a bit like a swarm of bees, where many interacting parts create the whole.

In daily life, this observing self becomes immersed in the attachments of the world and falls to sleep. We get lost in our desires and the world of commonplace things, worries, habits, misconceptions, and so on. This is the cause of our suffering and ignorance. Through the practice of yoga, we learn to become detached from the bondage of the banal, and we can free ourselves from the body and mind. In the Upanishads, this observing self is considered to be the true self, the *atman*. The Buddhist believe that even this is transient and illusory, and has no inherent, self-sustaining existence. They may be right, but from my own experience, there is something that does appear to persist after death, and I believe that this is the *atman*, clothed in the tendencies that we in the West call our personality. This witnessing self has its own feeling of uniqueness but is simultaneously omnipresent—existing everywhere at the same time and for all time. It is through it that the "I" experiences love and enjoys the eternal progress of the soul through the diversity of creation and unending perceptions, yet remains anchored in the infinite peace and stillness of God.

Whilst in Rishikesh I had lots of time on my hands to explore the sacred sites in the town and surrounding area. The place is sacred as so many great saints and gurus have walked its ground and infused their energy into every square inch of the landscape. In comparatively recent times prominent personalities such as Swami Vivekananda, Swami Rama Tirtha and Swami Sivananda have studied at Rishikesh and in February 1968, The Beatles visited the Maharishi Mahesh Yogi's ashram where John Lennon recorded many songs including "The Happy Rishikesh Song".

MAHARISHI'S ABANDONED ASHRAM

Places that a bus driver claims are impossible to get to suddenly become easy to access when you flash a few rupees. And when we were told by an "official" that he could not let us into the abandoned Rishikesh ashram of the Beatles' guru, Maharishi Mahesh Yogi, it's amazing how the padlock disappeared as soon as we "rupeed" him a little. (In fact we believe the guy was a complete impostor, who had just bought himself a padlock and a "uniform" to make a little cash from gullible Western yogis. But we didn't mind being ripped off a bit. These guys, like most people in India, are just scraping together a living.)

Maharishi Mahesh Yogi had, of course, brought the world Transcendental Meditation (TM), which gives each adept (for a price) a personal, secret mantra which they can chant to gain enlightenment. Problems occurred when the followers shared their secret mantras with one another, for they soon discovered that far from being their own personalized chant, most of the mantras were the same for everyone. As you may gather, I've never been impressed by Maharishi Mahesh Yogi's methods, but you do have to give him credit for encouraging over five million people to meditate, including many celebrities and pop stars. The most famous of these were the Beatles, who at this ashram wrote the music to the *White Album*.

The abandoned ashram was fascinating. It is gradually being overtaken by the jungle and is now the home of monkeys, cows, and the occasional leopard. Its most interesting features are the hundreds of meditation pods, which look a little like igloos and are dotted over the hillside that overlooks the Ganges. Exploring these, we discovered that each one is a self-contained unit, where a person could meditate, sleep, and cook their food. It is easy to see why the Beatles liked this place. It must have been a peaceful retreat from the madness of Beatlemania.

Where the Beatles Meditated

The Beatles' visit to the ashram had a big impact on their lives and creativity. But they curtailed their three-month course and suddenly decided to return home after a feud with the *maharishi*. During their time in the ashram they had written forty-eight songs, many of which became part of *Abbey Road* and the *White Album*. John Lennon considered the *maharishi* to be a money-grubbing, sex-obsessed fraud, who cynically abused his influence over the Beatles and other celebrities. George Harrison later felt regret, and in the 1990s he apologized for the way he and Lennon had treated the *maharishi*. Self-help writer (and one of the *maharishi*'s former disciples) Deepak Chopra claimed that the *maharishi* had actually ordered the Beatles to leave the ashram because they refused to stop taking drugs.

John Lennon wrote "I'm So Tired" at the start of his stay and says it was inspired by the fact that he was unable to sleep free of drugs.

"I couldn't sleep. I'm meditating all day and couldn't sleep at night. The story is that. One of my favorite tracks. I just like the sound of it, and I sing it well," he later said.

As they left Rishikesh, John Lennon began singing a song he originally titled "Maharishi," with lyrics expressing his disillusionment: "What have you done / You've made a fool of everyone." George Harrison, in an interview with *Rolling Stone* magazine, recalled those moments, saying: "Lennon had a song he had started to write, which he was singing: 'Maharishi, what have you done?' and I said, 'You can't say that, it's ridiculous.' I came up with the title of 'Sexy Sadie' and Lennon changed 'Maharishi' to 'Sexy Sadie.'"

Soon after the *maharishi* died on February 5, 2008, Paul McCartney commented, saying: "While I am deeply saddened by his passing, my memories of him will only be joyful ones. He was a great man, who worked tirelessly for the people of the world and the cause of unity."

The Beatles' interest in spirituality helped kick off the Age of Aquarius—a term that refers on one level to the cultural changes that happened in the 60s and 70s, as well as being a reference to the Western astrological term for the next *yuga*. The eon moves from Pisces, which coincided with the advent of Christianity, represented by the symbolism of the fish, to Aquarius, the water carrier. During these times, a profound change will take place in man's conception of himself and the universe. The psychologist Carl Jung spoke of how he believed that the changes soon to come would not only see changes in the world but also to mankind's psyche. In a letter to Fr. White written in 1954, he refers to the approaching change: "In the case of the Christian symbol, the tree, however, is dead, and man upon the cross is going to die, i.e., the solution of the problem takes place after death. That is so as far as Christian truth goes. But it is possible that the Christian symbolism expresses man's mental condition in the eon of Pisces, as the ram and the bull gods do for the ages of Aries and Taurus. In this case, the post-mortal solution would be symbolic of an entirely new psychological status, viz., that of Aquarius, which is certainly a oneness, presumably that of the *anthropos*, the realization of Christ's allusion, *Dii estis* ('ye are gods')."

Could this letter, written in 1954, perhaps have foreseen the advent of the West's sudden and widespread interest in Eastern spirituality and its core premise that we are all God? Dr. Tim Leary, the American psychologist and writer known for advocating psychedelic drugs, wryly called the Beatles St. John, St. Paul, St. George and St. Ringo. Perhaps if they were the heralds for the New Age, then Leary wasn't that far off the mark.

Western astrologers agree that the Age of Aquarius is imminent, but few agree on an exact date, and their predictions vary by hundreds—and, in some cases, thousands—of years. The new era starts when the vernal equinox point moves out of the constellation Pisces and into Aquarius. Astrologers maintain that an astrological age is a product of the earth's slow precessional rotation and lasts for 2,160 years on average (26,000-year period of precession, divided by twelve zodiac signs, equals 2,160 years). Some astrologers claim it started in 2012, and others, such as Rudolf Steiner, the founder of the anthroposophy movement, believed that the Age of Aquarius will arrive in A.D. 3573.

Seeing Maharishi Mahesh Yogi's ashram in ruins is in some ways a reflection of the disappointments of the flower-power era. Before leaving, we went into the remains of main buildings, which were in serious decay and had clearly been looted for anything of value. It was sad to see such an amazing place abandoned, but to lift the spirits of the past, we decided to burst into an energetic *bhajan* session. Once again the huge hall that once sat thousands now echoed to our fifteen enthusiastic voices.

THE ARUNDHATI GUHA CAVES

The Vashistha and Arundhati Guha Caves, just north of Rishikesh, have been a place of worship for over 7,000 years. Arundhati was the wife of the great sage Vashistha, who was one of the *saptarishis* (seven great sages) in ancient India. Vashistha is also said to be one of the authors of the Naadi leaves.

When I descended the steps to visit the caves with my fellow pilgrims, it was an atmospheric day, and the sharp, early morning light was fingering its way through the mist that still lingered on the Ganges. It was a place away from the bustle and noise of the gridlocked Indian roads, so you could clearly hear the sound of the holy river echoing through the vermillion forests that covered the nearby cliffs.

Breaking the stillness, a solitary *sadhu* began chanting the *Sutras* of Patanjali: "*Atha yoganusasanam. Yogah citta vritti nirodhah.*" The echoing sound was intoxicating, making me feel almost drunk with divinity, as the whole of sacred India seems to do to the open-minded traveler. The whole landscape was steeped in the vibrations of the enlightened people who had once practiced here.

The main Vashistha cave was closed, but we were shown the way to the Arundhati Guha caves, which most spiritual tourists miss. We scrambled across the rocks in our bare feet and along the muddy edge of the river, and entered a small, overgrown, insignificant-looking cave. We could still hear the *sadhu* chanting in the distance as we sat in meditation.

Inside we felt that we were swallowed by the consciousness of the past. Here great yogis had sat, and now we, too, sat in meditation and connected with our surroundings. I opened my mind and allowed the memories of the past to flood my awareness. Just as when I do psychometry as part of my readings for people, now my clairsentience was connecting to the cave's holy vibrations.

Here men had sat for years on end and had sealed themselves away from the world in meditation. I felt a spiritual presence that extended beyond space and time. I felt that these dedicated holy men had penetrated the mysteries of existence. I perceived that they were not only aware of the spirit world but had developed a telepathy that enabled them to communicate with their devotees in a similar way that spirit-guides communicate with mediums. What extraordinary states of consciousness had these yogis discovered in this dark solitude? What powers of telepathy, remote viewing, bilocation, and spiritual awareness had flowered in these ebony-black caves?

Although this was years before my first Naadi reading, I had an eerie feeling that I was in touch with the energy of people who had remotely guided the course of human history, not knowing of course that in the future I would have a very personal message from people associated with these caves. Here I felt something that I have sometimes experienced in my mediumship: guidance not just from the dead, but from living people, who in seclusion help spiritual aspirants to find higher awareness. When the mediumistic Theosophist, Madame Blavatsky, spoke of a White Brotherhood of Ascended Masters who guide the course of human history, I believe she, too, was touching this world of special guides, who work both within this world and the next. It could have been fantasy on both our parts, of course, for I had no way of verifying my experiences, but this is what my intuition was telling me. As a medium, I trust my intuition.

From the caves we picked our barefoot way across the rocks to another small cave in the cliff face. It was not easily accessed, had no temple entrance, was curtained by trees, and had a spectacular view of the foaming white waters of the Ganges. There were no sadhus chanting here—just the occasional monkey squawking in the trees and a few lonely birds hovering nearby. I discovered later that it was here that it is claimed Sri Isha lived for some time. Sri Isha is the name that legend says was taken by Jesus when he lived and studied in India. These stories were also channeled in the Spiritualist-Theosophical book *The Aquarian Gospels of Jesus Christ* by Levi H.

Dowling. According to Dowling, Jesus spent a lot of time in India, where he learned from the yogic masters. Claims about Jesus' life in India, Nepal, and Tibet were also made in 1894 by Nicolas Notovitch in the book titled *The Unknown Life of Christ* and, more recently, in *Jesus Lived in India: His Unknown Life Before and After the Crucifixion* by Holger Kersten.

The journey to find the Arundhati Guha caves

In the last century, Swami Rama Tirtha and Swami (Papa) Ramdas of Kananghad lived in this same cave and, at separate times, had visions of Isha meditating with them. Neither of these holy men had any prior knowledge that this was the place where Jesus had once resided. As we sat in silence, each of us contemplated the embers of the energies that permeated this extraordinary place of solitude.

Later, when I researched the history of the cave, I read that the last famous resident of the Vashistha cave during the 1930s was Swami Purshottamanand, who was a disciple of Swami Brahamananda of the Ramakrishna order, and had been initiated into monastic life by Mahapurushji, another direct disciple of Sri Ramakrishna. When Swami Brahamananda was still a young man, he had his palm read at Kanyakumari, and it was predicted that he would enter a cave and go on meditating and meditating!

Swami Purushottamananda had miraculous powers. He told one of the disciples to bring him pure water from the nearby Ganges in a silver container. Purushottamananda then stirred the water with his hand, and it was transformed into nectar, which his disciples used to make sweets (candy). In his lifetime, many people clamored to see this living saint, and to witness and share in his powerful psychic and healing powers

Sathya Sai Baba with Swami Purshottamananda 1957

Swami Purushottamananda lived in the cave for thirty years. Toward the end of his life, he was visited by Sathya Sai Baba, to whom he gave an incredible vision, as described by Sri Subbaramiah, president of the Divine Life Society, Venkatagiri: "Even now that picture is imprinted in my memory. I was standing near the entrance of the cave. I could see what was happening. Baba placed his head on the lap of Swami Purushottamananda and laid himself down. Suddenly, his entire body was bathed in divine brilliance. His head and face appeared to me to have increased very much in size. Rays of splendor emanated from his face. I was overwhelmed with a strange, inexplicable joy. The time was about 10:00 p.m."

"When pressed later to divulge the vision, Baba informed us that it was a vision of Jyothir-Padmanabha! (Lord Vishnu as the Flame of Love-Wisdom). What supreme *karuna* (compassion)! What immeasurable Good Fortune! Swami Purushottamananda passed away on *Shivarathri* night, 1961, four years later, during the *Lingodbhava Muhurtham*—the time Baba manifested the *lingam* that Shivaratri." (*Sathyam Shivam Sundaram*, volume I, by Prof. N. Kasturi, pages 111–113.)

A few days after our visit, we floated past the caves on the same stretch of the Ganges after a session of terrifying whitewater rafting—which, incidentally, is a lot safer than driving in India. After a white-knuckle ride on a rudimentary, safety-equipment–free dinghy, we emerged—shaken—into a quiet stretch of water near the turn in the river where the cave is situated.

Just a little further downriver, I saw long-haired forest yogis, their faces and near-naked bodies powdered with ash, meditating beneath the trees of the jungle and continuing the ancient traditions that had once been practiced in the sacred caves. High up on a road overhead, they would leave their begging bowls, relying on the good will of the community to support their austere spiritual efforts. Happily, this tradition of seclusion, which we had momentarily felt at the caves, continues to this day on the banks of the sacred Ganges.

It is a fascinating proposal that Jesus had come to this same place from the age of 14 and lived here many years under the name Isha Natha before returning to his own country to begin preaching. Surviving the crucifixion, he is also claimed to have returned to India via the Silk Road and was buried at a place called Khanyar Rozabal, in Srinagar. For me this does not negate the Christian message but instead brings it alive and makes it even more relevant to my spiritual quest.

In the next section we will visit another underground Christian site that is steeped in mystery and poses many more questions about the true message of the Christian Faith.

CATACOMBS AND ROME

The catacombs just outside Rome are a place where you can still feel the atmosphere of the people who knew the original Christian message. Like the Vashistha and Arundhati Guha caves in India, the walls of earth and stone seem to protect the knowledge of the past like a valuable old wine. Jane and I could feel this when we visited them with a small group of people, and had time to sit and take in the silence and the residual energy of this ancient mausoleum.

The families of these dead Christians used to come to these tombs to celebrate the anniversaries of the dead, to light small oil lamps, and have picnics in front of their loved ones' graves. It was here, too, that the first Christians sought refuge in this labyrinthine network of tunnels from persecution by the emperor Nero. In the hundreds of miles of tunnels, they created a maze of hiding places and underground churches, with some of the earliest examples of Christian art. Some Roman citizens believed that the Christians sacrificed their children and performed bizarre, secret worship rituals in the catacombs at midnight. It was rumored that they drank human blood, which was probably a misinterpretation of Jesus' command, "This cup is the new testament in my blood: this do you, as often as you drink it, in remembrance of me" (1 Corinthians 11:25). Today the catacombs are the property of the Catholic Church, and some limited excavation is permitted. Some say that the catacombs are the hiding place of the Holy Grail, which was hidden by agents of Pope Sixtus II underneath the Basilica of San Lorenzo Fuori le Mura, near the tomb of St. Lawrence, a deacon martyred in A.D. 258.

Of all the Christian sites in Rome, I felt that the catacombs were the place that brings you closest to the original Christian message. What we have in the Gospels today, I believe, is a shadow of the real teachings of Jesus. Apart from a few sections, such as the Sermon on the Mount, most has been tampered with to such an extent that the true message has been lost. The early Christians believed in all sorts of things that are far from what we have now in the modern version of the Gospels. For example, records show that the early Christian Church believed in reincarnation and the soul's journey back to union with God. This was all stopped five hundred years after the death of Christ by Emperor Justinian in A.D. 545. He used his power to insist that it be decreed that anyone who believes that souls come from God, and return to God, will be punished by death. As for the belief in reincarnation, he had written in the Fifth Ecumenical Council, A.D. 545 (given in the *Nicene and Post-Nicene Fathers*, 2nd series, 14:318): "If anyone asserts the fabulous preexistence of souls, and shall assert the monstrous restoration which follows from it, let him be anathema."

When I hear some modern-day Christian evangelists or hellfire preachers, I wonder whatever happened to the messages of love, tolerance, service, and forgiveness that are the simple but overwhelmingly powerful messages of this humble carpenter (more likely a stonemason) from Nazareth. Like all enlightened teachers, Jesus was a man who could present big ideas in a very clear way that everyone could understand, such as condensing the ten commandments of Moses to "You shall love the Lord your God with all your heart and with all your soul and with all your mind. This is the great and first commandment. And the second is like it: You shall love your neighbor as yourself. On these two commandments depend all the Law and the Prophets" (Matthew 22:36–40).

It was a Spiritualist classic from 1933, *The Rock of Truth* by Arthur Findlay, that first alerted me to the fact that Christianity had been butchered by the Roman emperor Caesar Flavius Constantine at the First Council of Nicaea in A.D. 325 and also by later revisions to Christian doctrine. Findlay shows how many of the Christian ideas propagated by Rome were in fact borrowed from Mithraism, which was a prominent belief system until Constantine decided to adopt Christianity as the Roman religion. Findlay points out that nothing was ever recorded in Roman archives or by Roman historians about what the Gospels tell us happened to Jesus. Nor do Plutarch, Pliny,

Seneca, Tacitus, Epictetus, or any others ever mention the miracles recounted in the Gospels. Like many Spiritualists, Arthur Findlay emphasizes the need to gain direct spiritual experience and, rather than relying on beliefs, take personal responsibility for our future. Findlay writes: "Each one of us is responsible for his own actions and thoughts. Our mental make-up determines our conditions hereafter, and no one need be deluded by the idea that belief in some vicarious atonement is going to alter the position each mind determines for itself."

Even the most basic of Jesus's teachings have been crucified, and their true meaning has been forgotten. Instead of an esoteric path to knowledge that awakens and celebrates the human spirit, we have now the work of prejudiced dogmatists with a blinkered understanding of the great truth that Jesus preached. We have Westernized Jesus, but he was in reality a God-realized Easterner, who spoke with the authority of God of the eternal principles of righteousness, which are common to all the great religions. When Constantine and his team intervened, we lost the original Christianity that I saw painted on the walls of the catacombs—a lost Christianity that now can only be found in the rediscovered Gnostic texts, such as those in the Nag Hammadi library, which are denounced as heretical by orthodox Christians.

It seems to me that the rebellious Jesus, who turned over the moneychangers' table in the temple and said all sorts of subversive things, is not the sort of person who would have wanted us to follow rules. He was closer to a hippy than to an archbishop or a pope. The big deal at the councils of Nicaea (A.D. 325) and Corinth (A.D. 381) was to elevate Jesus into the status of a deity, and by so doing they took his teachings away from the common people and put them into the hands of priests. The official teaching was now that Jesus was God. Not to accept Jesus as God was to reject God himself. This immediately isolated the Jews and would later isolate the Muslims, who regarded Jesus as a divine prophet but not part of the Godhead, and it had terrible consequences in the future for heathens and nonbelievers. Christianity now also had the power of propaganda and could be controlled more easily by the Roman state.

Editing Christianity reminds me of what TV editors can do to the work of mediums, since footage can be cut to look like whatever they want. Film of an accurate medium can be cut to make him or her look like a fraud, and a hopeless medium can be made to look brilliant. It all depends on what you leave in and what you leave out, what you re-shoot, and what material you emphasize. The only way to judge the truth and quality of the spirit communications is to see it live and unedited. When Constantine and his editors went to work on the Bible, Jesus had been dead for 325 years, and all the people who had witnessed the live events were now long dead.

What we are left with is not what Jesus taught. It is my understanding that Jesus wanted us to seek and find the truth for ourselves. He urged us that "He that believeth on me, the works that I do shall he do also; and greater works than these shall he do; because I go unto my Father" (John 14:12). He tells us that he is not God himself, but that God works though him, saying, "The words that I speak unto you I speak not of myself: but the Father that dwells in me, he does the works" (John 14:10). I believe he is saying here that once any of us surrender to the Divine, then God will naturally work though us. Jesus was an enlightened teacher, medium, and yogi, who spoke with the authority of the divine consciousness that flowed through him, and he was given the honorific title of Christ ("one who is anointed with divine knowledge").

Jesus had the same problems that other enlightened beings have encountered, since the knowledge of the Divine is impossible to express. The depth of that experience can never be communicated in words, and it is our highest destiny to attain that experience. But people have varying degrees of ability to understand this state, and they will interpret a spiritual message according to their limited understanding. This is parodied in a Monty Python sketch from the film the *Life of Brian*, when one follower hears, "Blessed are the peacemakers," and someone at the back hears, "Blessed are the cheesemakers." Buddha, who lived over five hundred years before Jesus, also understood how truth can quickly be misinterpreted. On attaining divine realization, he walked by the lotus ponds and initially felt that his awakening was impossible to teach, as no one could possibly understand. But then he looked at the lotus flowers. Some were open, some partly open, and some closed in a tight bud. He would teach to the flowers that were awakening to the light. In the same way, the teachings of Jesus are understood by some but missed by others. "He that has ears to hear, let him hear" (Matthew 11:15).

We all start to trip over ourselves when we use that word "God," because this is one of the most misunderstood words of all time. As I said in the chapter about Richard Dawkins, if people ask me if I believe in God, I have to question what we mean by the word "God." Many Christians believe the Roman councils' version and say that Jesus is God. Some see God as a separate being who created the world. Some envision God as a fatherly, Zeus-like figure, and others believe he is an invisible force that permeates all things. Jane also has her views, as she was taught in a Catholic school and was confirmed, and she has often asked me, "How can you believe in God without also believing in Jesus?"

The Naadi leaves expressed the difficulties I, too, would have explaining the nature of God. "Many people have a different culture. They have no understanding about what we mean by God—this divine energy. You know everything already and are connected to the universe. You are spiritual person. But normal person, it is not easy for them to open their third eye. It is not for them to understand spiritual things. Because many people have a different culture. They have no understanding about what we mean by God, or what we mean by energy. So in your destiny this is your duty. This is your purpose of this birth. You want to be of service to the people. You want to give the message to the people. What is meant by God? We can't see God, but how can we see God? What is the way of the God to see? People ask where God is. I don't know. I've never seen God. But you know. This is your duty. This is why God gave you this birth."

I believe that the truth is that God is both formless and has form. He is not elsewhere, he is not limited to being a man, he is not even an invisible essence, but he is *all* of it. God is both the creator and the creation. God is both light and dark. God is both the light of awareness and the darkness of ignorance. Everything is infused with God, and even that which is being infused is also God. This is what is meant when saints say that God is One. But also remember that you are God, too, just as I am God. Even the very idea of "I" is also God.

The universe is conscious. The planets, the stars, things with no life, and beings full of life—it is *all* consciousness. When we come close to this understanding in the stillness of meditation, or during an epiphany experience or a momentary oceanic insight, our initial experience of the totality of consciousness is of being immersed in endless bliss and light that stretches forever. We discover that we are embodiments of infinite love. Sometimes we may sense this truth and know it in its entirety, and sometimes we can go beyond these blissful limitations and directly know the true, ineffable experience of God that even the words "bliss," "light," and "love" fail to describe. All of us can do this. It is the reason we are here, for we *are* the formless God, finding expression through the diversity of creation, and nothing else matters. It is with this realization that the "I" becomes single.

Jane and I love Rome, as there are few places on Earth with such a link to the residual vibrations of the forces that have shaped Western civilization, from its foundation in 753 B.C. by the brothers Romulus and Remus, to its demise when it was sacked by the Visigoths in A.D. 476. After its fall, the popes now wore the purple robes of the emperors and set about tearing down much of what remained of the glory of Rome, or used the materials to build Christian churches. Buildings too large to destroy were given an *interpretatio Christiana* ("Christian reinterpretation") and converted into basilicas. Other prominent city features were rededicated to Christian saints. On the Roman Forum, the Curia Iulia or Roman senate building (Sant'Adriano in Foro), the temple of Antoninus and Faustina (San Lorenzo in Miranda), and the temple of Romulus (Santi Cosma e Damiano) were transformed into churches. The Pantheon was also spared, and even the Coliseum eventually become a church, after being damaged by earthquakes and used for a long time as a quarry. Nowadays, on each Good Friday, the pope leads a torch-lit "Way of the Cross" procession, which starts in the area around the Colosseum.

It is ironic that much of the stone from the Colosseum was used to build the Vatican's magnificent St. Peter's Basilica, designed by Donato Bramante, Michelangelo, Carlo Maderno, Gian Lorenzo, and Bernini. It is strange to think that great art and the central basilica of Christianity were built from the stone first commissioned by the emperors Vespasian and Nero, and splattered with the blood of thousands. It is, perhaps, symbolic of the argument that the version of Christianity we have today is an unhappy amalgam of the teachings of Jesus and Roman values. I hope that one day Christians will return to the original ways of Christianity, in which the individual seeks direct realization of the Christ-consciousness, which requires no intermediary or approval from anyone else. All we have to do is place our burdens on the formless God—or on the form of Jesus, if you consider him your Savior—and everything looks after itself.

When I think of Rome I am often reminded of the narrative poem *Lays of Ancient Rome* by Thomas Babington Macaulay that my father quoted when he was diagnosed with bone cancer and was soon to face a terrible battle and eventual death.

> Then out spake brave Horatius,
>   The Captain of the gate:
> "To every man upon this earth
>   Death cometh soon or late.
> And how can man die better
>   Than facing fearful odds
> For the ashes of his fathers
> And the temples of his gods,

In the narrative, Horatius stands to defend the Pons Sublicius Bridge across the Tiber against the army of Lars Porsena, king of Clusium in the late 6th century BC. For the Romans the Tiber river was not only a strategic defense for the city but they also considered it as a sacred river. It was here that the twin brothers Romulus and Remus, were abandoned on its waters and where they were rescued by the she-wolf, Lupa. The river is sacred to the legendary king Tiberinus who the god Jupiter into a god and guardian spirit of the river.

And all this brings us, with a cleaver little hook, to another sacred river that is the subject of my next spiritual enquiry: the Ganges.

MOTHER GANGA

The Ganges is the sixth most-polluted river in the world. In 2014 experts estimated that more than 3,000 million liters of untreated sewage from the towns along its course are pumped into the river every day. It is the repository for raw sewage, industrial effluents, human waste, chemicals from tanneries, partially cremated corpses, butcher's offal, chemical dyes from sari factories, and construction waste. Bathing in the Ganges is a must for any visitor to India!

We chose a sandy bank just upstream from Rishikesh, which is the first big town on the Ganges, so here the water is clean and safe to bathe in. It is believed that bathing in the Ganges washes away your sins, so my yoga teacher, Steve, grabbed me from my paddling spot and, doing his John the Baptist stunt, made absolutely sure I was completely submersed, and that I swallowed enough Ganges water to get me through this lifetime.

The water is surprisingly clean and had a slight emulsion feel from its many immiscible saturated salts, which it has carried from the Himalaya mountains. The water reminded me of when I bathed in the Dead Sea in Israel, where the water is so salty that you bob on the surface like a polystyrene float. The amount of sediment flowing down from the Himalayas in the Ganges is nearly 50% more than you would find in a normal river. Some of this is now being blocked by the dams built further upstream, and now not only are these dams silting up and damaging the quality of the river water, but forcing the water through turbines is also considered by many to be a sacrilege against this symbol of the consciousness of India.

As the riverbed sand squeezed between my toes in a viscous gel, it felt similar to the sand of the Dead Sea. There was something about the quality of the water at that place on the river that I find hard to describe. It certainly felt special.

Hindus believe that the Ganges is self-cleaning, and they often drink the water (*Ganga jal*). This holy water is drunk to ease the pain of death, and it is offered to household deities (*theertham*) or as a final elixir for a dying relative. People can, and do, get sick from drinking the waters of the Ganges, but far fewer than you would expect, and there are a great many who say that Ganges water can heal.

Bathing in the river causes the remission of sins and facilitates *moksha* (liberation). During the act of bathing, you are sin-free, but of course eventually you have to get out. Many also drink the water of the Ganges and believe that it can transform health, even though it is polluted.

The Ganges is sometimes seen as a symbol for the flow of the life-force through the human body, and in particular through the *naadi* channels that run along the spinal column. As I have mentioned before, the main channels for the subtle body are called *ida*, *pingala*, and *sushumna*. The word *ida* means "comfort" in Sanskrit. It is associated with lunar energy and has a feminine, cooling, moonlike quality. *Ida* corresponds to the Ganges River and controls all the mental processes. *Pingala naadi* controls all the vital processes and is associated with solar energy. The word *pingala* means "tawny" in Sanskrit. Like the sun, the *pingala* has an extrovert, male energy and corresponds to the river Yamuna—a tributary river of the Ganges.

Sushumna naadi connects the base chakra to the crown chakra and is the central canal in the subtle body which runs along the spine, and through which the kundalini energy travels during the process of enlightenment. It corresponds with the mythical river Saraswati, which is mentioned in the *Rigveda*, which says it was bigger than Indus and the Ganges, and flowed all the way from the mountains to the sea. Some historians say it was this river that allowed the growth of the great Indus Valley Harappan civilization, which flourished between 3500 and 1900 B.C.

Many theories have been put forward about this lost river, and some claim that it is an invisible river that still flows underground, possibly as a subterranean river beneath the Ganges. The Saraswati disappeared 4,000 years ago after a massive earthquake. Soon after the 2015 earthquakes in Nepal, people digging in in Mugalwali village of Yamunanagar district, which is believed to be part of the old river course, struck water at a depth of eight feet. Considering the spiritual significance of India's most holy river, this is an auspicious augury for the coming New Age. Many Indians say that when the Saraswati returns, then Rama, the seventh *avatar* of the Hindu god Vishnu, will also return.

Some legends say that the Saraswati River dried up at the end of the last *yuga* and prophesy that in the far future, the Ganges River will finally dry up at the end of *Kali Yuga*. We know that the Himalayan glaciers are melting at an alarming rate, so this is a possibility, but the *yugas* to come are predicted to be so blissful that we may have transcended the Earth altogether. Legend also has it that the first Vedic people lived on the banks of the Saraswati River 10,000 years ago, at about the same time as my Sushumna Naadi palm leaves were being written. Perhaps one day someone's oracle will reveal its whereabouts.

The Ganges is an incredibly beautiful river. When I stayed at an ashram on its right bank, we could watch the colors change throughout the day. At dawn, and in the morning when we did our yoga from the veranda, it foams white, and we could just hear the surge of river in the distance as it tumbles down cold from the Himalayas. The sound is gradually lost as India wakes up. As the day progresses, the river changes to a pastel turquoise, and it reminds of the coral seas I've seen in Thailand and the Seychelles. Come evening, the colors have changed to an indigo blue, reflecting the seashell white of the moon.

In places such as Rishikesh and Varanasi, there is always the feeling that the sacred river is somewhere in the background, like a holy thread that weaves its way through our lives. The river is linked both with life and with death, and it is a symbol of how we need to approach our time on earth. A river is constantly changing. When you put your foot in a river, it is never the same river, for already the waters have flowed past you toward the sea. In life, too, our problems occur when we grasp, control, and hold on to things.

In hatha yoga, when we force or become tense in a posture, we can cause ourselves physical harm. In life, as in *asanas*, we have to learn to flow and surrender into the place our soul tells us to be. The energy needs to fill us naturally, like a vessel being filled with holy water. When the water of life is free, we are healthy and energetic, and we function properly. When the life-force is frozen and compressed, we become fearful or ill. Yoga loosens up the spiritual energy of the body, so that we can be who we really are. Within us there may be blockages and tension—which is basically trapped and compressed energy—all of which can be set free and turned into vitality by opening our natural fluidity. When we flow like a river that fearlessly plunges from the greatest heights, or unhesitatingly fills the darkest depths, we become happy and free.

Rishikesh is a wonderful place to get to know the energy of the Ganges. At night the river is lit by the occasional floating light, and you can hear from the bank opposite where I was staying an echo to the rhythms of the *bhajans* and mantras coming from the *ghats* on the other bank. One of the most interesting I visited was the Triveni Ghat, with its giant archway depicting the chariot of Krishna, and its giant white statue of Shiva in the river. Some evenings, we joined the hundreds of pilgrims who attend the Ganga Arti. At this *ghat*, the air is electric with chanting from the orange-clad devotees and filled with the smell of incense.

We joined the ceremonies and released into the river flower-filled leaf boats, carrying tiny candle lamps as symbols of worship, remembrance, and hope.

For Hindus, the banks of Ganges are the most sacred place on earth and its spirituality is personified as a goddess known as Ganga. Few places have such an unbroken history of worship and put you in touch with ancient spiritual vibrations; except perhaps, the Temple Mount in Jerusalem.

TEMPLE MOUNT JERUSALEM

My first glimpse of Jerusalem in the 1970s was from the kibbutz's open-backed truck as it rounded a high corner on a small, quiet road into Jerusalem. This was a time before the new city towered behind the old city, so it must have looked much as it did hundreds of years ago, surrounded by the old city wall and dominated by the golden Dome of the Rock, which has sat since A.D. 691 in the Temple Mount area. The ocher colors of Jerusalem reminded me of hues of paintings by Paul Klee or Gustav Klimt, and the ancient city looked magnificent against the cerulean sky of Israel.

The Temple Mount is, of course, one of the most sacred places on Earth. Known in Hebrew as Har HaBayit and in Arabic as the Haram al-Sharif, it has been used as a religious site for thousands of years, and it is considered holy by Judaism, Christianity, the Roman religion, and Islam. For the Jews, this is the most sacred site of all. It is the place where God asked Abraham to sacrifice his son. It is Mount Zion, where the original Jebusite fortress stood, and it was from here that God gathered the dust used to create Adam.

According to the Bible, Solomon's temple, also known as the first temple (957 B.C.), stood here before its destruction by Nebuchadnezzar II after the Siege of Jerusalem of 587 B.C. The second temple (516 B.C.) was built in the same area and destroyed by the Roman Empire in A.D. 70. It is here that, according to the Gospel of John, Jesus Christ lashed out against the moneychangers.

Jewish tradition maintains that this is where the third and final temple will also be built, and it is the place Jews turn toward during prayer. Fundamentalist Christians believe that the third temple will exist during the Great Tribulation and will herald the coming of the Antichrist. I personally think it would be rather nice to knock it all down, dig it all up, then build a single, magnificent, pantheon temple to all religions—but that's a dream for a Golden Age that is still very far away.

Muslims believe that the Islamic miracle of the Isra and Mi'raj happened on Temple Mount. This is described as a night journey, which the prophet Muhammad took during a single night around A.D. 621. He travels on the steed Buraq to "the farthest mosque," where he leads other prophets in prayer. He then ascends to heaven, where he speaks to God, who gives Muhammad prayer instructions to take back to the faithful. To the majority of Muslim believers, Isra and Mi'raj were physical journeys, whereas others have argued that it was a dream or an example of astral travel.

At the time of my visit, there was a lot of tension, and at all four entrances were set machine-gun posts and heavily armed soldiers from the Israeli army. We visited the Al-Aqsa Mosque and then the Dome of the Rock, where we were escorted by an imam to view the foundation stone in the floor. Here, where the cool air offered a short respite from the hot sunlight above ground, we were told we may hear whispering voices from the roughly hewn, round hole at the upper left of the stone that penetrates a small cave, known as the Well of Souls, where medieval Islamic legend claims you can hear the spirits of the dead awaiting Judgment Day. Although the very idea sets the imagination afire, this was nonetheless one of the most eerie places I have visited, and it is a strange belief to place at the heart of one of the most holy places on earth. Clearly the cave was considered to be a sort of portal to the underworld.

The Jews believe that this is the spot that housed the Holy of Holies, the inner sanctuary of the Tabernacle, where God dwelt and where the Ark of the Covenant was kept during the first temple period. The Ark of the Covenant is said to have contained the Ten Commandments, which were given by God to Moses on Mount Sinai. Some say that the Ark of the Covenant remains hidden deep beneath the temple's foundation stone, and that stories of it being carried off to Ethiopia were a smokescreen to hide the real truth.

Conspiracy theorists believe that the Ark of the Covenant was a type of electrical capacitor from a space ship abandoned by aliens. These ideas were seeded by the movie *Raiders of the Lost Ark*, in which Harrison Ford's Indiana Jones goes in pursuit of the Ark, which is said to hold the key to human existence. The Indiana Jones story was loosely inspired by a real, intrepid British archeologist named Captain Monty Parker—no relation—who started excavations beneath Jerusalem in 1909 in search of the lost Ark. He was described by Simon Sebag Montefiore in his book *Jerusalem the Biography* as "an opportunistic but credulous rogue," who raised £74,000 and bribed Ottoman officials to turn a blind eye to his illegal excavations beneath Temple Mount. Eventually his dig was discovered by the proper authorities, and Parker made a run for it.

Captain Monty Parker was urged on by the Finnish spiritualist medium Valter Juvelius, who believed that the book of Ezekiel confirmed their intuitively received beliefs. Juvelius claimed to have received messages from the spirits about a "coded" passage in an ancient text of the book of Ezekiel that revealed the secret hiding place of the temple treasure in Jerusalem. The archeologist Silberman wrote: "The precise contents of this ancient depository remained Juvelius's closely guarded secret. By all accounts, however, it was of spectacular value, far beyond that of any archeological discovery made in Palestine—and probably anywhere else. By some later reports, based largely on hearsay, Juvelius's treasure was "the gold-encrusted Ark of the Covenant, brought by the children of Israel out of Egypt." In other versions, it was "the treasures of the Jewish kings, and ancient tables which will set to rest all doubts concerning the resurrection of Christ."

In 2014 these two nutty Spiritualists were vindicated, and their spirit-inspired maps of the cavernous tunnels beneath Jerusalem were discovered to be accurate when the archeologist Shukron and his team unearthed a shaft system, close to where Parker had been digging, that follows the course of the Gihon Spring. Shulron's team followed the maps Parker made of the watercourse, which led them to the site of what he believes to be the lost citadel of David. So far, no sign of the Ark of the Covenant has been found, but it is early days.

My intuitive feeling at the Holy Mount gave me the impression that this place is more than just a holy site. There was something about the energy that felt tangible and electric. The UFO theorists are stretching the imagination too far in thinking that Temple Mount hides parts of a spacecraft, though on January 28, 2011, two separate videos show a bright object slowly descending over the Dome of the Rock. A video taken from the Tzofim Mountain that overlooks Old Jerusalem shows a circular UFO hovering over the temple, while the second, taken from a different spot, shows a white light descending slowly and hovering directly above the Temple Mount. It then shoots up into the sky with a gigantic flash. Of course, these could be two fake videos, and skeptics argue that they are dubious, as nobody has laid claim to these anonymous and potentially very valuable videos. Also, moving lights are comparatively easy to edit in with software. If something on this scale had happened, then many more people would have reported seeing it. There has been no conclusive evidence to affirm or deny the UFO, and this, too, now joins the many beliefs and mysteries connected to the Temple Mount.

Old Jerusalem with its labyrinthine paths, narrow streets and alleys and its ancient shrines to three faiths is a place where you feel completely immersed in history. At every turn you catch a glimpse of unfamiliar ceremonies, rituals and prayer, get a whiff of incense and see people dressed in holy garb. We are just passing through history but this place is history. What we see here is the outward expression of religions but I fear that the inner, esoteric, aspect is missing. Some still practice forms of esoteric Christianity, Islam has its Sufism and Judaism has the Kabbalah but I fear all three of these great faiths do not have a simple yoga – a direct way to union with the divine that the individual can travel without the intervention of a clergyman, priest, minister, imam or rabbi. All rely on faith rather than direct experience.

YOGA IN THE HIMALAYAS

Rising at 2:30 a.m., we drove from Rishikesh for an hour or so and were able to ascend the steps up to the mountain temple well before dawn. We arranged our yoga mats in the temple courtyard to face the breaking dawn light, with a spectacular view across the valleys and purple foothills of the Himalayas. As the sun rose, we chanted our mantras to lead us from darkness into light and enjoyed yoga in the cool morning air. It gave a whole new meaning to the sun salutation series of yoga *asanas*, which we concluded as the sun fingered its way through the distant white peaks of the Himalayas. The colors and view were breath-taking. The temple bell tolled with the dawn and echoed through the purple mountains, majestic against the fiery orange sky. It was beautiful.

As the Naadi correctly noted, yoga has been part of most of my life and hopefully will, as the Naadi predicts, keep me healthy into my eighties. The first book I read about it was a Pelican book, published in 1959, which was *Yoga* by Ernest Wood. It was a great book but a nightmare to use, as it had no photos or illustrations. You try working out how to do the *ardha matsyendrasana* (spinal twist) without any illustrations to guide you, and we won't mention what happens when you try *jala basti* unaided. Today it's easy to learn, as we now have YouTube, local classes, and the rest, but in those days yoga was unheard of and a complete mystery to most people. Putting both feet behind my head (as I could do at the bendy age of thirteen), I asked our physical education teacher if I could do yoga like this instead of "mindlessly jumping over a stupid wooden horse." His response was simply to give me additional push-ups as punishment for being so cheeky. Twisting yourself around like a corkscrew would not equip a young man for society and would certainly not be part of *this* teacher's physical fitness regimen! He wanted to turn us into men, not sissies.

All this Far Eastern claptrap became more acceptable when it appeared on TV, and soon lots of people were bending along to Richard Hittleman's BBC program "Yoga for Health." It has been said that Richard Hittleman introduced yoga to millions of people. His method was to start with basic hatha yoga postures but to gradually introduce the more profound Yoga philosophy of *advaita vedanta*. In New York, "Yoga for Health" was screened for more than four-and-a-half years without a break. Richard Hittleman was a student of the great Indian spiritual master, Ramana Maharshi, whom you will recall Sri Sadguru Saravana claimed I had followed in a past-life.

Today yoga is everywhere, and it has become a fashionable form of physical exercise that is very attractive to women, fitness freaks on a low budget, and a few space cadets. But with "fashionable," the true message can get lost underneath in crazy Western yoga notions and bizarre new styles. Today everyone is trying to out-do one another with the latest new style or most grandiose-sounding lineage. There's some great stuff out there, such as aerial yoga, where people hang upside down in anti-gravity hammocks; hot nude yoga—yup, you got it, naked yoga in a baking-hot room; dog yoga, or "doga," which combines mediation, stretching, and massage for dogs; and, of course, tantrum yoga, which encourages its practitioners to scream their way to better health. I guess it's mildly better than jumping over a wooden horse. On a serious note, the mainstream styles of yoga are ashtanga, Bikram, Iyengar, vinyasa, viniyoga, prenatal, and jivamukti.

My feeling is that yoga has lost its way in the West. Often yoga teachers are on ego trips. Some see yoga as a competitive sport, and most think it is simply a cheap form of fitness for women. I was therefore supremely fortunate to find a superb local yoga teacher, who had not only mastered hatha yoga but also had an extensive and applied knowledge of the spiritual remit of yoga. Steve Harrison—a.k.a. Prem—helped me over many years to dive deep into yoga and its philosophy, and to explore the advanced *kriyas*, such as controlling the breath to move the flow of the energy in the spine, and tackling some of the more difficult techniques—such as *sutra neti*—all of which require a proper, sensible teacher. We learned to train the attention and dive into deep meditation.

Prem was taught by Nadu, a Persian teacher based in California, who then did further training in India at the Swami Sivananda Ashram in Rishikesh. He feels that his spiritual guru is Sri Yogeshwaranand Parmahan, a great yogi who died in 1985, having spent his life reviving the ancient science of yoga. Although Prem never met Sri Yogeshwaranand Parmahan, his dedication to his guru was such that he was given permission to spend an extended period of time in meditation inside in his master's *samadhi* tomb. This allowed Prem to connect to his master's *shakti* and perhaps also to his master's spirit.

In his book *The Essential Colorlessness of the Absolute*, Yogeshwaranand Parmahan explores some interesting ideas about the continuation of the human spirit after physical death that come very close to the philosophy of Spiritualism. He had a tremendous insight into the workings of the subtle body and subtle senses, and how they interact with the physical body. Yogeshwaranand Parmahan's psychic vision—called *prajnaloka*—could penetrate the human body, and also perceive the astral planes and gain direct insight into the progress of the astral and causal bodies after death.

Prem's primary yogic teaching is rooted in the world of the here-and-now, and he teaches that we should apply "living yoga" to everything we do and every aspect of life. We will find happiness if we open to the flow of life rather than resist it, and most of all if we move the focus of our attention from the head to the heart—from ego to love. Prem maintains a family, yet practices yoga from 3:00 a.m. until bedtime every day of the week except Sunday. His living example of dedication to yoga has been an inspiration.

My fashionable twist on yoga is to find ways that we can adapt the teachings of yoga for Spiritualists and mediums. Some of us are born to become mediums and give messages from the next world. Real mediums tend not to choose this difficult path, but somehow mediumship is thrust upon us, whether we like the idea of not. I have debated elsewhere the pros and cons of developing *siddhis* (powers) and the dangerous sidetrack of developing them for their own sake or as a way of glorifying the ego. In my case, I am stuck with them and am therefore compelled to use them in the service of mediumship and to help people know for certain that death is not the end of our story.

Mediumship brings with it a huge stress on the spiritual body. When a medium opens themselves as a channel for the spirit, all the illnesses and passing conditions of the dead spirit are, for a short while, impressed on their own spirit body so that the medium can gather clairsentient information about how the person died. This information is then passed on to the person receiving the spirit message as part of the verification of the identity of the communicating spirit. Similarly, when a medium's thoughts and emotions blend with the thoughts and emotions being projected from the spirit communicator, there is the danger of retaining the resonance of the spirit's problems and traits. When a communication is finished, the spirit guides and helpers will clear the medium's spirit body and aura of any residual energy and flush the aura through with healing light, but still there is the danger that a little negative energy can remain. It is the case that many mediums die too soon, and many Spiritualists believe that mediumship—and particularly physical mediumship—can trigger diabetes. Mediums who have abused their gift, or not managed it properly, have been known to be prone to alcoholism, chain smoking, depression, and promiscuity.

There have been no scientific studies to qualify what I have said, and a lot of these illnesses may be hearsay and misinformation, but it is certainly the case that mediumship can make you desperately tired, and sometimes, with extreme tiredness, the immune system breaks down and opens a door for illness. Yoga, I feel, has helped me remain fit, healthy, happy—and, of course, strikingly good-looking! All mediums should practice not only physical yoga but also some of the energy techniques that I describe in some of my other books, and teach in workshops.

Yoga is not just about the body and physical health. It is a method to help us move into the absolute stillness of being. It is best to get back to basics and see yoga as primarily a way to live in harmony with the universe and move toward an understanding of the way things really are, rather than what we think they should be. Keeping it very simple gets you to the Truth more quickly than clouding things with ego-trips. Even if you are on an ego trip, you can still use yoga to get to the knowledge, but it may hurt a bit, since the ego will drive you to want to be the great teacher. The cosmic joke is that it's the ego that has to be sacrificed on the bloody altar of Kali. The simplest way to get rid of egotism and its cravings and desires is to simply think about

God and surrender the expected fruits of your efforts to him.

In traditional yoga, the adept should first develop their spiritual code called the *yamas* (moral imperatives) and *niyamas* (duties or observances). It's same with people wanting to be a medium. The first question I have to ask is "Why do you want to develop these skills?" If there is no moral remit in the aspirant—such as wanting to serve spirit rather than the ego—then we will soon be in trouble. The *yamas* and *niyamas* cover all aspects of spiritual discipline and are a reliable rudder for those exploring the ultimate meaning of human existence. The same principles can be applied to those investigating or developing mediumship and healing, and I have shown how they can be adapted and applied in some of my other books about spiritual development.

When I took my yoga teacher training course with Prem, much of the emphasis in the 200-hour course was on showing how apply the *yamas* and *niyamas* to the *asanas* (postures). So, for example, we need to take a non-violent (*ahimsa*) attitude when melting into a difficult posture, or be truthful (*satya*) with ourselves when finding our limits. Being late for class is a form of stealing (*asteya*), as our disruption steals other people's time. In multiple ways, the main five *yamas* and five *niyamas* prepare us for the second rung of yoga, which is the *asanas*. (In some systems there are ten *yamas* and ten *niyamas*.)

If you work as a professional medium, healer, or a psychic, your spiritual body is constantly under assault from the vibrations of the people sitting with you or the deathbed memories in the astral shell of the communicating spirit. In Spiritualism and Reiki, healing practitioners are taught cleansing the aura, but in my opinion, this is not enough to safeguard the spirit body, which could pass on the vibrations to the mental and physical body and result in illness, stress, anxiety, tiredness, and so on. Physical yoga helps the life-energy to be restored and also loosens the compressed energy held in the joints and spine, which is the result of the traumas of this life and previous incarnations.

In my own mediumistic development classes, and watching awareness classes in Spiritualism, I am horrified how people looking to develop their spiritual skills slump in their chairs or immediately fall asleep when asked to meditate. Within most Spiritualist circles, there is absolutely no instruction about posture, breathing, concentration, or correct meditation. The ultimate yoga posture is simply to know how to sit with a straight spine, so that the aspirant can enter the next stages without distraction. Spiritualists could gain a great deal and have much more psychic energy at their disposal if they adopted some of the simplest teachings of hatha yoga.

In time the yogi will learn to use the breath with their movements until *pranayama* (breath control) goes hand in hand with the *asana* or pose. This has tremendous health benefits, as the breath moves the life-force (*prana*) through the body. This is the same healing energy used within Reiki and Spiritualism to fuel healing, psychism, and mediumship, but again it is often not given the emphasis it deserves. The breathing of a trance medium will deepen as the spirit communicator overshadows their body, perhaps as a means to control the spiritual and physical energy channels. It would be helpful if the medium and sitters were aware how breath and *prana* could be used more efficiently and safely. Similarly, Spiritualists generally have a rudimentary understanding of how the breath can link with the chakras, but most have no knowledge whatsoever of the thousands of years of research done within the tantric, *kriya*, and kundalini yoga systems. If we control the breath, we also control the attention and vice versa. It is madness to let loose the powers of mediumship without having some understanding of how the spirit body works. Within Spiritualism's circles, most of the adjustments to the medium's aura and spirit body are made by the spirit guides and helpers, so the work is safe, but we could advance much further if Spiritualism learned and applied the teachings from the East.

Real yoga begins when we learn to sit still and control and withdraw the senses (*pratyahara*). All the rest that went before is a preparation for this moment. What the yogi learns to do is to live from the inside rather than from the outside. We now start to live inside-out rather than outside-in. This internalization of the senses reveals to us that what he have previously known of ourselves is very little. Our material life is just the tip of an iceberg. Below the surface is a magnificent, huge inner world. This is what Jesus was talking about when he told us, "The Kingdom of Heaven is within you."

The Naadi oracle spotted my interest in yoga and told how I would help people to open their third eye. This is what I do in my psychic development workshops and circles, which are very different from Spiritualist groups because the emphasis is less on mediumship and more on developing consciousness. If you can develop spirituality and attain a higher consciousness, then the psychic powers will appear spontaneously, and the right guidance can be given to help the fledgling medium use their gift for the highest good. If we simply develop psychic powers and mediumship without spirituality, it is like a broken violin, which can squeak but never express the glory of existence.

In yoga training, once we learn to internalize the senses, the next step is to focus the attention. The methods used to do this are called *dharana*, which in Sanskrit translates as "immovable concentration of the mind." It sounds a bit fierce, but it is simply stopping the mind from wandering and wasting its power. If we can focus the mind in one direction, it can become like a laser of incredible power. This is done not by force, but by gentle and sustained training, until the mind comes under the control of the will rather than raging around like an out-of-control monkey. In turn, your own will becomes one with an even higher power. The famous yogi B.K.S. Iyengar states that the objective of *dharana* is to achieve the mental state where the mind, intellect, and ego are "all restrained, and all these faculties are offered to the Lord for his use and in his service. Here there is no feeling of 'I' and 'mine.'"

Spiritualists understand this message of service, which is talked about extensively by the spirit guides who have spoken through trance and physical mediumship. Some mediums may naturally have a good attention, but I often see people running off into all sorts of outlandish fantasy when you sit them down to meditate. They have no control over their revelries, and although spirit messages can sometimes get through this stream of consciousness, it would be far more powerful if the apprentice medium were to train his attention to remain in focus. Then they would then see clearly which thoughts are their own and which are given to them by the spirit communicators.

Mediumship requires the laser attention of *dharana* but also a super-passivity that allows the impressions from the spirit world to pass across the screen of the attention. Between *dharana* and the next step I'm about to talk about, *dhyana* (meditation), there's another state where the active mind is used to make a communication with spirit. The attention becomes alert and focused, while simultaneously there is a flow of consciousness in the background of the awareness, which enables a conversation to take place with the spirit communicators.

This is the state I call "sitting for spirit," which is not recognized in traditional yoga but has been accessed by some yogis.

I would recommend that Spiritualists interested in the yogi's take on life after death read *What Becomes of the Soul after Death* by Swami Sivananda (Divine Life Society Publications). As I have mentioned, Swami Sivananda was alive at the time news was in the Indian newspapers about the rise of Spiritualism in Europe. He was intrigued by the investigations of Sir Oliver Lodge, which attested that the human personality survives physical death, and he was pleased that the West was losing its atheism and accepting life after death. But he also had concerns that mediums had lost the power of self-control and could be in touch not with spirits, but with Earth-bound spirit imposters. Swami Sivananda was one of the greatest of yogis, but I feel he would have formed a better opinion if he could have directly witnessed physical mediumship for himself and directly heard the evidential mediumship that proves the spirits' identities. East and West have much to learn from one another.

The meditation we experience in yoga is different from the "sitting for spirit" in Spiritualist circles. Clearly we can prove that there is life after death and our methods work, but there are many misconceptions within Spiritualism as to what passes for meditation. It would be best if we could separate the ideas: sitting for spirit is a form of inner attunement to get messages from the spirit world, which at the start requires a circle setting, whereas meditation is a method for self-realization and something for you personally that can be done either in a group or alone.

Meditation (*dhyana*) is a state of mind that's hard to describe, because sometimes you don't realize you've been in the state until you come out of it. It is a deep awareness of oneness that lies at the very heart of our being, yet is inclusive of awareness of body, mind, senses, and surroundings, while remaining unattached to them. Meditation can be a process of stepping back, in which we consciously transcend the states of waking, dream, and dreamless sleep, until eventually we reach a state called *turiya*—pure consciousness. In Patanjali's *Yoga Sutras*, meditation is the last step before the final goal, *samadhi*, or the superconscious experience.

In India it is easy to become enveloped in meditation, since the whole country is steeped in the conducive vibrations of the great yogis, saints, and *avatars* that have walked on its sacred soil. It is incredible that a whole nation can be so devoted to the Divine and to thousands of years of meditation on the Infinite. The Sanskrit name for India is *Bharata*, from the root *bhr*, "to bear or to carry," with a literal meaning of "to be maintained" (of fire). This term also means "one who is engaged in search for knowledge," which is the reason I made this pilgrimage. If we find this knowledge, we take it with us and can carry India within us for the rest of our lives, for India is not a nation: it is an objective manifestation of a state of being.

   I will never forget the feeling of wonder and well-being that filled me as we left the mountain temple and descended the mountain path, through forests and steep, soft-earth slopes, back toward Rishikesh, since in this holy land every step felt like a meditation. We swam in pools beneath high waterfalls, trundled along viaducts and irrigation canals, sheltered beneath a *bodhi* tree, and scrambled down dangerous tracks, while far below us twinkled the Ganges, weaving its serpentine way through Rishikesh. This is truly a sacred land.

I have spoken here about Swami Sivananda's theories about life after death and how on 8 September 1887 he visited the Sri Aurobindo Ashram to study the idea of Punra Yoga or Integral Yoga. In the next section I will consider what Sri Aurobindo has to say about life after death and how they compare with the Spiritualist's stance.

SRI AUROBINDO'S ASHRAM IN DELHI

Sri Aurobindo's ashram in Delhi is spotlessly clean and is a friendly place where spiritual travelers can stay. As someone who has spent so much time involved with Spiritualism, I am intrigued by many of his ideas, which correspond quite closely, sometimes, with many of the things mediums have to say about the nature of soul.

Sri Aurobindo was an Indian nationalist, scholar, poet, mystic, philosopher, yogi, and guru. He taught a unique system of "integral yoga," and worked for the freedom of India and to bring to Earth what he referred to as the Super-mind. His integral yoga teachings included Psychicization, which is one of the most essential stages of the spiritual processes. In *The Life Divine* he talks of a spiritual movement inward, so that one realizes the psychic being or Divine Soul. Once this is discovered, the outer personality is spontaneously transformed. He believed in the cosmic evolution of the spirit, a concept which in some ways is similar to the Spiritualist principle of "the continuous progress of every human soul."

Sri Aurobindo also spoke of the five *koshas* or subtle bodies that we gradually shed after death. He claimed that we die step-by-step from each *kosha*, shedding one at a time, and that mediumistic communication takes place through the more Earth-like *koshas* of the astral body. I note very similar teachings here to the Spiritualist messages from the spirit of Silver Birch, who explained how he had to use the astral shell of a dead Native American and slow his vibrations in order to communicate with our world. Silver Birch was not actually a Native American: he was a being of light who had transcended earthly identity, but used this discarded *kosha* to communicate through the trance mediumship of Maurice Barbanell.

Sri Aurobindo does, however, differ from Spiritualists when it comes to the idea that the personality can persist after death. In his book *The Life Divine*, he talks extensively about the process of rebirth and the nature of the personality: "Personality is only a temporary mental, vital, and physical formation which the being, the real person, the psychic entity, puts forward on the surface. It is not the Self in its abiding reality. In each return to Earth, the person, the *purusha*, makes a new formation, builds a new personal quantum suitable for a new experience, for a new growth of its being. When it passes from its body, it keeps still the same vital and mental form for a time, but the forms or sheaths dissolve, and what is kept is only the essential elements of the past quantum, of which some will, but some may not, be used in the next incarnation. The essential form of the past personality may remain as one element among many, one personality among many personalities of the same person, but in the background, in the subliminal behind the veil of the surface mind and life and body, contributing from there whatever is needed of itself to the new formation; but it will not itself be the whole formation or build anew the old unchanged type of nature. It may even be that the new quantum or structure of being will exhibit a quite contrary character and temperament, quite other capacities, other very different tendencies; for latent potentials may be ready to emerge, or something already in action, but inchoate, may have been held back in the last life which needed to be worked out, but was kept over for a later and more suitable combination of the possibilities of the nature."

Sri Aurobindo is also credited with predicting the advent of Sathya Sai Baba and the coming of a new Golden Age. In 1910, he embarked on a mission to bring the Lord to Earth and to fill the whole world with bliss. With this in mind, he undertook spiritual practices for sixteen years. On November 24, 1926, he announced that Krishna had descended. Sathya Sai Baba was born on November 23, 1926.

Sri Aurobindo made a great contribution to Indian philosophy, and although I find that his writings are written in a style that is sometimes a little impenetrable, he has often proposed ideas that are unique and thought-provoking. His other great contribution to mankind is a spotlessly clean ashram with immaculate restrooms.

Now, I have seen some restrooms on my travels. The Beverly Hills Hotel restrooms were so enchanting that Jane videoed them and posted shots of the palatial privy on her Facebook page. In India it's a completely different story. My worst experience was at a hotel deceptively called "The Tourist Hotel." The restroom was dark and dismal, to say the least, and it had the shower directly next to the Victorian chain toilet, so of course I would sit on it naked after my shower. James Bond had nothing on me when a hairy spider, as big as my hand, landed beside the toilet and crawled its way toward me. Bravely, I leapt up and stood up on the toilet seat, shaking and shouting as it dashed across the floor, under the door, and into the bedroom, where my I heard my friends collectively scream as they jumped on the beds. Now when entering a tropical convenience, I contemplate the haunting possibility that a hairy Arachne leg may reach up and surprise me as I do my business.

Sri Aurobindo

I am grateful to Sri Aurobindo for the lovely clean facilities offered us in Delhi. I'm sure the spirit of Sri Aurobindo will not mind my levity, as in life he was known to have had a playful sense of humor. Mirra Alfassa ("The Mother"), who helped found the ashram, said: "He had a way of looking at things. . . . It's incredible. Incredible. But it seems that for him, the outside world was something . . . absurd, you know."

My stay in Sri Aurobindo's ashram in Delhi gave my friends and me a chance to visit the Akshardham temples, created by H.D.H. Pramukh Swami Maharaj in fulfillment of the wish of his guru, Brahmaswarup Yogiji Maharaj, the fourth successor in the spiritual hierarchy of Bhagwan Swaminarayan. This place is a huge, modern building complex built to traditional styles and incorporating traditional skills of Hindu carving. It is an astonishing group of buildings, ornamental walls, lakes, pools, and statues. The panorama stretches as far as the eye can see. It must have cost millions and millions of dollars to build. After visiting one breath-taking room after another, and gasping at the incredible gold statues, intricately carved ceilings, and beautiful paintings and sculpture, we finished the day watching their finale: a laser-lit fountain display. It's Hinduism with a Disneyesque twist.

My stay in Delhi gave me the opportunity to visit another of India's sacred places that commemorates the death of Gandhi who was shot on January 30th, 1948, aged seventy-eight, by the Hindu fanatic Nathuram Godse.

MAHATMA GANDHI

Visiting the Raj Ghat memorial to Mahatma Gandhi can either be a visit to a dead man's grave or a visit to an idea. As we took off our sandals and approached Gandhi's samadhi (memorial) to the father of the nation, I was inevitably reminded of his teaching of non-violent resistance that won victory over the British, and how he looked to the unity and common values of religions rather than to their differences. In My Experiments with Truth, Gandhi says: "My city is a Sea City. As you can see, it is full of Hindus, Muslims, Sikhs, Jews, Persians, and others. They all live like one family. My family was pranami. Even though we are Hindu by birth, in our temple, the priest used to read from the Muslim Koran and the Hindu Gita—moving from one to the other as if it mattered not which book was being read, as long as God was being worshiped."

The *samadhi* memorial is a black marble platform that marks the spot of Mahatma Gandhi's cremation on January 31, 1948, a day after his assassination. It is left open to the sky, while a perpetual flame burns at one end to mark the love and gratitude of the world for this man's example. There was a hushed, reverent air, and I noticed, sitting on the grass nearby, a woman spinning cloth in the traditional way—a poignant reminder of Gandhi's brilliant, non-violent way to wreak havoc on the British textile industry.

We also visited the nearby Gandhi museum, where I saw his simple bed, which we were allowed to touch. One of the foundation skills of any medium is the clairsentient ability called psychometry, in which memories recorded on objects are replayed through the medium's thoughts and feelings. It was one of the first skills I developed in circle, and it is a skill I teach all my psychic students and have demonstrated on a BBC television show about psychic archeology.

When my awareness opened, I could for a moment feel the vibrations of a man who set no limit to the suffering he was prepared to undertake in order to fulfill his purpose. Flashes of his extraordinary life played across the screen of my awareness. When I let go, I felt an overwhelming feeling of exhaustion and marveled at the incredible, single-pointed willpower of this great man.

The spiritual person will think of God at their passing moments. As the assassin's bullets tore through Mahatma Gandhi's body on January 30, 1948, his final cry was *"He, Ram"* ("Oh, God"). Clearly Gandhi was a man of exceptional spirituality and, according to the Hindu, these final words would have enabled him to merge with the godhead, and most likely he would not make any form of spirit communication with the living. So it was with some shock that Gandhi appeared to make his presence known some years later when I was demonstrating mediumship at a Spiritualist church.

I had just completed a communication for a lady in the audience, with some good, evidential messages, and with lots of factual information from the spirit of her grandfather. Very often in my readings, I ask the spirit communicator to show me something that is so weird and odd that nobody could accuse me of cold reading or the recipient of making things fit. I asked her dead grandfather to show me something as unusual as possible.

I had the sensation of him handing me something wooden. "He is handing me a wooden woodpecker," I said. "And he is showing me an Indian man standing with him. I cannot tell who the Indian man is, but he's tiny and has a mischievous smile and bright eyes."

To everyone's astonishment, and particularly mine, the lady explained that her grandfather had chaperoned Mahatma Gandhi when he visited England in 1931 and, as a parting gift, Gandhi had carved him a woodpecker. Clearly the man in the background was the great *mahatma*, yet I had been completely unaware of this significance.

While researching for this book, I also discovered that Gandhi's life and destiny had been foreseen. Some astrologers point out that he was born in a Gand Mool Nakshatras, and in particular the Jyeshth Nakhshatra, which traditionally Indian astrologers consider to be inauspicious. Yet from these dark stars, Gandhi became a light to the world.

I was particularly intrigued to discover that his Naadi leaf was found by the respected astrologer Bangalore Venkata Raman (August 9, 1912–December 20, 1998), who spent many years trying to unravel their mystery. He claimed that the Naadi leaves were not only written for those who will consult the oracle, but for every person who will ever live.

Raman's research concluded that the Naadi leaves were able to give detailed information of one's past up to the present, but only a few could accurately predict the future. The best system, he said, were the thirty-six Tantra Naadis. Each Tantra Naadi contains 1,588,320 astrological charts, which cycle every 360 years. He said: "The correctness of the forecasts depends upon the intensity of the rituals performed and recitation of the mantra to propitiate the *devata* [angelic beings]."

Bangalore Venkata Raman cites Gandhi's Naadi leaves, which appear to give an accurate précis of his life: "The native will be born in a holy city on the coast of the ocean. At the age of twenty, he will go to a foreign country. His mother will die at the age of twenty-two in his absence. He will marry at thirteen. At thirty-two, he will be a lawyer. He will always speak truth and will be pure in heart. There will be no distinction between his thoughts, words, and deeds. Before the age of sixty-five, he will meet the king of the white race. He will resort to fasting for the good of the world and will live beyond the age of seventy."

The Raj Ghat memorial to Mahatma Gandhi is located in Delhi, the capital of India, but my next stop was to the spiritual capital of India: Varanasi also known as Benares.

A CULINARY GUIDE TO VARANASI

The first glimpse I had of Varanasi was in a dream. I was walking with Sathya Sai Baba along a beautiful river, the sun was shining, and everything I could see was bathed in golden light. There were buildings around me, and I was surprised to see that they were all made of solid gold. We walked a little further to a temple that had sunk into a river. Here Sathya Sai Baba gave me some personal instruction and guidance about my life.

Our Varanasi "hotel," if you could call it that, was a half-built, half-derelict building that sat precariously overlooking the Ganges, right next to the Scindia Ghat, which was named after the after the Scindias who built it. It is one of the last *ghats* to still cremate bodies using wood. From my room, we had a fine view of the cremation area and an amazing Shiva temple that had, over the years, sunk into the river, until all that remained was the temple roof poking above the water. It was the exact same temple that Sai Baba had shown me in my dream.

The "hotel" had many salubrious, star-worthy additions, such as a half-built concrete staircase on the side of the building, which we had to climb up leaping across the gaps. There was no banister or landing lights, and in places you took your life in your hands as you went up to bed. Inside the main building, the stairs were also pretty dangerous and wound round a narrow corner that you had to squeeze sideways to get through, and the stairs were uneven, with the occasional, unexpected steep drop. Behind the "hotel," they molded cow dung into bricks for the funereal fires. The "restaurant" was hilarious. The huge, turbaned chef worked from a gas stove with just one working burner, and he would constantly shout at his tiny, bedraggled assistant and waiter. You never got what you ordered. I ordered soup and got a sort of pancake curry thing, so everyone present just agreed to eat whatever we were given, or we'd all go hungry. Someone else got my soup. Flies came as standard.

I had seen much better quality in the cheap hotel I stayed at in Bangalore with Jane. At least it had flock wallpaper and played "Hey, Margarita" at full volume. The rats tended to keep away from the main tables, with their sticky velvet seats. The most off-putting thing here was the fact that the head waiter looked like Mr. Bean (Rowan Atkinson), and as he stood there watching us eat, he casually picked his nose. When Jane called me in Varanasi, I explained that the hotel was even worse than the one in Bangalore and—knowing how much I like my food—Jane selflessly spent some time describing the Sunday lunch she was preparing and gave me a blow-by-blow description of what I was missing.

In old Varanasi itself, the restaurants were even worse. I remember sitting at a table drinking tea and feeling something cold touching my left arm. I looked around, and someone had laid out a corpse, which was covered in a bright red cloth with ornate golden threads and decorations. On their way to the *ghat*, the porters had stopped for *chai* and put down the corpse next to me. Her foot was sticking from beneath the funeral cloths and brushed against me as they laid down the corpse. I think the strangest thing was that I didn't leap back in horror. I had now gotten so used to surreal situations that I took no notice and just continued to sip my tea.

Aside from its culinary delights, Varanasi (Benares) is a magical place, mixed with chaos. Its labyrinth of narrow lanes and alleys are stuffed full with cows, goats, bikes, carts, people, and gold-clad corpses being carried on stretchers past fly-covered food counters. Apart from the occasional belching moped that forced its way through the jammed passageways, the scene we walked through to our lodgings had not changed for thousands of years. Mark Twain described it perfectly when he said, "Benares is older than history, older than tradition, older even than legend, and looks twice as old as all of them put together."

As my sandals hit another patch of lung-numbing effluent, I observed that if I fancied getting really, really sick, then this place had everything you could hope for. But of course once you see beyond the litter, dangerously built buildings, wall-to-wall cow pats, and grime, Varanasi reveals another extraordinary world. This is the world of Benares, the holy city that is to the Hindus what Jerusalem is to Christians. Varanasi is the golden city of Lord Shiva, the capital of spiritual knowledge, the city of light.

Dawn view of the sunken temple from my 'hotel' rooftop

The beauty of Varanasi revealed itself at dawn, as we practiced our yoga on the flat roof of the guest house. The early morning light revealed the opposite bank of the Ganges, illuminating in soft tones of purple and orange the flood plains and distant outline of trees. Closer to us we could see, as we stretched into our postures, sunken temples in the mud, and we smelled the last whiff of wood-fueled cremations. To our left, the cows were being milked, while all around ash-faced sadhus and beggars emerged from their slumbers.

As we moved into the somewhat vulnerable, full-reclining hero pose, a group of monkeys scrambled toward us over the rooftops and washing lines. Three big ones jumped up onto the veranda railings and looked down at me, lying flat on the floor with my ankles by my waist, and my crotch pointing at them in the come-and-hurt-me position. Fortunately, they scrutinized us for a while, decided we had no food, looked at us with perplexed disdain, and eventually left us alone.

By day you can sit by the waterside on the *ghats*, and India will come to you. It unfolds in a surreal pageant of orange-clad holy men, children selling postcards and *chai*, and women carrying enormous loads on their heads. I watched a man push a bike laden with fifteen Calor gas bottles, street masseurs and hairdressers touting for business, others sleeping on the floor, urinating on the sidewalk, or bathing in the soup of the Ganges. But it is at night that this place is most fascinating, for it transforms into an unfamiliar and eerie world, soaked in death.

At one time, I sat with my back to a wall, watching people being shaved, women carrying huge loads, people being massaged in the street, and so on. I noticed that people were putting food and water through a tiny slit in the floor beside me. I asked someone what this was all about, and they explained that just below where I was sitting was a cellar, where a holy man had been living in darkness for many years. It was considered auspicious to give him food and drink.

Strange things like this still go on in Varanasi. One of the weirdest holy men I encountered was sitting in the ashes of the funeral pyres by one of the *ghats*. He caught my eye with a quick glance, and it was as if someone had reached out at me and hit me in the face. I have never seen such dark and furious eyes—they were absolutely terrifying. There was a feeling that this man was trying to take my "power," like a spiritual thief who snatches the *siddhis* from strangers. Some years later, I saw this same man appear in my room at home—a story that I have already related in one of my other books.

I believe the man that did this was an *aghori*, a sinister and feared clan of sadhus who are said to have been practicing black magic for over a thousand years. They relish death. They will feast on rotten foods, food from trash cans, animal feces, urine, and putrefying human corpses, which are sometimes eaten in a cup made from a human skull. Eating terrible things and reveling in filth is said to kill ego, and it derails the perception of beauty, which in turn helps the *sadhu* to become liberated from attachment to earthly life. *Aghori sadhus* claim that they follow the "left way" to reach God, as it is quicker than the moral path. In seeking the "purity in the filthiest," they are able to concentrate on God while performing the most perverted acts. I'm not so sure that some of the foot-massaging, insipid, feel-good Western yogis I've met would enjoy this fast path to liberation!

Early one evening after supper, just as the sun was setting and casting its embroidered cloths of reds and golds across the waters of the Ganges, we boarded a rowing boat to take our group upriver to the temple dedicated to the woman guru Ananda Mayee Ma (1896–1981). The life of this woman saint is a fascinating story. As a young girl, she displayed an extraordinary spiritual awareness. Her parents made her marry at thirteen, but her husband, Ramani Mohan Cakravarti, or Bholanath as he was known, was soon to realize that this was not to be a traditional marriage. Whenever her husband tried to touch her in an intimate way, he would either be thrown to the ground by electric shocks, or Ananda Mayee Ma's body would fall into a corpse-like state. Initially fearing what was happening, Bholanath took his wife to an exorcist, but he was told that she was not mad in the conventional sense. The healer advised him that she had a kind of ecstatic God-intoxication—a divine madness for which there was no cure. (Eventually Bholanath became a devotee of his wife.)

She was known for her *siddhis* or yogic psychic powers. Before devotees could voice a question, she would read their thoughts and give an answer. Her telepathic powers were very advanced, and she could also intuit devotees' thoughts and feelings from a great distance. She could make her body shrink and expand in size and cure the sick. She brought one devotee back from the dead after a car accident. The devotee claimed that the saint grasped her "life substance" and brought it back into her dead body. Ananda Mayee Ma was also guided by inner voices that advised her what actions to take. Her body would spontaneously contort into advanced yoga positions without her ever having had any formal training, and at festivals she was known to materialize religious objects and produce spontaneous fire.

Despite her miraculous powers, Ananda Mayee Ma remained a deeply humble and pious woman. To Sri Ma, everyone was Father and everyone was Mother, for she always considered herself to be a little girl, a child of God.

By the time we docked at the *ghat* at this, the bad end of town, it was night. The temple-ashram was hidden in a network of dark, somewhat sinister lanes, full of "turbaned ruffians" (to quote Vivian Stanshaw). After some searching, we eventually found the temple door tucked away in an obscure alleyway. Here, in honor of the guru, we joined in with the *aarti*, chanted some of the saints' favorite mantras, and sat in meditation to absorb the *darshan* of this sacred place.

The boat was waiting to take us back down river to our guest house. The moonlit surface of the indigo waters of the Ganges was now a mass of floating candles, which drifted past us like the spirits of the dead on their way to Heaven. To our left, I counted fifteen funeral pyres, flickering against the backdrop of a carved temple, stained jet-black with smoke, and looking as if it had been lifted from a scene of Dante's *Inferno*. We could see, illuminated in the orange light of the fires, people tending the gold-shrouded dead and hear the solemn chant of requiem mantras, with the occasional crashing of bells and cymbals. Large and small wooden boats creaked past us, some being rowed, some motor-driven, and other pushed by boating poles, with young children swimming alongside in the filthy waters.

We gently chanted Shiva mantras as one of our group solemnly beat his *tabla* in rhythm to the oarsman. Here, by the burning *ghats* of Varanasi, there was certainly the feeling of being at a place where the world of the living met the world of the dead. As we passed again through another group of floating lights, and the mantras echoed from the buildings, I commented that I felt like a soul on its journey across the River Styx to Hades, the land of the dead. For a time, I silently contemplated my own mortality and also a story my father had told me, about how his grandfather, a fisherman, had said on his deathbed: "The boat's drifting portside, Don. There's fog on the water, and I have to go now." And with those words, my great-grandfather Daniel died.

I paid the boatman who, for an instant, looked to have the fierce, flashing, and feverish blue-gray eyes of the Greek god Charon.

When we cross to the other shore what sort of world will greet us? In the next section I explain what the next world is like. And what better place to set this theme than the paradise islands of the Seychelles.

PARADISE ON EARTH

A hotel is soon to be built on the tiny island of La Digue, which is the third-largest inhabited island of the Seychelles, so its colonial charm and deserted beaches will soon be gone. As Jane supported the local tradesmen and shopped at the few stalls selling shells and trinkets, I took a long stroll along the deserted beaches and found a spot under the palm trees where I could sit and meditate.

There's a form of meditation I like to do with nature, which starts by looking at everything around you with full concentration. Then you listen to every sound and become aware of any other sensations, such as your posture, the smells in the air, your breath, the breeze on your face, and so on. Then you close your eyes and do the same internally, watching the thoughts and imagery arising from the unconscious. Eventually, you step further back until you are even watching the watcher. This is all effortless, as you are simply sitting and being nothing else but what you already are. There's no pushing life away, as sometimes the eyes may open, and once again you let the world outside take you, or you slip again into the inner realm. Within and without are both the same thing. It's all you.

The beach at La Digue is a classic tropical paradise. Tiny crabs scamper across the soft, white sands, and the trees incandesce with emerald light. The breeze is soft on the skin and smells slightly of coconut husk, and the light feels just the right intensity, as it dances across the glittering waters of the Indian Ocean. Moving with the grace of contemplation, the mind and landscape become one. Are the waves moving, or is it the mind moving? I drop worthless thoughts and, for a while, settle into the glory of the world around me and just *be*.

Could this be what Heaven is like? When Jesus spoke about Heaven being within us, I believe he was talking about the state of being that transcends even bliss itself, where we and the Father are one. In moments of deep contemplation or meditation, we can float for a while on the edge of the oceanic experience, at one with all of creation. This is not just a fanciful thought, but a direct experience of transcendence, which leaves a residual feeling of having heard extraordinary good news. We all have this from time to time. Places of great beauty, or sudden release from a stressful experience, can sometimes trigger this inspired state. It is not enlightenment, but it somehow lightly touches enlightenment.

This is the life

From what I have gleaned from the spirts that have communicated through the mediumistic messages I have given at public demonstrations and private sittings, the experience of many spirits is described as a feeling of being at one with creation. The afterlife they describe is bathed in an ethereal light, and they say that time is experienced in a different way from how we understand it on earth. Spirits experience the next world according to their understanding of reality. For some, it is just like the world they knew here on earth and is filled with people, places, and situations that are familiar to them. For more advanced souls, the next world is a fluid reality, and for the near-enlightened it is a world of bliss and light.

From what I understand, everyone in the next life knows a reality that is a lot more fluid than here on earth. You can think of someone and be with them, you can think of a place and be there instantly, and you can relive your memories of earth in the blink of an eye and see the bigger picture of why things happened as they did. Enemies cannot come close, and people who love one another are attracted together in a natural, pure state of innocent love. We are told that the next world is just like the world we know on earth, and yet simultaneously it is impossible to describe because it is beyond our current experience. Yet when we enter the afterlife, everything is self-evident and familiar, as we realize that we have known these realms many times before. In short, the next world is like a lucid dream, from which realities emerge and fade, with landscapes and places that are both objective and subjective at the same time.

I have written extensively in my other books about proofs through mediumship and mused about what the next world is like. I have tried to build a detailed picture by looking at the common cultural beliefs and the reports given by people who have had a near-death experience, as well as by gathering evidence from materialization séances, out-of-body experiences, direct voice mediumship, remote viewing, Ouija boards, quantum physics, and the Naadis. The evidence taken as a whole gives overwhelming and irrefutable proof that life goes on after death.

All of the above I wrote about in my book titled *What to Do When You Are Dead*, so I was taken aback when the Naadi reader near as damn it named the actual book. He said: "After death the soul is going to where? After death what is the soul going to do? Is the soul going to reborn or not? What is the duty of the soul? Everything you can realize and give the message to the people. And also, you can write the books about the soul. The search related to soul. What is the body? What is the soul doing inside of the body? So what is the main thing? The body and soul are different things. So what are the activities of the soul in the body? How is this connected to the whole body? The soul is immortal. So you will research this type of thing."

"After death what is the soul going to do?"—I though this comment was amazing, as it pretty well paraphrased my book title.

Meanwhile, back in the Seychelles, at our hotel on the main Mahé Island, it was time to leave paradise. People leaving the heavenly paradise to reincarnate again and take a new human birth must grieve for the reborn, just as we grieve for the dead. When the karma that keeps you in the next world expires, for most spirits, the time comes to take a new human birth. Again we will suffer, grow, and learn new lessons, but we will also get another shot at using a human body to find enlightenment.

As we packed our bags and put them in the lobby, some of the Kreyol islander girls were weeping at the prospect of our leaving. While I'd been out, nobly contemplating my navel or losing myself in a book, Jane had been doing some real spiritual service. She'd got to know just about all the local shopkeepers and had been giving them readings and messages from the spirit.

While I was looking at paradise, Jane been showing these hardworking girls—who, we discovered, endured much poverty and abuse—some compassion and guidance and, in a few cases, given them a spirit message or two that told of the real paradise that awaits us after death.

In the next chapter I'm taking my story back to Varanasi to the place where the Buddha gave his first sermon. Buddhists also believe in paradise worlds but the emphasis is that all things are transitory so even the heavenly worlds can be a trap for the soul seeking enlightenment. Our progress after death is determined by karma which leads a person to be reborn in one of 6 realms which are; heaven, human beings, Asura, hungry ghost, animal and hell. None of these places are permanent and the soul does not remain in any place forever.

BUDDHA'S DEER PARK

I can understand why many Westerners find it hard to accept the gods, idols, and strange ways of Hinduism. The very idea of chanting before a graven image reeks of heresy, but scratch a little deeper and you soon discover that Hinduism is not so worried about outer form, but urges us to seek the God that lies beyond the form.

Hinduism is generally regarded as the world's oldest organized religion. It believes in one God, called Brahman, which is the unchanging reality of all things in this universe. God, to the Hindus, is not remote, but can be discovered by looking within. Some may know God as omnipresent and impersonal, the infinite light of existence that is the true nature of the Self, whereas others need to experience God on an intimate, human level. Yogananda tell us that God is both personal and impersonal, and he explains that Jesus was a personal manifestation of God. When Jesus said, "I and my Father are one," and, "These things that I do, you can do also," he was revealing to us that we are all made in this image of Divinity.

Hinduism believes in one God, but asserts that the one God can appear to humans in multiple names and forms. For the Hindu, chanting the name or worshiping the form of God is a valid way to experience contact with the divine. They may chant the names of Shiva, Krishna, Ram, and the many thousands of names of God, but would equally feel at home chanting the name Jesus or Buddha, as all holy personages are valued by this faith. Where they differ from other religions is that they do not consider their path to be the only way to God.

For Westerners who dislike the "idolatry" of Hinduism, the simple clarity of Buddhism has more appeal. In India, Buddhism all but disappeared because it was easily assimilated back into Hinduism. For many Hindus, Buddha is a valid teacher, and some recognize him as an incarnation of the god Vishnu. But there are many differences as well as similarities between the two faiths. As a Spiritualist, the most important difference to me is their attitude toward the immortal spirit. Buddhism does not believe in the existence of souls or the continuation of their identity after death. It also does not believe in a creator God. Hinduism believes in the existence of *atman*, the individual soul—the *jiva* or embodied soul—which, as I understand, equates to our concept of spirit; and Brahman—the supreme Creator. When Buddha was asked whether there was life after death, he remained silent, perhaps indicating that this could not be answered because it was beyond the listeners' comprehension or, as Carl Jung noted, he may not have known the answer!

It is a comparatively short journey from Varanasi to one of the most important holy sites of Buddhism, the "Deer Park," where the newly enlightened Gautama Buddha gave his first sermon about the basic principles of Buddhism. This is a site comparable to the Mount of Beatitudes in Israel, where Jesus delivered the Sermon on the Mount.

The Deer Park at Sarnath is surrounded by many temples, built by Buddhists from around the world. We enjoyed visiting the Tibetan, Chinese, and Japanese temples, as well as the main temple at the center of the complex, which housed beautiful frescos illustrating the Buddha's life and his temptations beneath the Bodhi tree. Dominating the skyline is the hundred-foot-high Dhamakh Stupa from the fifth century, built in brick in the shape of an upturned begging bowl, and marking the exact spot where the Buddha had preached. In the grounds, an open-air temple and ceremonial bell had been built around a tree grown from a cutting of a cutting of a cutting of the original Bodhi tree. I picked up a fallen leaf from the ground to add to my collection of precious things. Beneath the tree were carved the words of the Deer Park sermon, which first explained the Four Noble Truths about the cause and cessation of suffering, and the Eightfold Path of right views, right aspirations, right speech, right conduct, right mode of livelihood, right effort, right mindfulness, and right rapture.

Unlike many Spiritualists, Jane and I believe in reincarnation, and when we first met, one of our first dates was a visit to the Dalai Lama—not in Tibet or India, unfortunately, but at a public discourse he gave near St. James' Park, London. This was a spiritually themed event, where His Holiness spoke mainly about Buddhism and some of the more obscure texts in the *sutras*. As it was a day of intense spiritual attention and learning, the atmosphere in the building was charged with compassion and consciousness. When Jane and I left and walked back through St. James' Park, we were flipped into higher awareness. Our perceptions opened, to the extent that the world was bathed in beauty, and the movement of birds and dogs running past us left long-lasting, stroboscopic after-images. Jane has never taken psychedelic drugs, but to me this was like the first levels of a light acid trip, though one which had been induced not by chemicals, but by the quantity of spiritual energy we had encountered that day. It was one of our most interesting early dates.

More recently—as grandparents—we took our daughter, Willow, with us to see the Dalai Lama when he visited St. Paul's Cathedral. Willow (then aged four) became very excited about the idea of seeing the Dalai Lama, and when I lifted her up to sit on my shoulders so that she could see, she immediately put her hands together in the prayer position above her head, even though nobody else in the building was doing this. Although she eats meat now, she always insisted on eating vegetarian food when she was little, and she would put her hands together in prayer and bow whenever she saw a Buddha statue—all without any prompting from either us or her mother. As a newborn baby, she lifted her head when a bell rang in the ward, and I'm sure I heard her say, "Ommmm!" I wonder if a Buddhist has been put in our charge?

Who we were in a past life is a fascinating mystery and often a topic of wild speculation and fantasy. People will come up to Jane and me after a mediumistic demonstration and give us crazy readings about who they think we were in previous lives. I've been a Buddhist, a medicine man, an Atlantean, a space man, a Native American, a Nazi, and more. One good friend assembled loads of coincidences, similarities in circumstances, character, handwriting matches, and photographs that suggested that I was a famous socialist writer from the 1930s named Alfred Orage, who was a friend of the philosopher Gurdjieff, along with P. D. Ouspensky, G. B. Shaw, and H.G. Wells. In places it was persuasive evidence, but it just didn't feel right, and there was nothing in it that I felt could win me over. I've had dreams that are suggestive of past lives and been hypnotically regressed, but none of it was overwhelmingly convincing.

As I have already mentioned, the Naadi leaves have given me two very similarly themed past lives, both set in South India as a *rishi*—one as a bad-tempered male *rishi*, and the other as a female *rishi* who left her family to follow a spiritual life. The first said: "You were born in Sagura Geddi. It is in South India. You were born as a saint-man. You did lots of spiritual activities to the people. And you did lots of social service to the people. You were also worker in the temple, but in the temple, lots of arguments is there. There was lots of arguments, and you gave lots of troubles to the poor people, so they are angry, and they cursed you. That curse follows in this birth. That's why it has some health problems for you and your daughters, and your ambitions get blocked."

The first reader gave me a name—Kala Bhairava—but the second Naadi leaves gave no name, but told me the location of my past life: "In one of his past births, the native was born in a place named Kucherum, which is nowadays called Gujarat. The native was born in a caste named Yarava. In the previous birth, the native was born as a girl. The girl was very beautiful and was living with her parents. She was very beautiful and also very talented. The birth which is explained now is the native's fifth birth. The present birth is the sixth birth of the native. And also he has one more birth."

Of course, it is remarkably easy to believe wonderful things about yourself and your glorious past life. Cold-readers tend to hoodwink their clients with flattery. The Naadi readers are not cold-readers, but may sometimes over-egg the cake a bit to please you and make the reading as positive as possible. I expect that I was a spiritually minded person in my past life, as this would account for the mediumistic and clairvoyant powers the appeared in this life. But a *rishi*? A saint? I think not, though it does give me an ideal to strive toward.

My plan is to make a visit to Gujarat and see what happens to my feelings and intuition when I go there. I have already asked the Naadi readers to translate the chapters in the leaves that will give detailed information about my past lives, and I hope to include their insights and my visits to the relevant locations in my next book. I'll take a camera, so keep an eye on YouTube if this interests you.

Next stop Calcutta.

PARAMAHANSA YOGANANDA IN CALCUTTA

As our group lay on our pile of rucksacks on Varanasi station, watching the throng of people and the herds of cows wandering aimlessly on the rail track, the images of Varanasi floated through my mind. Even though we'd been advised that the train to Calcutta might be up to eight hours late, it didn't seem to matter. One of the things you discover in India is that schedules, like life, are subject to change. For the first time in many years, I was living fully in the present. This spiritual journey had become so enveloping that even a long wait at a train station could become a positive experience. If the train didn't come, so what? We probably were not going to sleep at all for the next three days, but so what? It was so nice to be without emails, phone calls, itineraries, schedules, and deadlines, just being here now. The past has gone, and tomorrow can wait.

If one book above all others has inspired me to look into yoga, then it is *Autobiography of a Yogi* by Paramahansa Yogananda. I consider it to be one of the most important books I have read, so it is not surprising that I was very excited when we were given a private invitation to visit what had been the home in Calcutta of this remarkable individual.

The family of Yogananda's brother, Sananda, continues to inhabit the home, which they keep as a shrine. We were greeted by his wife, who shared with us her stories about the house and also offered us a few sweet cakes afterward. It was here she explained that Yogananda spent his early years of spiritual seeking and, most importantly, the house also contains the attic meditation room where he attained full Self-realization. This was the place where he merged with God and had visions of the Divine Mother and Lord Krishna. In this same, sacred space, we were allowed to sit in reverent meditation.

Yogananda's own guru, Sri Yukteswar, also regularly came to this house to meditate with the family. In the room that had been Yogananda's bedroom, we were reminded of the story how, while lying in this bed, he had prayed to God to give him a sign as to whether he should go to the United States to share his teachings. Yogananda also had things to say about the spirit world: "If you were to behold the multitude of astral beings in the ether around you at this moment, many of you would be afraid, and some of you would try to seek among them your departed loved ones. If you concentrate deeply at the spiritual eye, you can view with inner vision that luminous world in which are living all the souls who have gone on to the astral plane. In human beings, the heart acts as a receiving instrument, and the spiritual eye as a broadcasting station. Even if you cannot see your lost beloved ones, if you can calmly concentrate your feeling on the heart, you can become aware of the reassuring presence of those dear to you, who are now in astral form, enjoying their freedom from flesh thralldom."

It was in this room at Yogananda's home that the *avatar* Babaji materialized to bless him at the doorway to his bedroom. (*Avatar* is a Sanskrit word that means "descent"; its roots are *ava*, "down," and *tri*, "to pass." In the Hindu scriptures, *avatar* signifies the descent of Divinity into flesh.)

Mahavatar Babaji is a remarkable person who, it is claimed, is 1,800 years old, still alive today, and maintains the form of a young man. He is only accessible to extremely devoted followers who are prepared to seek him out in a wild part of the Himalayan forests. He will occasionally materialize in the homes of his followers and is considered to be the guru of all gurus. Yogananda describes him also as the guru of Lahiri Mahasaya, whose home we visited in Varanasi.

Yogananda writes of him: "The *mahavatar* is in constant communion with Christ; together they send out vibrations of redemption and have planned the spiritual technique of salvation for this age. The work of these two fully-illumined masters—one with the body, and one without it—is to inspire the nations to forsake suicidal wars, race hatreds, religious sectarianism, and the boomerang-evils of materialism. Babaji is well aware of the trend of modern times, especially of the influence and complexities of Western civilization, and realizes the necessity of spreading the self-liberations of yoga equally in the West and in the East."

He's talking about the Brotherhood of Man. Again, we spent some time in silent meditation, tuning in to these remarkable people who had once graced this place.

In Varanasi we had also had the chance to make personal visits to two more of Yogananda's gurus. We visited the home of Lahiri Mahasaya and meditated in the rooms where this guru had lived. This same, small shrine housed a wonderful white statue of Babaji, which I believe is the only one of its kind. It also housed the only photograph of Lahiri Mahasaya. Normally Lahiri Mahasaya would not allow anyone to photograph him, but in response to pleas from his disciples, he eventually agreed to pose. Before the photo was taken, he asked the photographer Gangadhar Dey how photos were made. A few moments later, the photo was taken, but to everyone's astonishment the picture was blank. Lahiri Mahasaya chuckled and asked the photographer, "What does your science tell you?" Gangadhar prostrated himself before him and said, "My pride has been shattered." He asked Lahiri Mahasaya to pose again, and this time the photo came out perfectly. Strangely, when I tried to video the same picture, the batteries packed up, leaving me to puzzle about the strange story of Lahiri Mahasaya.

We also visited the Varanasi home of another of Yogananda's teachers, Trailanga Swami. We squeezed down some narrow steps into the cellar where this remarkable saint had spent his long periods in meditation. In this very cramped cellar, we meditated in front of a picture of the saint, placed on the spot where he used to sit.

Trailanga Swami was a fascinating man, who exhibited many supernormal powers, including the ability to bi-locate (be in two places at the same time). His psychic powers enabled him to gain mastery over the elements, and he would sit in meditation and, in front of thousands of people, levitate over the surface of the Ganges, sometimes disappearing under the surface for days at a time. He could read people's minds like a book. He could drink deadly poison, and while he seldom ate, he weighed over 300 pounds. It is claimed he lived to the age of 208.

In the tiny room, about eleven feet square, where this great—and fat—man sat, I thought about the stories of his life. Trailanga never wore clothes and remained completely nude, which was a big problem for the local police, who often unceremoniously committed him to jail. Although his cell would be securely locked and there was no mode of escape, no prison could hold him. Invariably the saint's huge, lumbering form would be seen standing on the roof of the police station soon after his incarceration.

Another story sees a skeptic offer him a bucket of lime whitewash and ask: "Master, I have brought you some clabbered milk. Please drink it." Without any hesitation, Trailanga drank the whole bucket of scalding lime, and as he did, the skeptic fell to the ground in pain. "Help, Swami! Help!" he cried. "I am on fire! Forgive my wicked test!"

"Scoffer," replied Trailanga. "You did not realize when you offered me poison that my life is one with your own. Except for my knowledge that God is present in my stomach, as in every atom of creation, the lime would have killed me. Now that you know the divine meaning of boomerang, never again play tricks on anyone."

The reformed skeptic recovered with Trailanga's words, now gifted with a lesson in the reality of the law of karma, its reason, and its effect. It's a shame Trailanga Swami isn't alive today, as I'd send along the bellyaching James Randi and Richard Dawkins for a few cosmic boomerang lessons!

Some of the places I have been describing are a tough journey and parts of India especially are not the sort of places Jane and I would take our mothers or young family. Our next sacred journey takes us to Thailand – with mother in tow!

THAILAND AND STUFFED MONKS

My mother (aged seventy-two at the time) is not the best person to take with you when touring the sacred sites and Buddhist temples of Phuket province in Thailand. Jane and I took her to the especially sacred area beneath one temple that was filled with hundreds of gold-plated tin Buddhas of varying size—made at a time when tin was considered to be a sacred metal. Poking one of them with her umbrella to see if it sounded hollow, she said, "Is this where they sell Buddhas wholesale?" She does have a way of gracefully upsetting people. It reminded me of the time when, among a group of bereaved Sai Baba devotees, she said: "Pffff! Well, he's had a good run for his money," or of the time in a hotel in Florence, when we found ourselves sitting by the soccer player Pelé, and she brushed him off, not knowing who he was. Pelé is widely regarded to be the greatest player of all time, and I think everyone on Earth knows his name—except my Mum.

Fortunately she kept quiet when we stood before the shrine where the mummified body of a great Buddhist abbot sat upright in a glass casket, surrounded by flowers, incense sticks, candles, and fruit offerings. Some Westerners may consider this to be a disturbing sight, but for Thai Buddhists the body of the mummified monk is there to be worshiped. Death is seen as an opportunity to be reborn into a better new life.

At the entrance to some of the temples, they had oracles who work by selecting a stick with a number on it. This is a form of sortilege—a way of foretelling the future by selecting something random from a collection. I believe that this method hails from

China, and it is practiced in many temples in the Far East. It is said in China that a person's "future becomes his past through the present, and the successful man is one who understands well what has happened, experiences acutely what is happening, and comprehends what is indicated in the future." With this in mind, we drew our sticks, and the temple priest translated the oracle from Pali and interpreted the numbers we'd drawn.

Jane's stick said something about signing a contract. Mine was pretty auspicious, too, but my mother's said all sorts of things that she didn't like, so she insisted the priest draw another until it said something acceptable. The flummoxed priest was charming, but part of me was praying that we wouldn't be thrown out of the temple and told to get stuffed.

This was not a "rucksack on my back" vacation. We visited Thailand soon after the tsunami of December 26, 2004, and we felt that we should still take our planned vacation despite the devastation. What the Thai people needed was foreign currency to help them rebuild, so we booked the best holiday we could afford and had a five-star hotel almost to ourselves. The gym and few auxiliary buildings had been washed away, but the rest of the hotel was intact. We spent what we could on the market stalls and never bartered, as it was clear that some of the people there were desperately trying to rebuild their lives. Jane befriended one lady who ran her market stall by day and, because her home had been swept away, slept beneath it at night, with her one surviving child. From what I saw, most of the ordinary Thai people are a very proud and honorable people, and they will never beg or accept handouts, so it seemed fitting to let Jane's shopping skills go into overdrive. Single-handedly, she planned to spend until the Thai economy came out of recession. I'm being flippant, but it is my belief that the best way we can help countries hit by disasters is to go there and spend our pounds, euros, and dollars. This will bring aid but not dependency, and being a friend at their side is one of the best ways to stop the poverty that has spawned terrorism in some countries. If, as the Naadi predicts, there are to be more environmental catastrophes ahead, we may want to consider direct ways we can help others that avoid the gross mismanagement, horrible marketing, and inflated executive wages that have become the hallmarks of many charities today.

The tsunami that swept over Indonesia and Thailand may be just the start of many global catastrophes that are to come. The Naadi oracle tells me that "In his sixty-two, the native will visit shrines and worship gods. The native will get the knowledge of both *yantra* and mantra, and also get the knowledge of ancient theories of *shastra* and also *sutra*—which means secrets. That is, the native will get knowledge of even those things that are kept as secrets by saints for centuries. Naturally, the native will get more knowledge about Lord Shiva." I am writing this in 2015, at the age of sixty-one, and already practice mantra and use *yantra* in the form of *trataka*. And as the oracle says, it has already been my decision not to follow any specific guru, even though I have what I believe are dreams and visions in meditation that are a form of help from holy people. The oracle says: "Without following a guru, the native will get the knowledge of spirituality and the knowledge about Lord Shiva naturally."

But right after this extract, the oracle continues to say that I will foresee natural calamities. I suspect that these will be on the same scale or bigger than the tragedies that beset Thailand and, more recently, Nepal. (This is a place I feel already will see a huge earthquake on an unimaginable scale, which will even rock India and China in years to come.) As I mentioned earlier on, the oracle says of events that are likely to happen after 2025: "In seventy, seventy-one, the native will fulfill all his responsibilities. The native will be able to foresee the natural calamities which will be coming in the future, and he would get this knowledge by the blessings of Lord Shiva and Goddess Parvathi. To protect the people from these natural calamities, the native would do some *pujas*, *yagnas* and *homas*. The native would be able to foretell about the natural calamities related to storm or rain, or related to waves or seas and oceans."

The responsibility that the oracle appears to put on my shoulders is daunting. At this stage in my spiritual knowledge, and without the "knowledge of even those things that are kept as secrets by saints for centuries," I am unable to see how *puja* (rituals) can protect people. I certainly believe in the power of prayer to God in whatever form people chose to believe, but how to specifically target prayer like a magical shield is, at this point, beyond any psychic powers I may have. I was as shocked as everyone else when the tsunami struck the day after Christmas. Could I possibly foresee similar disasters? On my website, I post predictions for the year ahead and did get it right about the uprisings they called "the Arab Spring," and correctly predicted the nuclear power station explosion in Japan (though I said, "somewhere like China"). But I also sometimes get things wildly wrong. I hope that in ten years' time, my accuracy will improve, if my destiny is to fulfill the remit of the oracle.

Now back to my vignette about Thailand. Buddhism in Thailand is largely of the Theravada school, which is followed by 90% of the population, and it is clear that the fortitude that the Buddhist teachings inspire is endemic. There is also a large Thai Chinese population that practices Chinese folk religions, including Taoism, as well as a significant Muslim population. While there, we also saw a number of small shrines to the Hindu elephant god Ganesha.

Beside all these lovely spiritual values, there is also a dark side to Thailand. We enjoyed a memorable elephant ride through the jungles, and it was brave of my frail mother to give it a try. But like most tourists, we were unaware of what terrible mistreatment Thai elephants endure. Wild elephants won't let humans ride on top of them, so to break its spirit, it is tortured as a baby. The process is called *phajaan*, or "the crush," which involves confining the baby elephant in a very small cage or hole in the ground, so that they are unable to move. Here they are starved, deprived of sleep, and beaten into submission with clubs and sharp bull-hooks. When it is old enough, mugs like me can enjoy a romantic elephant-ride through the jungle.

We witnessed the full horror of the mistreatment of elephants when we innocently went to watch the *Phuket FantaSea Show*, set in a 140-acre theme complex, which is described as "inspired by Thailand's rich and exotic heritage, and showcases the charm and beauty of Thailand, but also enriches ancient Thai traditions with the wonder of cutting-edge technology and special effects." We watched in horror as elephants performed death-defying tricks, which ended in a grand finale with dozens of elephants climbing on one another's backs to form a huge pachyderm pyramid. There was no limit to the cruelty on display, and the treatment of the animals, particularly the white tigers, deer, peacocks, and other birds in the pre-show exhibits was atrocious.

The sex industry in Thailand, of course, is also rampant, offering something for everyone. I must say I chuckled at Jane's reaction to the "Sin City" area of Phuket, where young girls were for sale, and lady-boys danced on open-air stages. One man got more than he bargained for when approached Jane and flipped open a photo album of naked photos of himself. "Get away, you filthy man!" she exclaimed as she slapped him around the face. She was also not impressed when a very old European man hobbled out of a seedy hotel with two young and stunningly beautiful Thai girls, one on each arm. "That man looks like he's in his nineties," I said. "He was thirty-five when he went in there," quipped Jane.

In a moment my narrative will return to India but before this I want to address the question of sexuality within Hinduism and some of the issues surrounding celibate gurus. In Sanskrit, sexuality is usually referred to by the word *kama* (not to be confused with the word *karma*) Kama is pleasure, and it refers to the desires of the mind and the physical body and the human desire for passion and emotion. It is one of four main goals of earthly life which include *dharma*, your religious, social and moral duty, *artha*, wealth and prosperity, *kama*, the fulfilment of sensual desires, and ultimately *moksha* which is liberation from rebirth. A balanced life is one in which all four goals are correctly pursued and attained. Hinduism accepts sexuality as natural but does not recommend unrestrained indulgence in sensuality.

In the *Bhagavad Gita* Krishna explains to Arjuna that sensuality is not in itself sinful, but can become one of the main causes of wickedness and a barrier to dharma. To the small group of people who wish to achieve moksha (spiritual liberation) in this lifetime celibacy is prescribed, as sexual desire is one of the most intense forms of worldly attachment.

In the next section I will be talking a little about Sri Ramakrishna who was a married celibate and had a very strange attitude to sexuality. He would enter periods of 'holy madness' and spout the most vulgar language imaginable and with a lot of additional references to defecation, saw the female body as being nothing more than "such things as blood, flesh, fat, entrails, worms, piss, shit, and the like" (Nikhilananda, 1984)

Aside from all of the above he was an enlightened teacher who attained the highest 'nirvikalpa samadhi' state and is considered as one of the most respected spiritual masters of the modern time in India. He is an amazing conundrum.

RAMAKRISHNA KOLKATA (CALCUTTA) ASHRAM

One place in Kolkata not to be missed is the Dakshineswar Temple complex, sprawling over forty acres of land on the western bank of the Hooghly River. It houses the living room and bed where the mystic yogi Ramakrishna Paramahamsa gave many of his discourses to his followers. His teachings emphasized that God-realization is the highest goal of life, and he spoke mainly about love and devotion for God, the oneness of existence, and the harmony of religions: "As many faiths, as many paths."

Ramakrishna also preached that money is an obstacle on the path of spiritual progress. In his living room, Sri Ramakrishna's disciple Vivekananda hid a coin under the bed to test if his guru really could not touch money. Throughout his later life, Ramakrishna refused to handle money, saying it was impossible for him to hold money or metal (which also symbolized coins), as he would feel pain, and his hand would be forced aside. In the past, while seated by the Ganges, Ramakrishna used to take a rupee in one hand and a clump of clay in the other. He would throw both into the holy river, reminding us that both are useless for realizing God.

When Sri Ramakrishna sat on the bed containing the hidden coin, he shouted in pain and was thrown to the floor, as if he had been hit by an electric shock. Sadly I noted that now there is a temple collection-box right by the side of the bed! It is also the only temple where you have to pay for the *prasad* (holy food that contains the blessing of the temple's deity or holy man). Nonetheless, the devotional love of Ramakrishna and his spirit of simplicity and surrender still permeate this temple, and it was an inspiring place to visit. I'm sure the residual energy of his spiritual influence is still in this place, and I certainly felt that it touched my soul.

Although Swami Vivekananda was a very powerful teacher, he never displayed any occult or spiritual powers in his lifetime. Swami Ramakrishna Paramahamsa forbade such display of powers, as they would pull the aspirant away from the spiritual path. In his article "Power of the Mind," Vivekananda tells how he tested the claims of a man who could read minds and foretell events, although nobody considered this man to be divine. He warns us that one has to be careful of such people, as there have been many cheats, since spirituality can be a very profitable business.

One of the commonest tricks is to read a man's mind and tell him about events which have taken place many years ago and which no one else knows about. Unfortunately, devotees mistake these powers as signs of divinity, and are impressed and influenced by them.

Just because a person has genuine psychic powers it does not necessarily mean that they are a spiritual person. Naive people will assume that if a person can reveal things about their life and past, then that person must also be a highly spiritual individual. Sadly my own experience of so many psychics and mediums shows otherwise. When I first started out working as a medium in Spiritualism for no fee or personal benefit, you could count the practitioners in the hundreds. Then mediums were seen on TV, and now there are millions claiming to be mediums. You only need to do a search with the hash tag **#psychic** on Twitter, and it will reveal an unbelievable number of supposed psychics and mediums. I have to ask myself where they all suddenly came from, and if any of these people have trained within Spiritualism or worked for years for free? Most of these are simply not genuine psychics or mediums, of course, and of those who do have the gift, there are a great many who are only in it for the money—or the glory of the ego trip.

Up to a point, I agree with Swami Vivekananda in that people have to be wary of people with powers but no divinity. I do, however, believe that most mediums working within Spiritualism are on a noble path and understand that what they do is a holy office, and that mediumistic powers can be used to bring great comfort and hope to the bereaved. The problem with our path is that it is so easy to fall into ego traps. The third chapter of the *Yoga Sutras* explains many methods of attaining psychic powers (*siddhis*), but also how these powers can create stumbling blocks in the path of enlightenment. On a divine path, powers arise naturally, but if you intentionally cultivate psychic powers for their own sake, you may get into difficulties. We do this, of course, within Spiritualism: we train new mediums to awaken their latent abilities for mediumship, though not as a means to self-aggrandizement, but as a means to give evidence of survival and bring forward the teachings from the spirit world.

Not all psychics and mediums are good people. Hitler employed mediums and astrologers and, together with Himmler, believed that through occult skills the "master race" could gain dominion over the world. When Hitler gave his thousands of public speeches, he would never become exhausted, but rather was invigorated and gained power, in similar way as a mediumistic address or demonstration can draw on the energy of the audience. People who met him face-to-face explain that they went away feeling drained and exhausted. He was an energy vampire.

I have not been able to find any references to Hitler in my research of the Naadi leaves, but it is interesting what Indian astrologers have to say about him. The famous Indian astrologer B.V. Raman said of him: "Hitler's great hatred of the Jews was probably due to the conjunction of the sun and Mars, and the conglomeration of evil combinations. The most significant combination in Hitler's horoscope is the absence of *dwirdwadasa* positions, which makes the native a remarkable one from an astrological point of view. The most powerful malefics—the sun, Saturn and Mars—have cantered their evil influences on the seventh house, or house of war. The sun is exalted, and Mars is in his own house, and Saturn casts his powerful aspect. This made Hitler excessively aggressive, delight in human suffering, and harvest death."

Hitler also consulted the writings of Nostradamus to plan his war and ran a secret sect for the S.S. called the Thulists, which practiced human sacrifice, black masses, and sexual perversions. Similarly, Rasputin was a healer with a ferocious sexual appetite, and Alistair Crowley was a sexual deviant who believed his powers came from a twisted amalgamation of kundalini yoga and sodomy.

There are people out there who have abused spiritual powers, and many who have turned spirituality into a lucrative industry. What is disheartening is that there are so many thousands of psychics swamping the world that it has become hard for the seeker to find real help. Just as there are many fake Naadi oracles in India who have obscured the true oracles, so now in the West fake and poor quality psychics and mediums have muddied the waters.

In Peggy Mason's book *Sai Baba, the Embodiment of Love*, Sathya Sai Baba was asked by the Spiritualist, "Is mediumship to communicate with those in the next sphere of life, provided the medium is honest and a pure channel, wrong?" "No, not at all," Swami replied quite categorically.

The words "honest and a pure channel" are important in Peggy's question. Jane and I were discussing this, and we talked about the many unspiritual mediums out there, who seemed to be out to milk the system and feed their egos. My questions are: "Would they still do it if there was no money in it? Would they still do it if they were ridiculed and jailed? Would they still do it if they could only work anonymously, and there was no personal glory in it?" I think most would stop in an instant.

At the Dakshineswar temple complex of Ramakrishna and his pupil Vivekananda, you can absorb the echoes of the sincerity, wisdom, and peace of these great men. A beautiful moment came when I sat quietly by myself on the temple *ghat* and watched the sun across the waters of Hooghly River transform the Kolkata skyline into a silhouette of deep violets and blues. A few lonely birds flashed across the crimson sky and, as darkness descended and a melancholy rhythm of mantras reverberated across the waters, I thought about how even the great men who once lived in this temple must pass away.

There was just time to charter a small boat to take us downriver to Vivekananda's ethereal Belur Math shrine and the headquarters of his monastic order. "The blazing light of universal harmony that will emanate from here will flood the whole world," said Vivekananda of this place where he spent the last days of his life. Thus was a place of extremely high energy, sculpted to represent the religious architecture of all the world religions combined, and the atmosphere was further enhanced by the thick incense and melodious deep mantras to Kali, the goddess who carries the severed heads (egos) of her devotees around her neck. Sitting in the glorious temple among the echoing tones and under the towering pillars in this mysterious setting, I had the feeling that I'd slipped into another time.

As we returned to the boat, we could hear strange, eerie mantras to Kali gliding across the jet-dark waters of the river and of course—this being India—the engine spluttered to a stop as we reached midstream. As the boat drifted aimlessly without an engine, it could perhaps be a metaphor for those ambitious, self-seeking psychics I wrote about earlier. Perhaps we simply just have to be like Siddhartha in the book of the same name by Hermann Hesse, and be content to simply be with the river.

Forget about trying to achieve anything; just go with it all, and flow as the universe intends. God is the boatman; he will restart the engine when he's ready. Why rush after goals and recognition? After all, as Ramakrishna said, "The goal of human life is God-realization."

In western culture, one of the most famous celibate aesthetics is St Francis of Assisi whose ideas I will be looking at next. Like Sri Ramakrishna he had a somewhat ambiguous approach to sexuality. Other Franciscan friars referred to him as "Mother" during his lifetime and he also liked to be greeted as "Lady Poverty." Some people outside of the church claim he was bi-sexual which, if it were proven to be true, would certainly cause the Catholic Church to wobble on its stance on Gay marriage. As with Ramakrishna, none of this, of course, reduces the tremendous spiritual legacy that St Francis has given to the world.

ASSISI, MIRACLES, AND THE TAMRAPOTHI ORACLE

My mother is probably not the best person in the world to take to Assisi, which is one of the holiest Catholic sites in the world. Her father—my grandfather, Francis Devonshire—had an Irish Catholic mother, and together with his army strictness, this may have created some resistance in her to religion.

In addition, she had a few unfortunate experiences with "enthusiastic" Christians when she was a young woman. For example, when I was a baby, my parents lived in lodgings owned by a Catholic religious maniac called Ivy. She would wear sackcloth, dust her hair with ash, leave notes about Armageddon on the walls, and play her piano and sing evangelical hymns late into the night. Throughout the day, she boiled a huge pot of clothes on the stove until the wallpaper fell from the walls, and at night she used the same stove to incinerate her turds. This routine was a 24/7 occupation. The stench and the noise, and the fact that she would wander into our upstairs part of the house, made bringing up a baby impossible. The last straw came when my mother caught her force-feeding me jam sandwiches. Apart from the danger of what she was doing, my brand new and expensive outfit was ruined by jam stains. Choking back the anger and tears, my mother hurried me down to her mother's house, and initiated desperate measures to get us out of the lodgings.

Part of me is strangely attracted to the Catholic faith, as it employs such exotic, ancient pageantry, and I love the stories about the saints and their miraculous deeds. I have a lot of issues with the authenticity of the faith, as you have read in my chapter about the catacombs of Rome, but none of this can detract from the fact the Catholicism has had some great saints and martyrs on its books. We tend to look to the East for great yogis and gurus, but Christianity has great teachers, too, and particularly the figure of St. Francis, whom I consider to be one of the greatest yogis ever to live.

The night before we set off for Assisi, I had a vivid dream of meeting St. Francis, and in the dream I ask, "How can you prove it is you?" He points to his tunic, and I notice that it is made from gray material. When I awoke, this struck me as odd, as I had always assumed that Franciscans wore brown cassocks—like Friar Tuck in the movies about Robin Hood. Franciscans do wear brown, to reflect the destitution of the peasants they serve, and their habits were usually made from old clothing donated by those peasants, who always wore undyed brown. But in the vivid dream, the man most definitely wore gray.

One of the first things we saw at Assisi were the gray robes of St. Francis. I was amazed at what I saw, to the point I would have seriously considered taking holy orders if asked. Could it be that this odd dream was a connection with the real spirit of St. Francis? With this in mind, I connected with Assisi on a deep level. As we had booked our own historian guide, I would learn a great deal about St. Francis, both from the guide and, with luck, from the spirit world, too.

We began our tour at Santa Maria degli Angeli (church of St. Mary of the Angels) in Assisi, which is much venerated as the place of St. Francis' death. Inside the grand Baroque basilica are two small, humble structures: the Capella del Transito and the Porziuncola. The Porziuncola is a chapel that was restored by St. Francis himself, and in it he founded the Order of Friars Minor, which would later be known as the Franciscans. We then saw the rose garden where he is believed to have taken roses to wear as thorns during his austerities, and went on to the Eremo delle Carceri, where St. Francis retreated and preached to birds. Our visit ended in the Basilica of San Francesco d'Assisi, where we could marvel at the architecture and the frescos by Giotto.

Giotto's frescos illustrate the story of the life of St. Francis, and some are set so that the golden Mediterranean light from the high windows highlights the paintings like spotlights. What interested me most were the stories of how St. Francis lived much like the yogis of India. He endured great austerity, and as a result would exhibit miraculous powers, which the yogis would call *siddhis*. In the process of his canonization, over forty miracles were reported and approved by the ecclesiastical authorities. He could heal the sick, drive out demons, carry out remote viewing, bring the dead back to life, and bi-locate.

St. Francis gained much of his power by devotion to God. He simply surrendered his being and tried to do whatever Jesus would have done in a situation. He believed in the physical as well as the spiritual imitation of Christ, and advocated a path of poverty and preaching like Jesus, who was poor at birth in the manger and died naked on the cross

Christianity is often mentioned in the Naadis, as sometimes the consultant follows the Christian faith, and the leaves will not try to shift the person from their chosen faith. In my own case, the oracle said that "the native is born in a reputed family which followed some other holy religion, but the native praises Lord Shiva and Goddess Parvathi." Which is true, as my family, although not particularly pious, would consider themselves Christians, though throughout my life I have been much more interested in Hinduism, Taoism, and Buddhism. As far as I am aware, the life of Jesus himself is not mentioned in the Naadi leaves, and there is no personal Naadi for him. There is a lot of evidence to suggest that he visited India, and he may have returned to Nepal and Tibet via the Silk Road after surviving the crucifixion. It would be impossible to ask the Naadi oracle, but there is another oracle in India that is just as mind-boggling called the Tamrapothi. This is a device which reads your thought-processes to get the questions you want to ask, and then provides answers to your questions on blank metallic plates. The answers are indented temporarily in the metal, and as soon as the Tamrapothi is closed, the plates become blank again.

I am sure that my now I am stretching your credulity to the limits, but many who have consulted the Tamrapothi give dazzling testimonials about its authenticity and accuracy. In the book *Compassion* by Kim Paisol, the author covers in detail the story of the reading given to Bishop Lewis Keizer on December 9, 2006. The bishop wanted to know the identity of the face on the Shroud of Turin and also asked questions about how best to reform Christianity. The reading was held in a remote and obscure Orissan village, and the bishop doubted if the reader would ever have heard of the Shroud of Turin or even seen a photo of it.

The bishop had a photo with him that he had cut out of *National Geographic* magazine, and he handed it to the reader as he asked his question. Tiny words appeared miraculously on the copper plate from the ascended master Achyuta, which said: "This man [the face on Shroud of Turin] was born by the blessing of the Almighty . . . by the blessing of God. The mission he had from God was to clarify his ways to the society and the human heart. The quality of this man is equal to the Almighty, realizing God within. The person had been born, but God also said that he cannot die. . . . This person is not dead. He will always live for the human society. The highest quality of the person was as a *mahaguru*, a teacher of teachers. Also, he knows past, present, and future. Throughout the life, he considered himself as a monk and a disciple. He has the highest quality as highest guru. His duty is to attach the people to spirituality and give the noble idea of the heart to each one. By the brilliant mastery of this man, people get the blessing of the Almighty. This person can't die but is covered up and hidden from society. He is not reached by the average man in society. He teaches how to be in the palm of the Almighty. These are his qualities."

There are some who claim that, like the 2,000-year-old saint Mahavatar Babaji, who was the teacher of Lahiri Mahasaya and is described by Paramahansa Yogananda in his book *Autobiography of a Yogi*, Jesus is also an immortal and continues to live in the Himalayas. The text here suggests that he never died on the cross but "is covered up and hidden from society." Of course, all of the above may upset some people and is perhaps pushing things a little too far. But who knows what other mysteries India may be able to tell us about Christianity. What is interesting here is that the oracle is suggesting that the Shroud of Turin is the real deal.

What really happened to Jesus after his death and when the shroud was placed over him is, of course, still a highly debated issue.

And of course, as with speculation about Sathya Sai Baba today, Christians pray for the return of their Savior. Some historians argue that there wasn't even a cross involved and claim that the Bible has been misinterpreted, as there are no explicit references to the use of nails or to the crucifixion. Jesus bore a *staurus* to Calvary, which is not necessarily a cross but can also mean a pole. Again, India gives some confirmations about the crucifixion. Sathya Sai Baba has materialized crosses for Christians to wear and given many Christmas discourses about what happened to Jesus.

Prof. Fida Hassnain, in his book *A Search for the Historical Jesus*, quotes an ancient Hindu *sutra* of the Nath Yogis, known as *Natha-nama-vali*, which gives a unique insight into the crucifixion of Jesus, who is often given the name Isha in other Indian texts. "After crucifixion, or perhaps even before it, Isha Natha (Jesus) entered *samadhi* or profound trance by means of yoga. Seeing him thus, the Jews presumed he was dead and buried him in a tomb. At that very moment however, one of his gurus or teachers, the great Chetan Natha, happened to be in profound meditation in the lower reaches of the Himalayas, and he saw in a vision the tortures which Isha Natha was undergoing. He therefore made his body lighter than air and passed over to the land of Israel. The day of his arrival was marked with thunder and lightning, for the gods were angry with the Jews, and the whole world trembled. When Chetan Natha arrived, he took the body of Isha Natha from the tomb, woke him [Jesus] from his *samadhi*, and later led him off to the sacred land of the Aryans."

Back in Assisi, I end this vignette with us gathered around a painting of the stigmata that appeared on St. Francis—the wounds of the crucified Christ. In 1224, while meditating on Mount La Verna, these appeared on his hands, feet, and side, and they are considered to be one of the holiest moments in the saint's life. We joined the hushed crowd of devout pilgrims, gathered around this holy spot, to glimpse the painting of the mystery of the five wounds, and my mother made a comment, "Do you think he pushed the nails in himself?"

I'm sure St Francis would completely ignore my mother's minor misdemeanor as he always said of himself that he was the "greatest sinner of all". In the next section I explain how I used the Naadi remedies to help mitigate my own sins.

COSMIC BOOMERANG REMEDIES

The objectives of the Naadi oracle are personal transformation the individual's freedom from their past karma so that they may realize their full potential and divinity. When Jesus said in Galatians 6:7, "Whatsoever a man soweth, that shall he also reap," he was highlighting the fact that results of our past sins follow us. The Hindus also say that the merit and sin from our actions can follow us to our next birth. The Bible we have today was edited at the Council of Nicaea to suit a Roman audience, but there are suggestions in the Gnostic texts, which were discovered in Upper Egypt in 1945, that many early Christians believed in reincarnation. The psychic seer Edgar Cayce also affirmed that Gnosticism is the highest form of Christianity.

The Christian idea of repentance from sin and the Hindu idea of freeing oneself from negative karma gathered in past lives are similar in many respects, in that both are an attempt to release us from the consequences of actions we have ourselves caused. Everyone has his or her own personal karma from the past, which determines our present and future destiny. The main culprits that cause the negative karma in our lives are wrong thinking, out of control emotions, and egotism. These lead to bad actions and ill-will toward others, which bounce back to us like a cosmic boomerang.

To cleanse the negative karma, we can use a spiritual practice which normalizes the emotions, strengthens the mind, and points us toward divinity. The *archana* and *puja* suggested by the Naadi serve as a form of repentance to free one from the negative energy, which is also reflected in the position of the planets in the horoscope. As my

Naadi said: "You also have some previous birth karma and also some bad planetary effects. In the present time, you have problems with Saturn. And also you have some problems with Jupiter. And besides this, there is previous birth karma. The planetary positions keep changing. When it comes to the bad things, it will make the bad things. When it comes to a good place, it will make the good things. This is normal for the human race."

Once we clear our karma and repent all small or big crimes committed against any living being, we place ourselves in a position where our full potential can be realized, and we achieve a life of spiritual significance and benefit to everyone. If there is deep remorse and love for the Divine, then the power of God's forgiveness comes to our aid, and nothing can prevent our progress. In addition to the rituals, it is of course important to continue your chosen form of spiritual practice. In my case, this includes creativity, writing, yoga, *pranayama*, meditation, and mantra, as well as service to others, particularly though spiritual teaching and using my mediumistic and psychic powers to help people. Each of us will have other qualities and practices that we can bring to bear to help ourselves and others, and to make this world a better place.

The enlightened yogi will not need to perform the rituals in the Naadi leaves. Devotees of Ramana Maharshi consulted the leaves for their guru, and he gave them permission to read them to him. However, he did not perform the prescribed *pariharam puja*, saying, "If there is no identification with body, mind, ego, and free will, then what is there to perform and for what reason?" (A detailed description of these ideas can be found in the excellent book *Compassion* by Kim Paisol. I highly recommend this book for its insights into the true purpose of the Naadis.)

As our own spiritual practice deepens, the material things of the world become less important to us, and the enlightened master becomes completely free of all karma. As the adept draws close to realization, the need for ownership, and the egotism that may have driven us in the past, drop away naturally, like the tail of a tadpole. It is the "I" that wishes to possess things, but the core of our soul is omnipresent and so cannot be limited by any desire. We come to understand that there is nothing greater than the Truth and no nobler accomplishment in life other than God-realization. Sathya Sai Baba says: "Desires directed toward worldly objects cause pleasure and suffering. But if a desire is directed toward God, then it gives bliss!"

The ego, of course, may be one of the things that the Naadis have in their sights, and it has been argued that sometimes a wrong prediction is made in order to create a wave of disappointment, questioning, and self-analysis that will cause a rethink and set the seeker on a path that requires a modest heart. This may help bring the seeker to greater spiritual maturity. Most people consult the Naadis for mundane reasons, and sometimes the remit of the leaves is not to solve all their problems, but to nudge them in a more spiritual direction. I am told that answers to spiritual questions tend to be much more accurately answered than questions about banal issues.

For those who are earnestly seeking spiritual truth, the Naadis will give highly accurate guidance and help restore the person's faith and motivation. But also, no matter how profound the Naadis may be, the seeker is advised not to rely entirely on them, or they can become a hindrance to Self-realization. The final step into divine consciousness can only be taken by you. No *avatar*, guru, or Naadi can take that step for you. Self-realization is yours and yours alone. The Naadi may be able to help to clear the way, and help you overcome karmic obstacles, but the Divine realization has to come from you.

The best way to clear negative karma is through spiritual practice and service to others. The Naadi oracle had also charged me to visit temples and ask the priest to do *archana*, and to have some of this done by proxy. The big problem with having someone do the *puja* by proxy is that there is no way to know if it has been done. My Indian friend Perminda told me that the problem is endemic, and she wouldn't even trust her own family in India to do it for her. I had heard a tale about a Naadi reader who had been taking money for *puja* but not performed any of the rituals. He met a terrible death by burning. When I narrated this story, Perminda's response was: "Well, their attitude is, 'Yes, there is karma, but we'll cross that bridge when we come to it.'"

I believe that my own proxy *puja* was done properly, but I have nonetheless continued to do the whole lot on my own as a personal discipline, and with the thought in my mind that if I am doubling the remedy, then may the spare spiritual energy go to help someone else in need. I see no harm at all in feeding people twice and doing the mantras—it's something I now love to do, and it keeps my mind focused on the spiritual. What we are talking about here is a form of prayer. *Puja* (also sometimes spelled *pooja*) is a Sanskrit word, which literally means "reverence," "honor," "adoration," or "worship". In colloquial Tamil, it is called *poosai*, with the same meaning.

Many Westerners would find the idea of doing rituals to Indian gods a little difficult to comprehend. Surely we got rid of all this nonsense with the end of the pagan gods, the advent of Christianity, and the idea of just one God. Hindus also believe that "God is One," and that the light of God not only shines through the idols, but also though our own hearts, too. In fact, everything is God, including us. We may know this intellectually, but we also have to realize the fact with our whole being. The Indian gods represent aspects and qualities of the one God. Some of these may manifest as male or female deities, and also in many different forms. We pray to the form that most represents the spiritual help we need at that time.

The Hindus believe that visiting the great temples of the gods changes the patterns of our personal karma that we acquired over many past lives. It helps to clear and clarify conditions that were created hundreds of years ago, which otherwise would remain as seeds of misfortune that could manifest in the future. Through the grace of the gods, the seeds are destroyed for the benefit of the evolution of the soul.

I have always been a bit anti-prayer. My argument is that if we are all God, then why pray to something separate from ourselves? I have always thought of God as the absolute and infinite awareness that lies at the heart of our being. The God I have described here is unmanifest, but God also takes form and becomes manifest. That's what this whole play of creation is—the unmanifest God becoming manifest, so he/she can become conscious of being conscious, though form—and we are all part of that form. In the Hindu religion, the many gods are seen as divine creations of the one Being. These gods are real beings, capable of thought and feeling that transcends the limited abilities of embodied man.

Multiple gods are therefore the manifest aspect of the one God—Allah, Yahweh, the Almighty, and the Great Spirit. For Hindus, God manifests as many gods but can also manifest as an *avatar*, which is God manifesting as a man, such as Sathya Sai Baba, Krishna, and Vishnu. *Avatars* may appear in other faiths, such as Buddha,

Muhammad, and Christ. The saints are mortal men who have ascended to Godhood.

I like to think of it as the same, one white light of God shining through many windows. Apart from a few misconceptions, most of the world's religions are compatible with one another when we drop the idea of exclusivity and accept that all are expressions of God. If we could see this simple fact, the world would find much more peace, and more people would seek direct divine knowledge. This would be the true Golden Age—a time when people become God-conscious.

Sathya Sai Baba expressed this beautifully:

There is only one religion, the religion of Love;
There is only one language, the language of the Heart;
There is only one caste, the caste of Humanity;
There is only one law, the law of Karma;
There is only one God, he is Omnipresent.

Whatever path we choose to connect with the God that is within us, it will always lead to the same place. If we choose the Christian path, then we must be a good Christian; if our path is Islam, then we should be a good Muslim; a Jew, a good Jew; and so on. All very, very simple, really. All is God—so no more arguments, please.

So *puja* is the Hindu form of worship to help negate problems in your life and, in my case, to clear the past karma that the Naadi identified.

Now consider all this from Jane's standpoint. Here is a husband who has accessed an ancient text and now believes that past sins can be negated by rituals and mantras. When I first told her about the Naadi reading and that I'd commissioned people in India to begin the mantras on my behalf, she initially pulled my leg: "Now you'd better take the trash out, or you'll need another hundred Brahmins chanting for your sins in your next life!"

When we went to the Festival of Mind Body and Spirit in London, we took a long detour on the way home to try to find the Shiva temple in Eastham, and asked if I could make a booking to do the *archana*, or whatever you have to do. It was a long drive though very heavy traffic, and Jane had that look on her face that Marge Simpson gives Homer when he has one of his hair-brained schemes. And, of course, to make matters worse, we arrived when a big festival was taking place, and there was absolutely no parking anywhere in the web of narrow streets that surrounded the temple.

After the first Naadi reading, it seemed to be an impossible task to do the *archana*, as the reader had given me a list of temples spread across India that I was supposed to visit. My new list also appeared to have a few problems, too. Fortunately, my friend Preminda at the yoga classes we attended suggested I try the local temple in Southampton and not worry about finding an exclusive Shiva temple. She went with me to make an arrangement, and I talked to the priest, who told me to come back later, and he would guide me through things.

When I looked again at the oracle, I noticed something. It said: "The next step is that the native has to visit a *nearby* temple of Lord Shiva and has to perform *archana* by telling the priest the native's name, moon sign, and birth star." It seemed to even know about my pointless running around by including the word "nearby," which I'd missed when planning my *archana*!

Although I had visited temples in India, it is still quite a cultural leap to go to an Indian temple and do a strange ritual, and I can imagine that Westerners who consult the Naadi and are less familiar with Indian culture will find it a big step. I am aware how daunting it is for many people to visit a Spiritualist church or make their first visit to sit with a medium. You just don't know what to expect. Visiting a Hindu temple for the first time has a similar feeling of exotic unfamiliarity.

In reality, it's all quite simple. The local temple priest at Southampton was very kind and helpful, and he guided me through the process. I was told to bring along milk, a white flower, dried fruit, and a piece of fresh fruit. We then stood in front of the shrine to Shiva, who is represented here by a Shiva *lingam*, which is a symbol of the energy and potential of the one formless God. With our hands in prayer, the priest then chanted to the sons of Shiva, his wife, and then to the *lingam*.

I give the priest my name and Indian star sign and then, using only my right hand, I pour milk and water, and place rice and flowers, on to the *lingam* as the priest chants the appropriate mantras. Next I hold an orange in my open hands and inwardly ask God for help with my problems. A small amount of orange paste is put in the middle of my forehead, some water wiped across my closed eyelids, and the procedure concludes with the priest tying a piece of red string around my right wrist.

The next part of the Naadi Shastra said I was to "visit a temple of any saint, for example Sai Baba, and there the native has to worship the saint according to the custom in the particular temple." I mentioned in the earlier section about Sathya Sai Baba that I took this to mean Sai Baba of Shirdi, since he was revered by both Hindus and Muslims as a saint. On the Internet, I discovered a brand new temple to Sai Baba of Shirdi had opened just three weeks ago, not that far from me, in Reading. So after a two-hour drive, Jane went shopping in Reading, and I went to the temple, which was located above a Primark store in the town center. The temple custom was straightforward. The priest made a mark with paste between my eyebrows and handed me a flower to offer to the golden statue of Sai Baba of Shirdi. I was then instructed to simply sit down and enjoy a meditation. I had my spiritual solace, while a few blocks away Jane enjoyed visiting lots of new stores!

I hope what I am writing now will help any Westerners who are unfamiliar with Indian ways to overcome any resistance they have to participating in Hindu rituals. The priest at Reading was another spiritual soul, and seeking out temples can be fun as well as spiritually uplifting. *Archana* and *puja* are not restricted to the Naadi leaves' prophecies. If you have any problem, you can call upon the power of God though the various aspects of God represented in the temple. The idea of multiple gods under one roof reminds me of the idea behind one of my favorite buildings on earth, the Pantheon of Rome, which was built by the emperor Hadrian. ("Pantheon" is derived from the ancient Greek *pantheon*, meaning "of, relating to, or common to all the gods.") It was one of the few Roman temples that was not destroyed by the Christians. Since the seventh century, the Pantheon has been used as a church dedicated to St. Mary and the Martyrs. You can also get an excellent pizza in the restaurants facing it in the Piazza della Rotonda!

Wouldn't it be marvelous if people in the future were to recognize that the one God could take multiple forms and were to see the common faith in all religions? Imagine a temple where Christians, Muslims, Hindus, Jews, and all faiths could feel equally at home, free to worship God in their own way? This is the idea of the Pantheon.

While I was in Haifa in Israel, I visited the shrine of the Bab, which is an exquisite shrine where the remains of the Bab, founder of the Babi faith and forerunner of Baha'u'llah in the Baha'i faith, have been buried. He said: "He who is your Lord, the All-Merciful, cherisheth in his heart the desire of beholding the entire human race as one soul and one body." The Baha'i faith has built temples around the world that reflect the idea of the oneness of God and religion, and the oneness of humanity free from prejudice. In a similar way, Hinduism is a pantheon of religions and, just like the Baha'i faith, is tolerant of all paths that lead to God.

The Indians believe the spirit of the god actually lives in the idol and responds to the offering, which is a symbol of love and devotion. It is the feeling of love from the heart that God takes into account and not the material that is offered. By doing the remedies, we bring the blessing of that aspect of God into our lives.

The next remedy on the list required a priest to perform *archana* to Lord Murugan and Lord Jupiter, and to do this the nearest temples to these gods, which was the Shri Sanatan Hindu *mandir* in Wembley, London. This roughly translates as the "All-Inclusive Hindu temple." It was opened in 2010 and is made entirely of imported Indian limestone. Among its carvings are portraits of Mother Teresa and the Sikh Guru Nanak. In 2012, in an act of great religious tolerance, the then–Archbishop of Canterbury, Dr. Rowan Williams, visited its sister temple in Leytonstone as part of the Near Neighbors Program.

On my way to the temple, I stopped at a motorway service station to buy some candy in the Marks and Spencer store. A smiling Indian man approached me and asked, "Are you a Hindu?" I was a little surprised at the stranger's remarks, as there was nothing about what I was doing or anything I was wearing or carrying to suggest an interest in Hinduism. I had to think: I was on my way to do a Hindu ceremony, but was I a Hindu? "No, I am not a Hindu," I replied. "As regards spirituality, I follow my heart, so I am open to all religions." The Indian man smiled and said: "That is good. Have you been to India?" I explained that I have visited Varanasi, Calcutta, and other Indian places. "And how will you support yourself when you go there?" asked the Indian. "By writing books," I replied. "That is good," he said. "Nice to meet you, sir." And with that, he gave another bright smile and went on his way.

Strange coincidences and synchronicity has always fascinated me, as there were some weird stories in my family as to how Edgar Allen Poe accidentally—and correctly—predicted that one of my family would be eaten by his shipmates. (See my book *Psychic Encounters*.) I have since read that many people who have consulted the Naadi have had odd synchronicities on their way to the temples to do the *puja* and *archana* remedies. It was odd that the man asked me a spiritual question and seemed to imply that I would go to India again. The event took me by surprise, so my answers leaped from my unconscious—I would support myself from my writing.

The Shri Sanatan Hindu *mandir* interior was beautiful, with intricately carved architecture that coiled in psychedelic patterns across its arches and buttresses. The priest did the rituals for me in front of the shrine to Murugan, and then to the *navagrahas* (nine planets), which included Jupiter. When we had finished, I walked around the temple paying my respects to each of the gods and to the shrine dedicated to Sathya Sai Baba.

It is interesting and inspiring to take part in the rituals of the Hindu temples, but I am reminded of verses 6:43–44 from the *Bhagavad Gita*, when Krishna talks about finding a fortunate birth in a good family where meditation is practiced: "The wisdom they have acquired in previous lives will be reawakened, Arjuna, and they will strive even harder for Self-realization. Indeed, they will be driven on by the strength of their past disciplines. Even one who inquires after the practice of meditation rises above those who simply perform rituals."

The remedies were now in place. Now the real, inner work must begin.

According to the Naadi, once the remedies are completed I will be able to fulfil one of my lifelong ambitions which is to set up a spiritual center and foundation that is focused on spiritual growth and the quest for the direct experience of higher consciousness. But before I tell you about this I want to scoot back 40 or more years and explain how this idea emerged in the mind of a young hippy drop-out.

COMMUNE AND KIBBUTZ

Once your celestial eyes have been opened, you never see the same world again. Not only are your perceptions changed, in that now you know that everything that surrounds you is a construct of the brain, but also all the pulls of the exterior world become less important, as the inner world becomes the real stage on which the story of our life is set. When we live internally, we naturally want to make the external world a better reflection of the inner values that we have discovered. No longer are we pulled off course by the trivial goals that most people seek. Now we hope to do something of significance that will help us and others to progress spiritually. This inner revelation also prompts us to change the world and set up new societies and perhaps—if there are enough of us—a new civilization as well.

During the psychedelic whirl of the 70s, some of us tried to put into practice the things that had been revealed to us through LSD. Our minds were alight with new ideas and new ways to approach the world. Not many years before, our parents had suffered from the conformist agenda, spiritual degradation, and the material poverty cast by the shadow of the Second World War. But now there was a baby boom, and an inspired and perhaps somewhat spoiled youth took the reins of society. We wanted something different, something optimistic, a society that valued creativity, freedom, and self-expression. There was no way we were going to get ordinary jobs, or plan a life from school to pension and to the grave. We had tasted the nectar of eternity and were wild with hope for a better world.

Fueled by crazy optimism, eight of us decided to see if we could do something different. We all quit art school, rented a big communal house, and made a bonfire of our exam certificates, which we lit with a five-pound note. The plan was to all get dangerous but highly paid jobs, such as industrial sandblasting or toxic waste disposal at the hospital, and pool our money to buy a farm in Canada, where land at that time was cheap. After work, we would study farming, building, electronics, and anything else necessary to make a self-sufficient community. And that's exactly what we did.

To save money, we all lived primarily on oatmeal, salad, and piccalilli. Piccalilli is an English interpretation of Indian pickles, a bright-yellow relish of chopped, pickled vegetables and spices. It is lovely by the spoonful, but foul by the gallon. One of our group, in a moment of stoned brilliance, decided that piccalilli had enough nutrients to fully sustain everyone, and there would be no need to ever go shopping.

My job was sewage-pipe laying and groundwork on a hospital construction site. It was a bitter winter, but we discovered a manhole that led to a warm, unlit vault beneath the hospital, where they stored brains in specimen jars. In this macabre but cozy place, we stopped for lunch. I can still recall the faces of my burly workmates as I opened my lunch box to reveal what looked like a small, open grave of luminous piccalilli sandwiches, lettuce, and oatmeal flapjacks. The combination of vinegar and sugar from the flapjacks gave it all a particularly arresting smell that could not be ignored.

Fortunately, one of our group managed to get himself a job as a butcher at a slaughterhouse, and he had the brilliant idea to take home the meat dust. Pets could eat it, so why not us? Of course, he forgot to mention that, as well as meat, it was also 50% or more bone, and we were all violently sick with what we euphemistically described as "vitamin poisoning." As we collectively threw up, we longed to return to our healthy piccalilli diet. Not only the food but the whole project was beginning to be more than any of us could chew. Here was a group of artists doing some of the toughest jobs and longest hours on the planet, becoming totally exhausted, and maybe even gradually losing sight of our objective. We had learned next to nothing about animal husbandry, crop planting, tractor maintenance, or high-density crop yields.

I think it was on a Sunday evening, with the prospect of another horrific week ahead, that our Jewish friend, Danny, called in to see us zombies. He'd grown his hair long, had a great tan, and beamed as he played his guitar and told us all about his travels to Israel and his stay on a kibbutz. It had the lot: sun, adventure, good food, and lots of women. And what's more, they'd already achieved what we were planning: a community based on shared values and no personal possessions. It was a no-brainer. We all quit our jobs and sold every possession other than what we could carry—including my precious and rare mono copy of *Sergeant Pepper*. Within a couple of weeks, we were on a flight to Tel Aviv to get some real experience of farming.

My job as a "volunteer" for the first month or so was emptying raw human sewage into the irrigation ditches, which fed water from Lake Galilee and around into the miles of banana plantations that surrounded Kibbutz Ashdot Ya'akov Meuhad. We'd rise at 3:00 a.m., work till noon, eat at the canteen, have a siesta in the afternoon, and go back to work until the early evening. They squeezed seven of us into a bare room meant for two people, and we slept on iron beds with straw mattresses. I think they'd bought them from a 1950s asylum surplus store. The toilet stank and was stained almost completely brown. They provided us with khaki clothes and a pair of old hobnailed boots, which they had painted with a sort of liquid tar. We looked and felt like prisoners of war.

Just as I was going off the idea of farming and wondering if there was an alternative lifestyle to this alternative lifestyle, they switched us from sewage duty to the banana fields. We were supervised by two very old-looking German Jews, Alfred and Namary, who worked us like slaves. Alfred was a huge man, but a little slow. Namary was a tiny little man, but very sharp, and definitely the one in charge.

One of the few words I learned in Hebrew was *hashigah*, which means "rest break." "*Hashigah, hashigah*, Namary—we need a rest!" I moaned. "Rest! Rest!" exclaimed Namary. "In Belsen, we never rested. We worked day *and* night, until we were dead!"

So much for a holiday break.

It is surprising how you do eventually adjust to long, grueling hours working at break-neck speed, and although we all now unanimously agreed that farming was not for us, our time in the fields was definitely a character-building experience—and eventually it became fun, too. And the girls outnumbered the guys by three to one, so it was fun in lots of ways. During our time off, we were also taken to see the sights of Israel from the back of a flatbed truck. We saw Ein Gedi, Jerusalem, and Mount Sinai, dove in the Red Sea, and the Israeli army escorted us with armored vehicles and waved us under the noses of the Jordanian troops as we sang, "*Hava nagila, hava nagila, hava nagila ve-nismecha*" on the Golan Heights.

Golan Heights Vacation

Whenever we were shown the sites, our visit tended always to have a Six-Day War theme. We'd be presented with a load of burned-out tanks and told how the glorious Israeli soldiers, under the brave leadership of Moshe Dayan, had fought off the Syrian invaders. We'd swiftly bypass Bethlehem or Nazareth in preference for battlefields. The kibbutz still showed the scars of war. In places it was surrounded by barbed wire, and it had machine-gun posts, watchtowers, and air-raid shelters. The movie theater was a converted airplane hangar. On one occasion, four of us accidentally wandered into a minefield when we were showing a new recruit around the kibbutz perimeter. My friend Mike, who was very tall and had long legs, decided he could make it back to the road in three paces, so he took a chance. As Mike had taken huge strides, which we couldn't match, the rest of us had to jump to reach his footprints. I have never seen anyone shake as much as the guest we were showing around. Perhaps jumping up and down in a minefield is not a good introduction to kibbutz life.

Apart from the ever-increasing gunfire coming from the border, the low-flying jets breaking the sound barrier as they flew past the pool, and the tanks moving through the kibbutz at night, everything was beautifully peaceful. I wrote to my parents to reassure them that everything was fine in Paradise, and meanwhile reached for my copy of the *I Ching* to decide whether I should stay.

The *I Ching* gave me an unequivocal answer. "He crosses the great water and thunder breaks behind him."

I bought an air ticket to Athens and left. The next day, the Yom Kippur War broke out and, as the kibbutz next to us also harbored a secret arms factory, it was all a prime target for the Egyptian air force. As my friends crouched in air-raid shelters, the *I Ching* oracle guided me to the safety of Athens.

The kibbutz I saw in 1973 was driven forward by men and women with high ideals, whose souls had been steeled by the Holocaust, and who were now hell-bent on carving out a new life in Israel. Aside from whether this was a fair deal for the Palestinians, the settlers on Kibbutz Ashdot Ya'akov Meuhad were trying hard to build a socialist society, with Judaism as its foundation. I think if I'd been Jewish and had experienced the Holocaust, I would have considered this a potential utopia. As an outsider, I could see flaws. Not everyone was prepared to share, and it was apparent that some kibbutzniks were "more equal than others." Some had curtains, personal TV sets, a bath, and other luxuries. And the young kibbutzniks yearned to have motor scooters and listen to *Sergeant Pepper*. It was clear to me that this society could probably not work, for the young would leave and the old would hoard.

On the kibbutz, my friends and I learned all about farming, and now we were experts at growing bananas. Somehow I don't think this would have been a suitable crop for our planned Canadian farm. We gave up on the idea of setting up a farm, but it was a nice try, and it was one of the best times of my life.

THE FOUNDATION

"Don't let the karmic tendencies described in your horoscope, no matter how valid the prediction, enslave you to anything that your will rejects. The prediction made by our family astrologer was accurate according to the stellar positions, but that didn't mean I had to accept it as cosmic dictate." So says Yogananda in *Conversations with Yogananda* by J. Donald Walters. Yogananda—whose own guru was Sri Yukteswar, one of the most accomplished Vedic astrologers who ever lived—resisted the whole idea of astrology. To prove the reality of astrology, Sri Yukteswar foresaw in the horoscope that Yogananda would have a serious liver complaint and prescribed an amulet/bangle he should wear as a remedy to minimize the impact of the illness. A month later, Yogananda became very ill, as predicted, and had agonizing liver pain for weeks, which only stopped when Sri Yukteswar intervened.

Nonetheless, to prove his sincere faith in God, Yogananda would often have astrologers select the worst dates to accomplish specific tasks, and he would go about accomplishing them anyway. He admitted that sometimes this fight with the stars did create problems, but all the difficulties were overcome, and fate could be transcended. To illustrate his disdain, Yogananda burned his horoscope in front of his devotees. Perhaps his resistance is understandable, as Yogananda had his moon in Leo, and that also rests in a smaller sign called Magha—a demonic influence, but in a spiritual position—all of which can make for people who are very stubborn!

I, too, have always believed in the power of the will to transcend destiny, and it is not my intention in the future to make the Naadi predictions fit, or to force my life to follow a certain path. Providence expects us to make choices and difficult decisions, as this life is not just a free ride. But with this in mind, the Naadi did make some predictions about my life that reveal and clarify my deepest spiritual hopes. It washed the mud from my eyes and helped me see the path ahead.

All my life, I have wished there was a way that money could be taken out of the equation. In Israel, I had hoped to find a model that I could learn from to build our hippy ideas. As an artist and painter, I wanted only to paint and produce inspired works and not to have to worry about flipping burgers to keep the studio going. When I met Jane—who had similar ideals—I was quick to drop my corporate communications business to follow a spiritual path. Similarly, when we did a theater show for the BBC, we both agreed the proceeds should go to a children's cancer ward and the fees from the "Spirit of Diana" show would go to a Diana charity. Our years of work for Spiritualism cost us more in unclaimed expenses than anything we ever made from television.

When I met Jane, she was giving all of her readings for free. People were waiting in line down the street to get readings, and she would often work late into the night helping people in distress. Of course, we still had to live, and my eventual solution came when I monetized my website, and I insisted Jane charge at least the same price per hour as the mechanics who fixed my car. But often people would come to visit and, when their terrible circumstances were revealed, she not only didn't charge them but gave them her housekeeping money. To help a lady with a disabled daughter get a computer and enable her to find specialist American doctors via the then-new Internet, she handed over all the money we'd been saving for a holiday. I joke in the stories here about Jane and her "shopping powers," but the reality is that most of this is just fun bargain-hunting, and a large part of what she buys is given away to others as gifts.

Things were to change for the better. The website started getting millions of hits, and I was approached by a company that persuaded me to add their psychic phone line services to the site. As an affiliate, I would get a commission. The readers were being selected and trained by a Sai Baba devotee, and once I was absolutely sure they were up to standard, I put the phone number on my website and overnight had a livelihood. For a number of years after that, the website generated a very good income, and I was soon in the luxurious position of being able to give all the proceeds from my workshops and circles to Spiritualism, as well as helping to raise thousands of dollars in additional funds through my online community.

When the Google ranking problems hit me, my model fell apart, and this meant that we could no longer support our free services. Jane and I both disliked the idea of becoming theater mediums, since we felt this was being badly abused, and many mediums were milking people. It was also becoming more about entertainment than getting a real message across. Many of the theater mediums were arrogant; some were only in it for the money; others were complete fakes and amateurs. It's a small world, and I know of one theater ghost hunter and medium who was putting plants in the audience to receive messages—something I've had confirmed now from three different cameramen. This "medium" is now a millionaire.

Meanwhile, Jane and I were in a fix and didn't know what to do. We had both become disillusioned with the way the media were promoting the wrong mediums, and we felt that Spiritualism was out of date, out of touch, and refusing to change. Nice as many Spiritualists are, it seemed pointless to demonstrate in shabby churches, with their ghastly rummage-sale decor and 1950s mentality. Here we were preaching to the converted rather than reaching out to the world, and although I will always try to do some work for Spiritualism, it could no longer be the main driving force of my life. I will still do what I can for Spiritualism, since at its best, it is tremendously uplifting for the bereaved and a great starting place for many people's spiritual quest. However, Jane and I felt it offered limited opportunities to express our own, unique spiritual message. We needed a new model and new places where we could teach our unique ideas, reach out further, and include in our messages guidance for the development of higher consciousness and a broader understanding of the purpose of spirit communication and reincarnation.

I am a Spiritualist medium, but I'm also a Hindu yogi—not an easy combination. This is what I believe the Naadi meant when it said, "You are born into a different religion," as I can feel the echoes of the worship from my past life. Strictly speaking, it was the pull of the universal religion that I felt. This was the call of the ancient *sanatana dharma* that is the source of, and yet transcends, all religions. Sathya Sai Baba once asked a scientist, "Did gravity exist before Newton discovered it?" His point was that gravity has always been there and is everywhere, and that none can claim to own it. And so it is with divine knowledge. It is not just for Hindus, but for all. Spiritual realization comes not from a limited intellectual or doctrinal viewpoint, but directly from the heart. It is an "inner-standing" rather than "under-standing." The Truth is self-evident.

Just before consulting the Naadi oracle, I had expressed to Jane my feelings about wishing we could be in a position that enabled us to work for free in the theaters and on TV, so that we could read for whomever we felt was in the most need. Demonstrating in a public setting, rather than by private reading, means the maximum good can come from every message given. If you took away all the fame, money, smug self-satisfaction, self-importance, glory, and kudos, would we still do mediumship? Our answer was yes—we'd even do it if we were working anonymously, so that no one would ever know who gave the messages from spirit. Would some of these other mediums do the same? I think not.

Perhaps the timeless God heard our hopes and took our dreams back though time to influence the *maharishi* as he wrote the Naadi palms all those centuries ago, for in the writings was the perfect expression of the model I had dreamed of—and the means to achieve it.

According to the first reading, rich and influential people will support our work, and this will result in forming a charitable foundation and building ashrams around the world. The second Naadi interpretation calls these centers temples. "All of your businesses are going to do very well. Financially you will have no major problems. And you are also going to elaborate your ashram, not only in your country, but you are also going to build some ashram in foreign country, also. So in the foreign country, every year you can receive people from your country. You are the master of your language-people. You can give the way for the people, and all the people follows you."

When I asked where these ashrams will be built, the first reader interpreted it as "whichever place you like. This is all about you. Wherever you like, you can do it. So in the future, not only in one place, you can also go to different countries. Not only the same country. It's like America, Asia, India, wherever, like Germany in Europe side, you can develop."

Jane and I have often talked about setting up centers where people could watch mediumship and learn. We talked of having a fund that could be used to help us tour the world giving lectures, doing demonstrations of mediumship and workshops, and building this fund until it gets to a point that we can set up centers where people can visit. Together we would raise money through our work to make this happen, and once a month we would demonstrate for free so that it would be available to everyone.

We want these "ashrams" to be family-oriented havens, where safe mediumship can be presented in a spiritual atmosphere. We did not "see" huge buildings, but spiritual villages set in tranquil meditation gardens. These places would be family-friendly and aimed at the householder—people with families, who want to live a spiritual life, but who also have commitments. With programs in place to entertain, amuse, and spiritually inspire children, the adults could meditate while the children have fun. Music would also play a part, with concerts, songs, *bhajans*, and group chanting. We would also do *havan* and the Atri Rudra Maha Yajna—sacred, world-peace fire ceremonies. Rituals performed with divine intent and devotion send out ripples that will help the world in times of calamity and cataclysm. They elevate not only the participants, but the whole world.

To maintain our personal livelihood, Jane and I would continue to maintain the website and its psychic phone-reading affiliation, and still do the occasional private reading to pay for our personal bills. Our theater and public work would fund the foundation. The Naadi oracle spotted the fact that we could help people for free once a month, on every full moon—which energetically is the ideal time for doing mediumship. "And also every full moon day you receive lots of poor people, so people who want anything without any money, you can give free spiritual consultation to the people, so they like, and whenever they see you, they are crying, happy tears. When they meet you, they get relief from their problems." To me this sounds exactly like the free public demonstrations of mediumship and clairvoyance I had spoken about with Jane.

At first, Jane and I will struggle to do this on our own and with the help of a few close friends, but the oracle sees that we will get the support from rich and famous people, who will contribute to the foundation that also directly helps the poor. "And also you can give the dress and the book for the orphanage people, some adopted children, and poor children. So in your name, you can make some organization. Every year you can give lots of help to the poor people, not only from you—lots of rich people help you. They give money so you can organize things."

Modern charities make me angry. Most of the money we donate is wasted on administration and gross marketing that relies on guilt and shame by showing starving people as we eat our TV dinners. If you give a donation, you are mail-bombed and leafletted for more, and to me it looks like more is spent on doing this than the original donation we sent. Whatever happened to giving money simply out of love? I believe that if people are spiritually inspired, then it becomes natural to give whatever we can in money, but also as service to others. Service to others actualizes the good we have developed inside us and helps it to manifest in the world. We can share our material resources, but also our inner wealth, to make this world a better place. If after death we were to meet God in the anthropomorphic way, he would not ask us how much we have eaten during our lives, but how many others we have fed. God will run away if we come to him as a beggar with a list of wants, but when he sees us doing service, he falls over himself to help us.

According to the first oracle translation, many people will get to know of Jane's and my work and will want to help: "And besides that, lots of people are going to support you. In this period you make a big ashram; you have lots of followers. And you have followers from foreign countries also." In the second translation, it suggests that we also build a temple. "The native will donate some materials, which are used for building a temple or a shrine. . . . In sixty-eight, sixty-nine, the native will worship Lord Shiva and get more and more spiritual knowledge. In this period, the native will sit in a temple. The native would understand the problems of the people who come to him, and the native will guide the spiritual ways by which the people can get eradicated from their problems."

Some of the money will be raised through what appears to be fire ceremonies to clear people's personal karma, and other spiritual people will help with the work. "It means that all the spiritual people will help you—they will give the money to you, but with that money you cannot use for your own purpose. That money will be used for social service. So in the foreign country you can give the dress and the food for the old people and poor people. Some village people you can help in the rural area, and go help the people and make some small, small cottages for the village people. . . . So also you can elaborate your ashram, you will enjoy your life. All your spiritual activities are going to be very good. This is the purpose of your birth."

I believe most of the funds needed will come through the conferences that the first Naadi reader describes. These, I believe, will be lectures and demonstrations of mediumship. My intent is to use some of the funds to travel around the world and book venues where Jane and I can share our knowledge and spiritual gifts. In addition, the Naadi explains that our teachings will be enhanced with the help of astrologers, Naadi readers, and yogis from the Himalayas. "So after you get lots of spiritual experience in the astrology. Beside the astrology, you can do lots of conferences. Every day you do lots of conferences, [in] different, different cities. And you can speak about the spiritual, and you can speak about the astrology. And if any people have a problem, you can give the proper solution for them. And not only this. You make some spiritual tours for the people. So you are the head of the people, and you can make spiritual tour, so you can arrange spiritual tour. You can give lots of spiritual places to the people. You can give lots of spiritual service to the people."

I am writing this at the age of sixty-one in the year 2015, so if the oracle is right, it will be a few more years before the full effect of what we envision comes to pass. We have, however, made a start and begun our work to raise funds. If you are interested in finding out more about our foundation conferences, or would like to help or contribute, you can find out more at our website, **psychics.co.uk**.

WILL THE PREDICTIONS COME TRUE?

For many Westerners, the fatalism that is evident in the Naadis is unnerving. It suggests that we have little or no control over our destiny and that our path ahead is determined almost entirely by karmic influences from our past lives. I wonder if I would have written this book with such enthusiasm if the Naadis had predicted misfortune in my future and said that I was a half-wit in my past lives. When we hear prediction of good things, we want them to happen and sometimes unconsciously try to make them come true.

From what I have read of other people's predictions, the Naadis do often come true, to the letter, and with astonishing accuracy. Some say that the short-term predictions happen, but the long-term predictions fail to materialize. Others say that their Naadi predictions did not come to pass at all.

From what I have observed, the Naadis fail for people who do not do the *puja* remedies. This is not because of the cost of having it done by proxy, as often, in other people's leaves, it says not to trust Naadi readers who charge high fees. The *puja* can be done yourself, so this is not an obstacle. I have also noticed in other people's readings that if the *puja* is completed for the first reading, then subsequent readings show an improvement in circumstances, such as a longer life. Also, the materialistic needs of a person, such as wealth, are less likely to be fulfilled, whereas the road opens when a person seeks spiritual things. It is claimed by some that, as we live in the age of *Kali Yuga*, very few people live to high moral standards or have good human values, so they do not apply the advice to their lives. And, of course, a bad reader may misinterpret the written text or tell you what he thinks you want to hear, whereas the Naadi leaves in the hands of a spiritual reader are miraculous, for through the Naadis we get to talk directly to the saints who, through their grace, want to help us to remove the darkness of ignorance.

I marvel at these superhuman *rishis* who wrote these prophecies so long ago and seem to know minute details about our world now. I am told that some leaves say they are over eight million years old and claim to be from a time when the continents of Africa, India, and Australia were joined together as one landmass. If this really is the case, then the mind boggles as to who these writers were. It leads me to think of the pseudoscientific claims of Erich von Daniken, who claims that mankind is descended from superbeings from another star who visited earth millions of years ago. Perhaps also there is an influence from the spirit world, as in some people's Naadis there are references to enlightened beings communicating from the *lokas*—the Indian name for the multiple spirit worlds. Some also talk of other types of advanced living beings that live on earth—some manifest and others who live in a non-physical form.

The Naadis are a type of time-machine, in that they seem to know if you have made the changes in your life and done the *puja* remedies, so that Naadis that are consulted a few years later change. For example, the Naadis predicted that one person would be seriously injured in a car accident, but he did the remedies, and when the car accident happened, he got out of the terrible crash without a scratch. Sometimes, the day of death is predicted at sixty-five, but gradually, as more remedies are done, the date changes to up to ninety. There have been cases where a blank leaf has had writing appear from nowhere with a new prediction, or the writing has changed as it is being read. These miracles were witnessed by everyone present. It's as if the *rishi* is writing the leaves in the past at the same time as events take place in the present. These supermen clearly had such an understanding of time, and lived so close to the eternal Now, that they had a knowledge of time that is beyond our comprehension.

Using the Jiva Naadi, it is possible to ask questions in real time, and this oracle gives answers to very specific questions in great detail. In the right hands, these are "alive" and directly connected to the Divine Mind. Only highly evolved people can use these Naadis, and again there are thousands of fraudulent Jiva Naadis in India, and it is near impossible to find the real one. As I write this, I have networked my Naadi contacts and this—together with further Naadi predictions from my about the world, the other *kandams* (chapters) from my leaves, and some encounters with physical mediums and gurus—will become the basis of my next book.

It is also apparent that the destiny revealed in the Naadis can change, and there may be multiple paths though this multiverse. One person who consulted the leaves noticed that, during the identification process, all the information was right except the important fact that he was married to the person described in the leaf. This leaf was discarded in favor of the next one, which started with the same identification information, mother's name, father's name, and so on, except in this one he is married. Could it be that the Naadis are tapping into the multiverse, where infinite copies of "you" are playing out every possible story of your life? A fully conscious being who transcends all of the universes can advise us to do something that would could not have happened through the current flow of cause and effect in the universe we currently live in. A remedy is a magical act, as it would not have happened if I had not consulted the Naadi leaves, so it disrupts the flow of cause and effect and flips us into another universe—a version where I experience an almost identical but slightly more positive life. We have altered reality.

Supposing the Naadi leaves contain multiple destinies and have information about the roads we almost traveled in life. This suggests to me that our destiny can change, or rather that our path through the multiverse can change, and that we do have free will and can influence the fate that is determined by our karma. The remedies serve to eliminate the sins of past lives through *pujas* and, if ignored, the promised results are not achieved.

It is interesting also how the Naadi will spot connections between people. The Ganesh Naadi in particular will, if consulted when others who are close to you are also present, mention everyone present by name, and you may be told about previous connections in another life.

Indian astrology is called *jyotish*, which means "the science of light," a phrase that implies the subtle light of the universe and also the inner light of realization. The influences of the planets are seen as a reflection of the law of karma which create our fate, but our future is shaped by our actions in the present. Spiritual practices such as meditation, yoga, chanting, and *puja* help to neutralize and negative karma.

I believe that the Naadi oracle offers us a potential blueprint for our lives based upon our current karma. Perhaps we should not see them as predictions, but as revelations about what will happen if we do not take actions and make spiritual changes to our lives. Good karma is like having money in the bank that can be used wisely or squandered, and this is where the power of choice and free will come in. The objective of the oracle, I believe, is to push people to seek out a spiritual path. Then all the other positive predictions will also happen, and the bad will fall away. It's much the same as when Jesus advised, "Seek ye first the Kingdom of God, and his righteousness; and all these things shall be added unto you" (Matthew 6:33).

NAADI READINGS AND REMEDIES

The Naadi leaves predict that I will help people clear their karma through my spiritual work and writings, and maybe part of this service is to help some people find their leaves: "In the olden times, all the *rishis*, all the spiritual people, they write all the things in the palm leaves. But since ancient time, you are going to write everything in the notebook—this is the difference. So Alta, he says you are also one of the *rishis*—saints—you are also blessed by the gods. You are an ambassador of the gods. So why you get this birth? Like Alta, you want to give a message to the people. And you want to clear all the karma of the people."

If people come to me in search of their leaves, I may be able to help, but I anticipate that this book may open a floodgate of interest that I may not be able to cope with. I will not, therefore, help idle curiosity-seekers or people who want to use the leaves in inappropriate ways. I get this a lot through my website. "Please, can you tell me the lottery numbers?"—you'd be surprised how often I get asked that—and people are dead serious!

If you would like help from me, then I will keep a list of names and will try to point you to a proper, spiritually inspired Naadi reader, and at the same time ensure that the reader is also not flooded to the extent that his or her job becomes impossible. The leaves have already anticipated a huge upsurge in interest in these times, as there are more leaves available in the libraries for the coming years than at any time in their long history. Then they all stop after 2050, and there are no more leaves after that date. I am hoping that this will be the start of a new Golden Age, when humanity will know its future by other means—perhaps through some discovery about time and consciousness that comes about by peering into the quantum world.

I will help the serious seeker to find their leaf, and I also hope to have something in place to help with the *puja* and *archana*. Finding the leaf may become part of a greater long-term process of developing a person's spiritual understanding. Vivek is working on something at the time of writing, and you would need to initially get in touch with me about this via my website at **psychics.co.uk**.

Accessing your Naadi—if it's there—is no small undertaking. It takes time, and there is a frustrating lack of organization among the readers. When a Naadi reader says "tomorrow," he may mean just that, or next week, or months away—or "not until you pester me again." There is the process of finding the leaf and also the matter of the translation. I have noticed that Indian Internet providers are a bit slow for some Skype connections. So if you do ask, expect delays and hassles!

I am also planning to take people to India and other spiritual places around the world to get their readings and also to perform the necessary *puja* in suitable spiritual locations (as specified by the oracle). Again, if you would like to take part in these spiritual endeavors, you can find the information you need on my website.

Hopefully this book has also given you some idea of what the Naadi is all about and the type of things it can help with. The *rishis* who wrote these leaves were enlightened beings who did not give a hoot about our greedy, worldly desires. They wrote the leaves to elevate people. The answers they give require a complete transformation of your nature.

APPENDIX

Throughout this book, I have often referred to my readings with the Naadi oracle and used the readings as a platform to explain some of my ideas about mediumship and spirituality. Of course, it could be that I am reading things into what was told me, or my ego could be distorting the message for its own nefarious purposes, or I could have simply misunderstood what I have been told. For those of you who would like the exact details of what I was told, I have included here the transcripts of the sessions.

THE TRANSCRIPTS

My first reading was recorded via Skype, but some of the sound was poor on my end when I asked questions. Apart from this small blip, I was able to make a complete, word-for-word transcript of what was said. I have not edited the grammar and have transcribed the conversation "warts and all," exactly as it was spoken on the recording. The first reading was comparatively interactive, though you will notice that I hardly spoke at all throughout the reading. As I have explained in the earlier chapters, Vivek and I went to great lengths to ensure that the reader knew absolutely nothing about me.

The second reading was done just from my thumbprint and was a Maha Suksuma Naadi, which has no chapters and is presented as a long conversation between Shiva and Parvathi. There was an initial consultation by Skype to find the right page in the Naadi leaves. This was a long process in which leaves were rejected. At no time did they ask me leading questions or fish for names and so on. It was a simple yes/no session. Most of this I was unable to record, as we were having connection problems. I did, however, manage to record some of it, including the exciting moment they found my leaf, and I have included a small part of this so that you can get some idea of how the session progressed. I will add that it was very exciting for everyone, including the Naadi reader, who saw special significance in my thumbprint, since it identified a particularly interesting group of leaves, which is a group for people who will have a spiritual influence on future events.

Taking part in this second session was the Naadi reader, a professor, and a translator. Once the leaves were found, the leaf was translated in my absence, and a recording was made and then sent to me by email.

The audio file was huge, and there were problems getting it to me. Eventually they managed to split the file into nine sections and email them to Vivek, who also had problems forwarding them to me. The Naadi reader found it all very funny, as he pointed out that the leaves had predicted that there would be a delay in my reading the predictions. At the time he didn't understand what the leaf had meant, but now it all made sense. (You can read this in the transcript)

The second reading is much more literal and is a direct translation of what is written on the leaf. The person consulting the oracle is called "the native," and you will note that this second reading is full of references to Shiva and the gods. I think that if I had had this reading the first time around, I would have found it a lot harder to understand. As you have read already, I was most interested in getting confirmation, or otherwise, of the first reading. You will see that, although the two readings differ in tone, they contain pretty much the same information.

THE REMEDIES

I have also included the remedies from both readers and the cost. You will note that the first reader—who has Western clients—charges far more than the second reader, who is a traditional Naadi reader. I paid for the remedies with the second reader, though I feel that even the first reader's higher costs were acceptable when you consider what an influence and positive benefit the leaves have had on my life.

It may be the case that the *maharishis* included the remedies simply to allow the oracle to exist. If there is a profit available to the custodian, then the leaves are less likely to be used as tinder. It is said that the gambling with the tarot cards—which eventually evolved into playing cards—was encouraged so that the spiritual message behind them could be taken forward into the future.

Although I paid the cheaper option, I did feel honored to make the payment for the remedies. By doing this, I was helping keep alive one of the great wonders of India. The money also supported the Naadi reader, fed children, and supported the traditions of the temple priests. I believe in the power of prayer, mantra, and *puja* to mitigate past lives, but even if you don't, and you believe that the remedies only help feed the poor and keep traditions alive, then surely it is money well spent.

NAADI READING 1 (BY SKYPE)

[Tamil speaking.]

NAADI READER: That is finished [finding the leaf]. Now I want to give you the prediction. After the prediction, if you have any doubts or questions, then you can ask me. Now just listen to your prediction. *Shiva mayam.*

[Tamil speaking.]

This is God's prayer. Prayer to Lord Shiva. Prayer to Lord Shiva and Parvathi. They will give you a prediction. Before giving the prediction, Maharishi is saying lots of indications about you.

The first indication is your right-hand thumb impression. That thumb impression name is Irue Suri Neruleka. In that thumb impression, there are six dots. So who are the people who have these six dots? They are people who are going to be involved in the spiritual or media field, so they are very popular to the people.

On this basis you were born 24th January, 1954. The day was Sunday, and your birth star is Hastum. As your Vedic astrology, your birth star is Hastum. Your moon sign is Virgo.

You were born in a good family. You are a very kind person. And also talented and intelligent person. In the future, you are going to get name and fame in the spiritual field. And, by God's blessing, you are going to give lots of messages related to life. What is meant by a life? How we can go with the life in this world? So this type of message you will give to the people.

So why do we get this birth? What is the purpose of this birth? What is the reason and what are you going to do? So you are going to give lots of messages to the people. And also you are going to communicate with the universe. Sometimes you are in deep thinking, and in deep meditation you are connected to the universe. So you give messages from the universe. So in that message, you going to share with the people.

So with this type of messages you are going to get from the universe, you are going to write the books. Everything. All the people like your activities. All the people like your messages.

In the present, your mother is alive. You have one brother and one sister. They are married, but the sister is a widow. You are married twice. First wife is divorced. With the first wife, you have one daughter. With the second wife—the present wife—you have two daughters?

CRAIG: [My voice on the Skype did not record, but I explain one daughter with each wife.]

NAADI: You have total two daughter?

CRAIG: Yes.

NAADI: The first daughter is married. And you are involved in the spiritual field?

CRAIG: Yes.

NAADI: And also you know about astrology? And you have written lots of books related to the spiritual?

CRAIG: Yes.

NAADI: And also you are doing the business related to media production with your wife?

CRAIG: Yes.

NAADI: And also you are doing spiritual conferences and consultant?

CRAIG: Yes.

NAADI: Your name is Craig. Your father's name is Donald. Your mother's name is Ethel.

CRAIG: Yes!

NAADI: Tina—your first wife's name?

CRAIG: Yes.

NAADI: And Jane—the present wife's name.

CRAIG: Yes.

NAADI: These are shown in the palm leafs. So this prediction is for you. This is the witness for your prediction your father's name, your mother's name—all the details. So as you listen to the prediction, your age is sixty-one running. Your age is sixty-one, sixty plus.

CRAIG: I am sixty.

NAADI: Yes, sixty plus. So in the future, you are going to get a peaceful life, happy life, and you are going to share your enjoyment of life with the people. So in the future you have lots of experience of the life.

What about the past? What about the future? What is the past of the human beings? What is the future of the human beings? You can go to discover about this. And also you can get answers from the universe.

After death, the soul is going to where? After death, what is the soul going to do? Is the soul going to reborn or not? What is the duty of the soul? Everything you can realize and give the message to the people. And also you can write the books about the soul. The search related to soul. What is the body? What is the soul doing inside of the body? So what is the main thing? The body and soul are different things? So what are the activities of the soul in the body? How is this connected to the whole body? The soul is immortal. So you will research this type of thing.

So you can cover everything. You can research all the people's activities. Then you can get the answers and write the books related to soul.

So what are the activities of soul in the next birth? The soul is going to be reborn or not? You have everything you know. Suppose people do some mistake. So in the next birth, is it a peaceful birth or not? Everything you can calculate.

So what is the solution? You want to be reborn very peaceful. There is a solution in this birth. What is the remedy in this birth? You can give this to the people.

In the future, you are going to get fame and name in the spiritual field. And also, you are going to get a good name from the people. You will learn lots of things related to astrology. You will give a message of astrology to the people. In all your activities, your wife is going to support and help you.

Everything is going to be very well, but you are also going to become a good spiritual person in the future. Now you are a spiritual master, but in the future you will get lots of character from the universe. You become a good spiritual master. You give lots of messages to the people.

You have some previous birth karma. You also have some previous birth karma and also some bad planetary effects. In the present time, you have problems with Saturn. And also you have some problems with Jupiter. And besides this there is previous birth karma. The planetary positions keep changing. When it comes to the bad things, it will make the bad things. When it comes to a good place, it will make the good things. This is normal for the human race.

The previous birth karma—when you was born, in that onwards the karma follow you. So that's why the karmas sometimes make problems for you and make some confusion for you, and you have some thinking, but in that time you cannot get the proper answer. So it will make lots of problems for you, and in your personal life, and family—like that.

So what can we do? Maharishi recommends that you can go and do the remedies and clean the karma. Remedy means what temples you can see, how you can do the *pujas* and you can do the proper remedies and the *pujas*. So that all the people can clear their karma. It's like that you also have some karma. So you can go and do the remedies properly and clean the karma.

So after you clean the karma, you are going to direct your character to the universe and get lots of experience, and you will refresh your body and mind. Then you can write lots of things related to spiritual. You can write on chakras, some spiritual messages for the people, what are the duties for the people, and how we can use the third eye, how we can open the third eye, and what is the process and how we can do. Everything comes to your knowledge. So when this comes to your knowledge, then you can say to the people. But people may not listen, because it is difficult for you, and the people, because you are already a spiritual person. But for a normal person, it is not easy for them to open the third eye. It is not many that understand spiritual things.

Many people have a different culture. They have no understanding about what we mean by God, this divine energy. You know everything already and are connected to the Universe. You are spiritual person, but [for a] normal person, it is not easy for them to open their third eye. It is not for them to understand spiritual things. Because many people have a different culture. They have no understanding about what we mean by God, or what we mean by energy. So in your destiny, this is your duty, this is your purpose of this birth. You want to be of service to the people. You want to give the message to the people. What is meant by God? We can't see God, but how can we see God? What is the way of the God to see? People ask where God is. I don't know. I've never seen God. But you know. This is your duty. This is why God gave you this birth.

So you want to go and give this message to the people. Every day, you will give lots of conference, but you give the message, but lots of people cannot get the message from you. They don't understand, so have lots of long ways to clear the people.

So by God's grace, by the *maharishi*'s grace, you are going to give everything to the people. And Anasha Maharishi says you are not a normal person. You are one of the *rishis*. You are one of the saints. You are the rebirth of saint. That's why from childhood onwards you have followed the spiritual.

In the olden times, all the *rishis*, all the spiritual people, they write all the things in the palm leaves. But since ancient time, you are going to write everything in the notebook—this is the difference. So Alta, he says you are also one of the *rishis*—saints—you are also blessed by the gods. You are an ambassador of the gods. So why you get this birth? Like Alta, you want to give a message to the people. And you want to clear all the karma of the people.

You want to clear everything to the people. So you want to give the message to the people. Please don't do any mistake. You don't give troubles to people. You allow everybody. When you allow everybody, then automatically they allow you. Don't fight, don't do mistake, don't do angry, everything. This is your message to the people.

After some years, you are going to buy some properties, make the ashram, and you become a master, and you are sitting, and you are doing spiritual activities to the people.

But take care at the age sixty-three. Sixty-one, sixty-two, sixty-three. This is some bad period for you. In this period, you are going to lots of activities, and you want to do lots of service, but it is not easy for you, because your body is going to be very tired. You cannot travel to lots of places. You cannot speak lots of times, so you are going to tire. So, beside that, your mother also going to have some breathing troubles. And beside this, your mother has problems related to digestion. And you wife is going to make some blood-related problems and skin-related problems. Your family are going to protect you.

In this period, you are going to be involved in palm-leaf research. You are going to research lots of things to palm leafs, lots of things to *rishis*, and lots of things to palm-leaf prediction. And you are also going to be seeing some foreign countries related to spiritual. And you are also going to visit some foreign countries to do the remedies. And you are going to meet lots of spiritual persons. And you will get lots of blessings, lots of messages from the spiritual person.

So after, you get lots of spiritual experience in the astrology. Beside the astrology, you can do lots of conferences. Every day, you do lots of conferences, [in] different, different cities. And you can speak about the spiritual. And you can speak about the astrology. And if any people have a problem, you can give the proper solution for them. And not only this, you make some spiritual tours for the people. So you are the head of the people, and you can make spiritual tour, so you can arrange spiritual tour, you can give lots of spiritual places to the people, you can give lots of spiritual service to the people.

So all the people get relieved from their problem. They worship you, and they look to you like master. So everyone come and get blessing from you. And besides, that your wife is also going to support you in the spiritual fields. And you and your wife, both are going to do the spiritual service. All the spiritual persons call her like Mother, and you they also call you like Father in the spiritual field. So easily you can do the spiritual service to the people.

All of your businesses are going to do very well. Financially you will have no major problems. And you are also going to elaborate your ashram, not only in your country, but you are also going to build some ashram in foreign country also. So in the foreign country, every year you can receive people from your country. You are the master of your language-people. You can give the way for the people, and all the people follows you.

You are also going to visit the Himalayas in India. In the Himalayas you are going to meet lots of *rishis*, so also you are going to start some "argony" session. [The recording here is unclear, but I take this as *agni*—fire ceremonies to clear past karma.]—non-profit "argony" session. It means that all the spiritual people will help you—they will give the money to you, but with that money, you cannot use for your own purpose. That money will be used for social service. So in the foreign country, you can give the dress and the food for the old people and poor people. Some village people you can help in the rural area, and go help the people and make some small, small cottages for the village people.

And also you can give the dress and the book for the orphanage people, some adopted children, and poor children. So in your name, you can make some organization. Every year, you can give lots of help to the poor people. Not only from you. Lots of rich people help you. They give money to you, you can organize things. You get fame, name with the people. So also you can elaborate your ashram. You will enjoy your life; all your spiritual activities are going to be very good. This is the purpose of your birth.

Beside that, both of your daughters are going to get a peaceful life. They'll not have any major problems, and first two daughter carry a child, and you are also going to enjoy your time with your daughters and grandchildren. And all the time, you wife is going to support you, take care of you, and you are a good couple, and also going to enjoy the spiritual field in this birth. You do not know any major problem.

Also, by doing the yoga and the meditation, you are not tired, and are health, and are happy. All of your ambitions are going to be successful.

Sixty-four, sixty-five, sixty-six, still sixty-seven, you do not know any major problem, and you can continue your spiritual service to the people. You also have lots of fund. You can use that fund to help the poor people. Whenever people have any natural problem in the world, immediately your organization is going to help there. Your organization, your people, and your fund are going to relieve the problem for the people.

You will be happy, and still you cannot stop your writing. All the time, whatever your experience, everything you will write in the books, all your life: like life-history, whatever your ambition, whatever your dreams, all about God and everything you can go write. All the books are going to sell, so whatever money you get, you are also going to give it to the poor people and give to children. They also get support from you in the future.

Money ways, you do not have any major problem. Health ways, you do not have any major problem. And spiritually, you are going to get fame, name, not only in your country. You'll get fame, name in the foreign country also. And besides that, lots of people are going to support you. In this period, you make a big ashram. You have lots of followers. And you have followers from foreign countries also.

And lots of people like your books, and your books are going to be printed in so many languages. For people, it is necessary to want to use your books, for they want some message from the soul from the life. What is meant by life? Why are we living? Everything they want.

Lots of people will research your books. So they will get some masters like that. So in your books is going to be help for the next generation also. So in the next generation, it is going to develop everything so already they know, so already another person [hard to understand voice here]. They said everything already. So what Shiva says in the past, that is going on now in this life. So they will get everything from your big book.

All the people read your books. All the people use your books. Lots of students research your books, not only in your country, lots of countries are going to do research related to your books.

After sixty-seven, you are going to retire, but you are going to continue your spiritual activity. You are not traveling to lots of places, only sitting in the ashram and giving blessings to the people, and writing the books with your wife, and you are going to enjoy your life in the spiritual field.

And also, every full moon day, you receive lots of poor people, so people who want anything without any money, you can give free spiritual consultation to the people, so they like, and whenever they see you, they are crying happy tears. When they meet you, they get relief from their problems. They want to see the master face. When they see the master face, they get relief from their problems. They are happy and healthy. You don't speak anything, but your face, eyes, everything speaks to the people.

They understand everything from your eyes. They understand everything from your face and your eyes. It will make people happy. So many people from such a distance, they are traveling to meet you. Whenever they have any problems, they come to you. Once they meet you, they get relief from their problems.

So after, also, you are going to give help to the people until the end of your life.

Sixty-eight, sixty-nine, seventy, still seventy-two, continuing to do spiritual life activities. You have not any major problem, and you have good activities, and your wife also going to have good activities, your second daughter also going to get a good life. She also not know any major problem.

All your ambitions are going to be successful. What is the meaning of life? Why God give this birth for you? Everything is going to be proper for this birth. You can't go to do any mistake, because all the time God is watching you. They will give you the right energy. When you go to write the books, all the messages that you want to say to the people, all the messages put in the right places in your book. Everything is going to be successful for the people. So there is no major mistake in your life.

So without any major problem you are going to be living in this Earth more than seventy-eight. Still seventy-eight, you don't know any major health issues. All your ambitions are going to be successful.

Still seventy-eight, your wife also going to be living with you. She also going to support and take care of you, all your children, and your grandchildren. Everybody is going to make a happy life for you. And as a spiritual master, you are going to make a good life for them without any major problem.

But only one thing is, you have some previous birth karma. That karma will make some problem, some disturbance for you. It cannot give the development for you—you have lots of development in your life related to spiritual. So in the future, you are going to get a peaceful life, and you are going to develop into the spiritual field. Maharishi says please do the remedies and clean the karma. After clean the karma, everything is going to do very well in this world. You are also one of the *rishis*, you are also a spiritual person, and even though you know everything already, so you can do that, the *maharishi* says to go and do the remedies and clean the karma.

This is your prediction. [Puts his hands together.] *Subah*.

Now if you want to ask any questions? Ask to me.

CRAIG: [Voice did not record but asked about a call we had to go to America to make a TV show presentation.]

NAADI: Yes it is good but not now—after June. After June you can go and can definitely be successful, but this is the proper time for you can go to America and do spiritual service. After 19th June. You can go and be successful with this plan.

The last several years have been a bad period for you. You have money, but you have lots of expenditure. You do the hard work, but you cannot get the good name. Financially, this year has been a bad position, but after June everything goes to a high level. You get fame and name. After June, all your energy is going to get a good energy. You have lots of energy, but all the energy cannot be successful. You can speak, write, everything. It is not good because of the bad karma. After June, everything is going to be successful, and you get fame, name, whatever project, whatever ambition, everything is going to be successful.

CRAIG: Where will I build these ashrams?

NADDI: Whatever you may do. Whichever place you like. This is all about you. Wherever you like, you can do it. So in the future, not only in one place, you can also go to different countries. Not only the same country. It's like America, Asia, India, wherever like Germany in Europe side, you can develop.

CRAIG: My second daughter has some health worries. Can you tell me about these?

NAADI: What is her date of birth? What is the problem she has?

CRAIG: [Answers.]

NAADI: In the future, it will clear everything. It is not going to be serious. After her birthday, everything will go very well. Still some fear, 22 after June, everything is going to be normal.

CRAIG: Can you tell me more about my past life?

NAADI: You were born in Sagura Geddi. It is in South India. You were born as a saint-man. You did lots of spiritual activities to the people. And you did lots of social service to the people. You were also worker in the temple, but in the temple lots of arguments is there. There was lots of arguments, and you gave lots of troubles to the poor people, so they are angry and they cursed you. That curse follows in this birth. That's why it has some health problems for you and your daughters, and your ambitions get blocked. So if you want to achieve your ambitions and have a peaceful life, the *maharishi* says to do the remedies and clear the karma. What are the remedies? I will write and send it to Vivek, and he can explain the process and everything.

CRAIG: What was my name in my past life?

NAADI: Your name was Kala Bhairava.

REMEDIES AND PUJA FOR NAADI READING 1

Sir, I was finish reading with Craig. He was happy, and I write his remedy to you. You will give to him and give the definition to him.

POOJA DETAILS FOR CRAIG

Bring flowers, sweets, fruits, candles, dresses, and donation of 120 euros (£85 or U.S. $129).

Visit Alangudi in South India. Do *puja* to Jupiter

Visit Suryanarkoil in South India. Do *puja* to nine planets, and give dress and food to 108 poor people.

Visit Thirukkadayur in South India and do *ayush homa* and *puja* to Shiva and Parvathi. Give food to forty-eight people.

Visit Swamimalai in South India. Do *puja* to Karthick.

Visit Rameswaram in South India. Do *puja* to Shiva.

Visit Thiruvenkadu in South India. Do *puja* to Mercury.

Mantra *puja* in India Navgraha Mantra. 240 days *puja*. Twice daily *puja*.

Puja expenses = 100 INR per day. Total 240 x 100 = 24000 INR.

[At time of writing, 24,000 Indian Rupees = £253 = U.S. $381. In addition, there is the cost of the reading itself, which was around £25 = U.S. $38. Although sometimes it can take many hours of searching to find your leaf, it is standard practice with Naadi readers not to charge if your leaf is not found.]

NAADI READING 2 (BY SKYPE AND EMAIL), MAHA SUKSHMA NAADI

PART ONE

Namaste. May the blessings of Satguru Sri Aruhahum be showered. Today's date is 13th March, 2015. With the help of Mr. Craig's right-hand thumb impression, Swami Shiva Shakti has found out the inscription engraved by a saint of ancient period, and from this, the first chapter he's found out and has explained.

Lord Shiva, who is in the form of atom, in the form of matter, and in the form of elements, and who is in the form of universe, and who is in the form of emotion, in the form of light and in the form of darkness, and who is in the form of divine sound "Om Kara," who is in the form of divine sound, time, and period, and who is in the form of Shiva *linga*. Goddess Parvathi prays Lord Shiva and accepts the native as her own son and asks about the native's life. Goddess Parvathi asks about her own son, who is born in this universe. Goddess Parvathi accepts the native as her own son and asks about the native's future and asks Lord Shiva about the native's future.

Lord Shiva, who is in the form of atom—that is, atom is the base of life. Atoms become matter, and with the matter, Lord Shiva is able to create the creatures in the universe. Goddess Parvathi prays that Lord Shiva, who has given feelings and emotions to the living things. Lord Shiva, who gives light to the universe. Lord Shiva, who relieves us from the darkness named *maya*, and who blesses, "Om Kara," Goddess Parvathi prays to Lord Shiva and asks about the native's future. She prays Lord Shiva, who is in the form of *lingam*, and who protects the universe. Goddess Parvathi prays Lord Shiva with pleasure and asks about the future of her own son, and also she requests Lord Shiva to explain about the native's future in a very elaborate and precise way. Lord Shiva explains about the native's future in such a way by listening to that Goddess Parvathi, as well as the native would be pleased.

The conversation between Goddess Parvathi and Lord Shiva engraved by Saint Shivavakier Maharishi on the palm leaf. This palm leaf is found out by the process by which this particular palm leaf is being found out is explained.

PART TWO

The first evidence that proves that this palm-leaf inscription is written for the native is the native's thumb impression. Sulle Sutra Sankrika is the name of the native's right-hand thumb impression. There are three coil-like shapes in the thumb impression and also a shape of shank (Valampuni Shank), that is, a shank which is open in the right side. In the thumb impression, there are three dots which give good luck to the native.

The people in the world have the two different styles in the two parts of their life. That is first part of their life and the second part of the life. The native would have the power of knowing the future of other people.

In the beginning, the native would be interested in spirituality, and later he would be fully involved in spirituality. He would get spiritual knowledge. With this knowledge, the native would be able to know about the obstacles which are yet to come in the life of the people, and he would guide those people to the way by following, which they can get eradicated from the problems which are yet to come.

And this guidance is given by the native, and such nature of the native is indicated by the third dot in his thumb impression. The third dot indicates the third eye of Lord Shiva. So the third dot in the native's thumb impression gives sudden changes in the native's life and sudden fortune in the native's life. The third eye of Lord Shiva is to perish the evils, devils, and demons. With the help of the third eye, Lord Shiva created Lord Muragan to perish the demons and to protect gods of the Heaven. So because of the third dot in the native's thumb impression, the native would do many favors to many people, and the native would lead a life of high status.

The native is born in a reputed family. According to Tamil Almanac, there are sixty years which come in cycle. The native is born in the year named Vijaya, which means victory and success. According to the Tamil manuscript, the native is born in the Tamil month named Tai. According to Tamil Almanac, the native is born on 11th. The native is born on a Sunday. His birth star is Hastam. His moon sign is Kanya, that is, Virgo. Palm-leaf manuscript was not written in the current *yuga*—that is, *Kali Yuga*—but it was written in *Dvapara Yuga*—that is, the previous *yuga*. Saint Siva Vakiyam Maharishi being in the state of meditation, and through intuition, and when Goddess Parvathi and Lord Shiva conversed, the saint got the *gnaynum*—that is, divine spiritual knowledge—and wrote this manuscript. The tasks that the native expects to accomplish and the thoughts that the native wants to accomplish may in times not be materialized. How and when these tasks and desires would be materialized, in what way, and with the help of which person, seek answers of these questions the native seeks the Naadi prediction.

Saint Shivamakia Maharishi explains the planetary position at the time of the native's birth. The planetary position at the time of birth of the native is as follows. The ascendant is Scorpio, and Venus and Varhu are in Sagittarius. Sun and Mercury are in Capricorn, Jupiter is in Taurus, Katu is in Gemini, moon is in Virgo, and Saturn and Mars are in Libra. This planetary position is given as the evidence which prove that this palm leaf inscription was written for the native.

[Note: I am an Aquarius and was born on January 24, 1954, and not January 11, as stated in the horoscope. I was able to ask the translator about this, and he said: "The astrologer says that the Tamil date of 11 coincides with January 24, 1954. The placement of the sun will change from the angle of the continent."]

[Speaking in Tamil.]

PART THREE

The native is born as the first child for his biological parents, and the native is born in a hospital. The native is born as a healthy child. The native is polite in nature. He is very talented. He is intelligent. He is healthy and has good guessing power. By nature, the native has good knowledge.

In this birth, the native cannot get any favor from other person. Only the native can do favor to many people. The native has good knowledge and is very talented, but in times the native is short-tempered. That is, the native was short-tempered at very young age, but not at present. The native must have had some confusions in his mind at very young age, but at present not. The native has done his academics in school. When the native is listening to this prediction, his mother is alive. His father is no more. The native has a brother and a sister. The native's brother is leading his own family life, and also his sister is leading her family life. The native's sister has lost her husband.

The native is married twice. The native has parted his way from his first wife. The native has one child through his first wife. This child is leading their own family life.

The native has his own house, and the native is deriving income from his own business. The native does his own business with his wife, and the business is related to art and teaching. That is, the native teaches some art to many people. Those arts are related to spirituality. This teaching is also related to physical health. It is also related to science of curing. It is also related to morals and ethics.

Till now the native did not get saturated knowledge about these arts. The native wants to know the time period when he will accomplish in getting the complete knowledge of these type of arts. How he would accomplish in getting this knowledge, and the native seeks this Naadi prediction to know about the future.

The native would worship gods and goddesses in shrines. And the native has power and good luck to meet a few gurus, but because of some ladies or girls, there will be some obstacles, so the native should be very careful. While teaching spiritual arts to people, the native must be very careful. The native should also be very keen about the way the spiritual arts are taught to the people.

The native has a daughter through his second wife. The native's daughter is leading a family life. The native has got his prediction without any obstacle, but it will take some time for the native to know his future.

Craig is the native's good name. Donald is his father's name, and Ethel is his mother's name. Tina is the name of the native's first wife, and Jane is the name of the native's second wife.

The native is living in his own house and deriving income from art of teaching, with the support of his wife. The business is related to spirituality and God. The native is teaching and also doing consultations related to spirituality.

The native's desire is to be in the stage of a guru, and also the native is trying to get more and more spiritual knowledge. By doing penance and by doing meditation, the native will get the blessings of Lord Shiva, says Lord Shiva.

At the time when the native is seeking his prediction through Naadi astrology of Shivavatchi Maharishi from Atisuchma Naadi, his running age is sixty-two. When the native seeks his prediction from the manuscript written by Shivavachi Maharishi, Rahu is in Virgo, and Katel is Pisces. This planetary position is according to Guchara.

[Tamil talking.]

Goddess Parvathi prays Lord and requests him to divulge the native's future in such a way that by listening to the future, Goddess Parvathi and the native would be pleased.

Lord Shiva says that he has . . . [End of tape.]

PART FOUR

[Tape starts.]

. . . given some evidence about the future of the native, but the native would come to know about his future from Shivamaka Maharishi.

The native got this birth because he prayed gods and goddesses that he would have to take a birth like this. The native got his birth because in one of his previous births he prayed to Lord Shiva and Goddess Parvathi that he would like to take another birth like this. He prayed that he has to take another birth in a particular place. He has to lead such a life, and he did penance and meditation, and after that, and because of that this life, this birth is blessed by Lord Shiva to the native.

So this birth is very, very special for the native. In this birth, the native would not harm anyone. He would do many favors to many people. He would serve many people, and he would lead his life with virtues.

After his parents, Lord Shiva and Goddess Parvathi would guide the native in his life. Lord Shiva and Goddess Parvathi would be like the native's parents in this birth. Lord Shiva and Goddess Parvathi would give the native more spiritual knowledge. According to the native's prayers, penance, and meditation and worship, the native has got this birth. Lord Shiva and Goddess Parvathi would guide you and also bless fortunes, as this is said by Lord Shiva, but Lord Shiva and Goddess Parvathi would bless good luck to the native.

By visiting shrines of Lord Shiva and Goddess Parvathi, there are developments in the native's life. The native would worship Lord Shiva and Goddess Parvathi in this birth.

The native is born in a reputed family, which followed some other holy religion, but the native praises Lord Shiva and Goddess Parvathi. Goddess Parvathi has become one with Lord Shiva.

The native would get unforeseen friendship with good people and great people. The native would also get the blessings of Saint Siva Vakiya Maharishi and also the blessings of the Naadi *shashtris*. By getting the blessings of Siva Vakiya Maharishi, there are a few turning points in the native's life.

The native seeks more and more spiritual knowledge. The native has attachment with the worldly life, but the native daily worships Lord Shiva, but the native did not get the fame that he deserves for his service to the people. The reason is the bad effects of the previous birth's karma.

Goddess Parvathi again prayed to Lord Shiva, who is explaining about the life of the native. There is development, prosperity, and success in the life of the native in the future. But till now, the native is leading his life without a completeness in spiritual knowledge. The native has not so far attained the state that he actually deserves. So for that Lord Shiva gives the reason. Then Goddess Parvathi asks about the native's karma, and about one of the past births, and where he was born in one of his past births, and what is the karma of the native, and what are the bad effects of those karmas in the present birth, and what are the ways and remedial measures by following which the native get eradicated from the problems which the native is facing in the present time, and also the problems that are yet to come in the future.

And also Parvathi Devi requests that Lord Shiva guide the native in the right way.

[Tamil talking.]

[Something missing?]

. . . and separated from his first wife, and after that the native married another person, but he would not be satisfied in this family life, too. The native would not get enough income, and also he would not be satisfied in the current family life.

Unknowingly the native had committed some sins in one of the past births . . .

[Something missing?]

PART FIVE

[Tamil speaking.]

In one of his past births, the native was born in a place named Kucherum, which is nowadays called Gujarat. The native was born in a caste named Yarava. In the previous birth, the native was born as a girl. The girl was very beautiful and was living with her parents. She was very beautiful and also very talented. The birth which is explained now is the native's fifth birth. The present birth is the sixth birth of the native. And also he has one more birth.

She got married, and she lived a pleasant family with her husband and her children. She was very much interested in spirituality. She was worshiping Devi Durga. After that, there were some changes in her life, and she almost became a saint. And at a very young age, she left her family life, and she did not fulfill the responsibility toward her husband. Later, she did not fulfill the responsibilities towards her family members, and she also almost became a saint.

So her husband was badly affected, and he cursed the lady. That is the native. And apart from this, a few ladies cursed her. The lady left her husband and children, and led a spiritual life.

The native has got the curses of the husband and also the children. After that, the lady realized that what she did in her young age were sins. She admitted that what she'd done in her young age—that is, the sins she committed in a young age—and wanted to get eradicated from the bad effects of the sins. And she realized that what she'd done was unfavorable to her husband and her children, [and] were sins. In the past, the lady was interested in family life, she got married, she was blessed with children, but after entering into spirituality, the lady got the curses of the husband and also her children.

She also prayed that, in the coming births, she would lead a family life and fulfill all the responsibility toward the spouse and children and then involved in spirituality with the spouse. Like this, the lady prayed to Lord Shiva and Goddess Parvathi, and got such a birth as a male child.

So by praying daily, the native has got this birth.

The native is born in a country and in a family which followed some other holy religion. So because of this, the native would at first fulfill all his responsibilities to his family members, and later he would shine in the field of spirituality by doing the services related to spirituality.

After that, the native would get interested in *sannyasa*. With the blessings of Kaylinattan—that is, Lord Shiva—the native has got this birth. In this birth, the native is leading a life of good status, but in one of the past births the native has got the curses of the spouse and also of their children. So because of this, the native would be neither satisfied in his family life nor would he be satisfied in his spiritual life.

The native at first got married and had a child and separated from his first wife. And after that, the native married another person, but he would not be satisfied in this family life, too. The native would not get enough income, and also he would not be satisfied in the current family life.

Unknowingly the native had committed some sins in one of the past births . . .

PART SIX

[Something missing?]

[Tamil speaking.]

Goddess Parvathi asks Lord Shiva that, though he had committed some sins in one of the past births, later he realized and was fully involved in spirituality, he admitted his sins and he wanted to get eradicated from the curses got from his spouse and children. So Goddess Parvathi asked Lord Shiva to guide the ways by following in which the native can get eradicated from the bad effects of the curses he has got in one of the past births, and by following which he can get eradicated from curses and he would be able to fulfill all the responsibilities towards his family members, and also accomplish the spiritual services and attain the stage which he desires.

So for that, Lord Shiva says that the native has to get rid of the previous birth curses which he had got by committing sins in the previous birth. By following the remedial measures, the native would get rid of the previous birth curses and the bad effect due to those.

The first step is that the native should get the blessings of the Naadi reader who has expounded the native's prediction, and also the details about the past life sins, curses and bad effects due to those.

Actually, the native has to get the blessings Siva Vakiya Maharishi, but it is not possible to meet him and get blessings from him, so instead the native has to get blessings from the Naadi reader who has explained the prediction, previous birth address, one of the past birth detail, the sins the native had committed and the curses he had got and the bad effects in the present birth due to those.

So by doing a *puja* before the palm-leaf inscription itself is a way to get blessings of Saint Siva Vakiya Maharishi. The native has to offer fruit, sweets, flowers, banana, beetle leaf, coconut, and lemon. And also he has to offer dresses of saffron color to five saints. That is the native has to offer five shirts, five *dhotis*, and five towels of saffron color. And also the native has to offer the copper kettle used by saints Brahmadandum and Vardaractsha, that is, wooden shoes. And also the native has to offer an umbrella and a set of chapel [?]. And the native has to offer money equal to the number of times the mantras are chanted. That is the native has to offer money equal to 1,008 rupees.

The native has to offer these things and get rid of the previous birth sins, curses due to those, and bad effects due to those. After that the native has to visit a few shrines. There is a teaching in spirituality which says that first we have to worship saints, and then we have to worship gods and goddesses. So we have to worship monks, saints, yogis. It is said that after worshiping saints, monks, and yogis, we can go for worshiping gods and goddesses.

At first we have to worship, then who have guided us toward spirituality and toward divineness and toward gods and goddesses.

The next step is that the native has to visit a nearby temple of Lord Shiva and has to perform *archana* by telling the priest the native's name, moon sign, and birth star. Then the native has to light a lamp and also offer flower garlands to Lord Shiva. After that, the native has to visit a temple of any saint, for example Sai Baba, and there the native has to worship the saint according to the custom in the particular temple. After that the native has to visit a temple of Lord Kartikeya—that is Lord Muruga—and the native has to perform *archana* by telling the priest his name, his moon sign, and his birth star. And also he has to offer flower garlands to the god and also light a lamp.

After that, the native has to visit a temple of Lord Shiva, and he has to perform *archana* by telling the priest the native's name, moon sign, and birth star. And also the native has to perform *archana* before Lord Jupiter by telling his name, moon sign, and birth star to the priest. And also the native has to offer flower garland to Lord Jupiter, and he has to light a lamp.

After that, the native has to worship Lord Jupiter by raising and joining both the palms above his head, and also after that he has to sit down and meditate.

By doing this, the native would get the blessings of Lord Shiva and Goddess Umbal. By getting the blessings of Lord Jupiter, the native will get more spiritual knowledge. By doing all these, the native, who is really the son of Lord Shiva and Goddess Parvathi, will get success in all his tasks. He would worship Lord Shiva and also get more knowledge about the arts related to spirituality. After that there is development in the native's life.

[Tamil speaking.]

PART SEVEN

[Tamil speaking.]

In his sixty-two, the native will visit shrines and worship gods. The native will get the knowledge of both *yantra* and mantra, and also get the knowledge of ancient theories of *shastra* and also *sutra*—which means secrets. That is, the native will get knowledge of even those things that are kept as secrets by saints for centuries. Naturally, the native will get more knowledge about Lord Shiva.

Without following a guru, the native will get the knowledge of spirituality and the knowledge about Lord Shiva naturally. "When will the native get this type of knowledge?" asks Goddess Parvathi to Lord Shiva.

"The time when the native will get such a knowledge is a time when the sun sits in in its 'enemy' place."

The month is Vaikasi. In the month of Vaikasi, the sun sits in a place which is its enemy. Vaikasi month comes between May and June—that is after 15th May and before 15th June, approximately.

The native will teach some arts related to bodily health, and also the native will serve people as consultation related to spirituality. The native will do some service related to consultation related to physical health.

Lord Shiva says that the native will get the blessings of Lord Shiva till the end of his life. The native will get the blessings from Lord Shiva, who is the guru of the native. Then, further, Goddess Parvathi asks how the native's family life will be.

Lord Shiva says that the native's family life would be very pleasant. There will be love, affection, and unity between the family members. There would not be any misunderstanding between husband and wife. There will be unity among the family members.

The native will get success in all his tasks. The native will get all favors and also the blessings of Lord Shiva and Goddess Parvathi.

The native's daughter's family life would be pleasant. The native will get love and affection from his family members.

[Tamil speaking.]

By the end of sixty-two and in sixty-three, the native would worship Lord Shiva and get blessings from Lord Shiva. The native would donate and also do charity and get blessings because of that.

There will be some obstacle in getting blessings and *deeksha* from guru. For that, Goddess Parvathi asks how the native can win over the obstacle and getting blessings and *deeksha* from guru—that is, Lord Shiva. Lord Shiva says that the native should offer food to poor people according to the age of his present wife—that is present spouse.

[Tamil speaking.]

In the native's sixty-four, sixty-five, the native will do meditation seeing a round figure—by that the native will get more spiritual knowledge. By doing meditation and chanting, the native would see a form. He would see energy in a form of a shadow. After seeing that shadow the native would get more spiritual knowledge. The native would get some message . . .

PART EIGHT

. . . from a saint. The native would get the knowledge of Veda and *shastra*. In this period, the native will fulfill all responsibilities towards his grandchildren. The native will travel to different states, different cities, and different countries. The native will teach the art of spirituality to many people.

The native will teach the art of living without medicine by doing some exercises or yoga or energy healing. The native will teach the arts related to meditation, vibration, and yoga.

In this birth, the native will fulfill the needs of others and do this as a service. The native can get a profit by selling materials related to *puja*, *homa*, and also he can sell gems. Or the native can sell materials and metals used for *puja*.

In sixty-six and sixty-seven, the native will have all comforts. The native will use his knowledge about *shastra* and arts related to spirituality to fulfill the needs of others and solve the problems of others.

There will be some misunderstandings and arguments between the native and his spouse that may grow into a big problem. While in deep sleep or deep meditation, the native will get the vision of Lord Shiva and Goddess Parvathi. After that, both the native and the native's spouse would lead a healthy life.

The native will donate some materials which are used for building a temple or a shrine.

In sixty-eight, sixty-nine, the native will worship Lord Shiva and get more and more spiritual knowledge. In this period, the native will sit in a temple. The native would understand the problems of the people who come to him, and the native will guide the spiritual ways by which the people can get eradicated from their problems.

Without the support of a lady, the native can't get spiritual knowledge in his life. After fulfilling all the responsibilities in the family life, the native would get more and more spiritual knowledge.

In this age, the native will have some problems related to bones and also to his internal parts or private parts. By getting proper treatment, proper medicines, and also by using the spiritual arts, the native will be healthy.

Friendship with other ladies would not be permanent. It would be now and then.

[Tamil speaking.]

In seventy, seventy-one, the native will fulfill all his responsibilities. The native will be able to foresee the natural calamities which will be coming in the future, and he would get this knowledge by the blessings of Lord Shiva and Goddess Parvathi.

To protect the people from these natural calamities, the native would do some *pujas*, *yagnas*, and *homas*. The native would be able to foretell about the natural calamities related to storm or rain, or related to waves or seas and oceans.

Some countries may face some problems related to toxic air or toxic storm, and the native would be able to foresee and foretell those problems to people. This would happen in the north or northeastern side of a country, which the native would be able to foretell to people. To protect the people from this calamity, the native would perform some *pujas*. Like this, the native would use two or three ways to protect the people from natural calamities.

In seventy-one, seventy-two, and seventy-three, the native would do some consultation. The native would be very famous for his services related to spirituality, but still there will be some obstacles in going ahead in spiritual knowledge.

These problems occur because of conspiracy of some people. By worshiping God, by following the remedial methods given by Shiva Vakiya Maharishi, all these obstacles can be eradicated from the native's life.

In seventy-four, seventy-five, the native will get some knowledge related to universe. In this period, the native will teach the art of spirituality to many people. In this period, the native can build a shrine for some saints who lived in the past.

[Tamil speaking.]

The native can foresee what is going to happen in his life after seventy-five. So the native can make his way according to his future and lead his life.

[Tamil speaking.]

In seventy-six, seventy-seven, many people would appreciate the native because of his spiritual knowledge and spiritual services.

In the Tamil month named Tai, comes between December and January [Wikipedia says mid-January to mid-February], in the star of Lord Shiva—that is on an Ardra Nakshatra day. On a day when sun and moon are in the same sign, there is an *amavasya* or a new moon day, there are some obstacles in getting the blessings of Lord Shiva.

[Tamil speaking.]

In seventy-eight, seventy-nine, in the day of your birth star, seventy-eight, seventy-nine . . .

PART NINE

. . . in a day of the native's birth star before the [unintelligible], the native will be healthy. The native will do some charity, and later the native will get eradicated from all the obstacles and get the blessings of Lord Shiva.

Prediction given by Lord Shiva about the native. Lord Shiva says that the native would not attain salvation by this birth, and the native has another birth. The native will take another birth, and he will attain salvation or *moksha* at the next birth.

Then Goddess Parvathi asks about the ways following which the native can attain salvation in the next birth. Goddess asks about the ways by following which the native can lead a very pleasant life in the next life and attain salvation. Following the remedial measures given by Lord Shiva is enough for the native.

[Tamil speaking.]

The astrologer who has explained about the native's future has to perform a *puja*. A *puja* or *Panchatcharam* mantra. The *Panchatcharam* mantra should be written on a noble metal like silver or gold. The mantra *puja* should be performed for three *mandals*—that is, one *mandal* is forty-eight days, and three *mandals* are 144 days. For 144 days plus six days—that is, 450 days—the *puja* should be performed, should be chanted 108 times.

This *puja* should be performed by keeping *kalashas*—that is copper pots—that is, five *kalashas* should be kept, which indicate five elements. Five elements like soil, fire, water, air, and sky—that is, ether—should be filled in these five copper pots.

This mantra *puja* should be performed before Lord Shiva, and after that the native should get this metal plate and put it into a metal amulet and wear on his physique. After that, there will not be any problem in the native's life. There would not be any obstacle.

There is more development in the native's life, and the native would lead a life of very high style.

The native's life span is more than seventy-eight, and even after seventy-eight, the native would lead a life with luxury, spirituality because of the native's spiritual services and the blessings of Lord Shiva the lifespan of the native is more than eighty.

Lord Shiva showers his blessings on the native. By giving a lot of blessings, Shiva Vakiya Maharishi completes the native's Atisushumna Naadi prediction.

To know more about the native's life, the native can see the other chapters of this Atisushmna Naadi. By giving a lot of blessings, Lord Shiva and Siva Vakiya Maharishi conclude the Atisushmna Naadi prediction of the native.

Thank you.

REMEDIES AND PUJA FOR NAADI READING 2

POOJA DETAILS FOR MR. CRAIG

Shanti Chapter
Gurudaan: Fruits, flowers, banana, betel leaf, and betel nut, lemon, coconut, saffron color clothes for five saints. INR 1,008 = £11 = U.S. $17.

Go to a Shiva temple, offer flower garland, and do *puja* and *archana*.

Go to a saint's temple, and do *puja* according to the custom of the temple.

Go to a Murugan temple, offer a flower garland, and do *archana*.

Go to a temple where nine planets are there. Perform *archana* to Lord Guru. Meditate there for a few minutes.

Diksha Chapter
Panchakshara mantra should be engraved on a noble metal foil.

By keeping all the *puja* material, the *Panchakshara* mantra should be chanted 108 times per day for 144 days (3 *mandals* = 48 x 3= 144).

Mr. Craig can himself do the remedies explained in *Shanti* chapter.

Diksha mantra *puja* can be done for him.

[The cost would be 80 INR per day. 80 x 144 = 11,520 INR. 11,520 Indian Rupees = £122 = U.S. $183. The cost of noble metal (gold), 4200 INR = £45 = U.S. $67. In addition, there is the cost of the reading itself which was around £25 = U.S. $38.]

EPILOGUE

A few weeks before completing this book, I consulted the Naadi again and asked for a translation of the Gnanam Kandam, which is the chapter of the leaves that deals with spirituality and the seeker's divine destiny. Not everyone who consults the oracle has this chapter, so I was pleased that it existed, and could be translated and sent to me by email as an audio file.

I had intended to include it in this book, but the leaves gave instructions that the completed translations should first be put on a Shiva altar for a number of days. While I waited, I came close to finishing the last few sections of this book. The file was sent to me by email, but it was corrupt and could not be opened. I continued writing. The next file and the one after that also had different problems. I completed the book, did a final check of all the contents, and decided it was complete and could be now sent to my editor.

I added the final period and put a photo of Sathya Sai Baba in front of me. I closed my eyes and chanted a mantra to bless the completed project. As I said the last syllable of the mantra, my computer pinged to announce that an email, with a working file of the Gnanam Kandam, had arrived in my inbox.

My Gnanam Kandam is not included in this book, but it may be included in my next project. It tells of my spiritual work in the future and gives instructions about how to find divine knowledge, how to activate the third eye, and how to rediscover secret methods of clairvoyance, mediumship, and healing that are hitherto unknown to most people. It tells of how I will discover and use yoga techniques that will enable me to retain a youthful body into my old age. All these methods I will teach to others.

Later, I am told I will use the Naadis to help protect individuals from evil spirits and will warn people of environmental calamities. It tells also of the gurus and teachers I will meet and, in particular, of a meeting with Shiva, who will materialize and dematerialize himself, and who will appear to me in the form of hermaphrodite on one of my future pilgrimages. There are also instructions about the charitable foundation, with a renewed charge to build a temple and ashram.

Clearly, there is much more to come, and I will share my insights and spiritual adventures with you in future books.

Sai Ram!

DID YOU ENJOY THIS BOOK?

If you enjoyed this book, please leave a testimonial and rating on amazon.com or amazon.co.uk Your positive comments help me to reach more people and share the philosophy of spirit.

GLOSSARY

Archana A special, personal, abbreviated *puja* done by temple priests in which the name, birth star, and family lineage of a devotee are recited to invoke individual guidance and blessings. *Archana* also refers to chanting the names of the deity, which is a central part of every *puja*. The Sanskrit meaning is "honoring, praising."

Diksha (also spelled *deeksha* or *deeksa*, translated as a "preparation or consecration for a religious ceremony"). Giving of a mantra or an initiation by the guru

Guru dana or *daana* is the virtue of generosity or giving, a form of alms.

Kala Bhairava A fierce manifestation of Shiva associated with annihilation. He originated in Hindu mythology and is sacred to Hindus, Buddhists, and Jains alike. He is worshiped in Nepal, Rajasthan, Karnataka, Tamil Nadu, and Uttarakhand.

Kundalini The primal energy, or *shakti*, located at the base of the spine.

Moksha (also called *vimoksha*, *vimukti*, and *mukti*). Liberation, emancipation, Self-realization, or release.

Murugan (Kartikeya) The god whom the Tamils regard as their own. He is the same as Subrahmanya, Skanda (Kanda), Karttikeya, or Kumara. The name means "beautiful." A lot of Tamil hymnal literature is devoted to him, of which the Tiruppugazh is particularly famous. Lord Murugan was born by the divine spark from Lord Shiva, and he is very popular among Tamil-speaking people. He is worshiped for prosperity and protection from evil. He is the second son of Lord Shiva and Goddess Parvathi. He is often shown as having six faces. His chariot is driven by a peacock. He is the general for warriors of the angels in the fights against evil. He is worshiped for health and wealth.

Naadi Naadi is an ancient astrology, which has been composed by great *maharishis* of ancient India, using their precognitive spiritual powers. The sages recorded these predictions for every individual for the betterment of humanity and to safeguard *dharma* (righteousness). There are two types of Naadi—Maha Sukshma are written as one long dialogue between Shiva and his consort Parvathi; the others are divided into chapters.

Panchakshara mantra (also called the *Panchakshara stotra*). The *Panchakshara* literally means "five letters" in Sanskrit and refers to the five holy letters "Na," "Ma," "Si," "Va," and "Ya." This is a prayer to Lord Shiva, and it is associated with Shiva's mantra "Om Namah Shivaya."

Puja A religious ritual performed as an offering to various deities, distinguished persons, or special guests. Some Hindus perform *puja* every morning after bathing and dressing but prior to taking any food or drink. *Puja* is seen as a way of linking humans to the divine, and it can be performed for anything considered holy.

Rishi A holy Hindu sage, saint, or inspired poet. *Maharishi*—great saint. *Saptarishi*—the seven patriarchs of the Vedic religion.

Sadhana (Sanskrit, "a means of accomplishing something"). An ego-transcending spiritual practice.

Sannyasa The final life-stage of renunciation within the Hindu philosophy of four, age-based life-stages known as *ashrams*, with the previous three being *brahmacharya* (bachelor student), *grihastha* (householder), and *vanaprastha* (forest dweller, retired).

Shanti (also *santhi* or *shanthi*, from Sanskrit meaning "be calm"). Peace, rest, calmness, tranquility, or bliss.

Shastra The knowledge which is based on principles that are held to be timeless. It is also a byword used when referring to a scripture such as a treatise or text written in explanation of some idea. The palm leaves are often called the *Naadi Shastra*.

Shiva (Sanskrit, "The Auspicious One"), also known as *Mahadeva* ("Great God"), is one of the main deities of Hinduism. Shiva is worshiped as the destroyer and restorer of worlds and in numerous other forms. Shiva is often conceived as a member of the *Trimurti*, along with Brahma and Vishnu.

Swarga (or *svarga*), also known as *swarga loka*, is one of the seven *loka* or planes in Hindu cosmology, which sequentially are *bhu loka* (*prithvi loka*, Earth), *bhuvar loka*, *swarga loka*, *mahar loka*, *jana loka*, *tapa loka*, and the highest, *satyaloka* (*brahmaloka*). It is a set of heavenly worlds located on and above Mount Meru. It is a heaven, where the righteous live in a paradise before their next incarnation. During each *pralaya*, the great dissolution, the first three realms, *bhu loka* (Earth), *bhuvar loka*, and *swarga loka*, are destroyed. Below the seven upper realms lie seven lower realms of *patala*, the underworld and netherworld

Theertham The physical, holy-water body associated with a temple or deity.

Trataka The practice of fixed gazing at an external object to achieve single-pointed concentration, strengthening the eyes, and stimulating the *ajna* chakra (third eye).

Turiya The background that underlies and transcends the three common states of consciousness, which are waking consciousness, dreaming, and dreamless sleep.

MANTRAS

Nishprapanchaya

Nishprapanchaya is a description of one of the aspects of God—bliss—in the sequence "being-consciousness-bliss" in Hindu monotheism. As such, it is sung daily in some Hindu temples and ashrams.

Om Namah Shivaya Gurave
(Om. Salutations to the guru, who is Shiva)
Satchidananda Murtaye
(His form is being, consciousness, and bliss)
Nishprapanchaya Shantaya
(He is transcendent, calm)
Niralambaya Tejase
(Free from all support, and luminous)

Gayatri Mantra

The Gayatri Mantra is a highly revered mantra from the Vedas. Like all Vedic mantras, the Gayatri mantra is considered not to have an author, and like all other Vedic mantras, is believed to have been revealed to a brahmarshi, in this case Vishvamitra.

Oṃ bhur bhuvaḥ svaḥ

tat savitur vareṇyaṃ

bhargo devasya dhimahi

dhiyo yo naḥ pracodayat

We contemplate the glory of Light illuminating the three worlds: gross, subtle, and causal.
I am that vivifying power, love, radiant illumination, and divine grace of universal intelligence.
We pray for the divine light to illumine our minds.

PUBLISHED BOOKS BY CRAIG HAMILTON-PARKER

Hamilton-Parker, Craig & Jane (1995) *The Psychic Workbook* Random House ISBN 0-09-179086-7 (Languages: English, Chinese)

Hamilton-Parker, Craig (1996) *Your Psychic Powers* Hodder & Stoughton ISBN 0-340-67417-2 (Languages: English)

Hamilton-Parker, Craig (1999) *Timeless Wisdom of the Tibetans* Hodder & Stoughton ISBN 0-340-70483-7 (Languages: English)

Hamilton-Parker, Craig (1999) *The Psychic Casebook* Blandford/Sterling ISBN 0-7137-2755-1 (Languages: English, Turkish)

Hamilton-Parker, Craig (1999) *The Hidden Meaning of Dreams* Sterling imprint Barnes & Noble ISBN 0-8069-7773-6 (Languages: English, Spanish, Portuguese, Russian, Israeli, Greek Icelandic.)

Hamilton-Parker, Craig (2000) *The Intuition Pack* Godfield Books ISBN 1-84181-007-X

Hamilton-Parker, Craig (2000) *Remembering Your Dreams* Sterling imprint Barnes & Noble ISBN 0-8069-4343-2

Hamilton-Parker, Craig (2000) *Unlock Your Secret Dreams* Sterling imprint Barnes & Noble ISBN 1-4027-0316-3

Hamilton-Parker, Craig (2002) *Fantasy Dreaming Sterling* imprint Barnes & Noble ISBN 0-8069-5478-7

Hamilton-Parker, Craig (2003) *Protecting the Soul* Sterling imprint Barnes & Noble ISBN 0-8069-8719-7

Hamilton-Parker, Craig (2004) *Psychic Dreaming* Sterling imprint Barnes & Noble ISBN 1-4027-0474-7

Hamilton-Parker, Craig (2005) *Opening to the Other Side* Sterling imprint Barnes & Noble ISBN 1-4027-1346-0

Hamilton-Parker, Craig (2010) *What To Do When You Are Dead* Sterling imprint Barnes & Noble ISBN 978-1-4027-7660-1 (Languages: English, Dutch, Portuguese)

PUBLISHED ON AMAZON & KINDLE

Hamilton-Parker, Craig with Kipling, Violet (2014) *Psychics & Mediums Network Training Manuals* Amazon.com ISBN 1503126048

Hamilton-Parker, Craig (2014) *The Dream Handbook* Amazon.com ISBN 1503004309

Hamilton-Parker, Craig (2014) *Psychic Protection* Amazon.com ISBN 1501005642

Hamilton-Parker, Craig (2014) *A Medium's Guide to Psychic Dream Interpretation* Amazon.com ISBN 1500924474

Hamilton-Parker, Craig (2014) *Psychic School* Amazon.com ISBN 150247798X

Hamilton-Parker, Craig (2014) *Psychic Encounters* Amazon.com ISBN 1500759228

Hamilton-Parker, Craig (2014) *Tibetan Buddhism in Daily Life* Amazon.com ISBN 1502554933

Hamilton-Parker, Craig (2014) *Your Psychic Powers* Amazon.com ISBN 1500807230

Hamilton-Parker, Craig (2014) *Common Dream Meanings* Amazon.com ISBN 1502775778

Hamilton-Parker, Craig (2014) *Real Ghosts* Amazon.com ISBN 150247798X

IF YOU ENJOYED THIS BOOK YOU MAY ALSO ENJOY:

WHAT TO DO WHEN YOU ARE DEAD

Craig's book that explores mediumship and the nature of life after death. Available now on Amazon.com and Amazon.co.uk Or from Craig & Jane's website: psychics.co.uk

ONLINE PSYCHIC SCHOOL

At our Online Psychic School we have classes, courses and circles happening most week days as well as a thriving community of spiritually minded people.

Join our Online Psychic School: psychics.co.uk

CLAIRVOYANCE SERVICES

Craig & Jane Hamilton-Parker offer psychic and mediumistic readings from their website. They also have an online community where you can ask questions and share your paranormal dreams and psychic insights with likeminded people.

Visit: psychics.co.uk

If you would like a reading today you can call their telephone psychics and book a reading on the numbers below:

UK: 0800 067 8600
USA: 1855 444 6887
EIRE: 1800 719 656
AUSTRALIA: 1800 825 305

Callers must be 18 or over to use this service and have the bill payers permission. For entertainment purposes only. All calls are recorded. PhonePayPlus regulated SP: StreamLive Ltd, EC4R 1BB, 0800 0673 330.

THE HAMILTON-PARKER FOUNDATION

The Hamilton-Parker Foundation has the key objectives of spreading the teachings and messages of Craig & Jane Hamilton-Parker to the masses; establish Meditation Temples, Spiritual Education Centres, and to contribute for the causes of helping the poor, care for the environment, spiritual healing for all creatures and the safe practice of mediumship.

The Hamilton-Parker Foundation provides a family orientated haven where safe mediumship can be presented in a spiritual atmosphere. Though a worldwide network of meditation villages, trainees are invited to raise their consciousness through the powers of **concentration**, **meditation** and **mediumship**. The organisation also encourages a spirit of **service** with part of its resources used to directly feed the destitute and homeless.

If you would like to help with our cause, please see the page on our website:
psychics.co.uk/foundation

ABOUT THE AUTHOR

Craig Hamilton-Parker is a British author, television personality and professional psychic medium. He is best known for his TV shows *Our Psychic Family*, *The Spirit of Diana* and *Nightmares Decoded*. On television he usually works with his wife Jane Hamilton-Parker who is also a psychic medium. Their work was showcased in a three part documentary on the BBC called *Mediums Talking to the Dead*.

They now have TV shows in the USA and spend a lot of time demonstrating mediumship around the world.

Born in Southampton UK, Craig was convinced at an early age that he was mediumistic. He became a well-known as a platform medium within Spiritualism and in 1994 left his job as advertising executive to become the resident psychic on Channel 4 television's *The Big Breakfast* making predictions for upcoming news stories. He wrote a regular psychic advice column for *The Scottish Daily Record* and regular features for *The Daily Mail*, *Sunday Mirror* and *The People*.

His first book about the psychic genre was published in 1995 and are now published in many languages. You can find out more and join Craig & Jane's work and Spiritual Foundation at their website: **psychics.co.uk**

Printed in Great Britain
by Amazon